Euro Bonds
Markets, Infrastructure and Trends

World Scientific Series in Finance
(ISSN: 2010-1082)

Series Editor: William T. Ziemba *(University of British Columbia (Emeritus), ICMA Centre, University of Reading and Visiting Professor of University of Cyprus, Luiss Guido Carli University, Rome, Sabanci University, Istanbul and Korea Institute of Science and Technology)*

Advisory Editors:

Greg Connor *(National University of Ireland, Maynooth, Ireland)*
George Constantinides *(University of Chicago, USA)*
Espen Eckbo *(Dartmouth College, USA)*
Hans Foellmer *(Humboldt University, Germany)*
Christian Gollier *(Toulouse School of Economics, France)*
Thorsten Hens *(University of Zurich)*
Robert Jarrow *(Cornell University, USA)*
Hayne Leland *(University of California, Berkeley, USA)*
Haim Levy *(The Hebrew University of Jerusalem, Israel)*
John Mulvey *(Princeton University, USA)*
Marti Subrahmanyam *(New York University, USA)*

Published

Vol. 1   Bridging the GAAP: Recent Advances in Finance and Accounting
edited by Itzhak Venezia & Zvi Wiener (The Hebrew University of Jerusalem, Israel)

Vol. 2   Calendar Anomalies and Arbitrage
by William T. Ziemba (University of British Columbia, Canada & ICMA Centre, University of Reading, UK)

Vol. 3   Social Security's Investment Shortfall: $8 Trillion Plus — and the Way Forward
Plus How the US Goverment's Financial Deficit Reporting = 64 Madoffs
by Nils H. Hakansson (University of California, Berkeley, USA)

Vol. 4   Stochastic Programming: Applications in Finance, Energy, Planning and Logistics
edited by Horand Gassmann (Dalhousie University, Canada) &
William T. Ziemba (University of British Columbia, Canada & ICMA Centre, University of Reading, UK)

Vol. 5   Managing and Measuring Risk: Emerging Global Standards and Regulations after the Financial Crisis
edited by Oliviero Roggi (University of Florence, Italy & New York University, USA) & Edward I. Altman (New York University, USA)

Vol. 6   Investing in the Modern Age
by Rachel E S Ziemba (Roubini Global Economics, UK) & William T Ziemba (University of British Columbia, Canada)

Vol. 7   Euro Bonds: Markets, Infrastructure and Trends
by Marida Bertocchi (University of Bergamo, Italy), Giorgio Consigli (University of Bergamo, Italy), Rita D'Ecclesia (University of Sapienza, Rome, Italy), Rosella Giacometti (University of Bergamo, Italy), Vittorio Moriggia (University of Bergamo, Italy), & Sergio Ortobelli (University of Bergamo, Italy)

World Scientific Series
in **FINANCE** vol. **7**

Euro Bonds
Markets, Infrastructure and Trends

Marida Bertocchi
University of Bergamo, Italy

Giorgio Consigli
University of Bergamo, Italy

Rita D'Ecclesia
University of Sapienza, Rome, Italy

Rosella Giacometti
University of Bergamo, Italy

Vittorio Moriggia
University of Bergamo, Italy

Sergio Ortobelli
University of Bergamo, Italy

World Scientific

NEW JERSEY · LONDON · SINGAPORE · BEIJING · SHANGHAI · HONG KONG · TAIPEI · CHENNAI

Published by

World Scientific Publishing Co. Pte. Ltd.

5 Toh Tuck Link, Singapore 596224

USA office: 27 Warren Street, Suite 401-402, Hackensack, NJ 07601

UK office: 57 Shelton Street, Covent Garden, London WC2H 9HE

Library of Congress Cataloging-in-Publication Data
Bertocchi, Marida.
    Euro bonds : markets, infrastructure and trends / by Marida Bertocchi (University of Bergamo, Italy), Giorgio Consigli (University of Bergamo, Italy), Rita D'Ecclesia (University of Sapienza, Rome, Italy), Rosella Giacometti (University of Bergamo, Italy), Vittorio Moriggia (University of Bergamo, Italy), & Sergio Ortobelli (University of Bergamo, Italy).
        pages cm. -- (World scientific series in finance, ISSN 2010-1082 ; volume 7)
    ISBN 978-9814440158 (hardcover : alk. paper)
    1. Euro-bond market. I. Title.
    HG3896.B47 2014
    332.63'23094--dc23
                                                                2013034281

British Library Cataloguing-in-Publication Data
A catalogue record for this book is available from the British Library.

In-house Editor: Monica Lesmana

Printed in Singapore by World Scientific Printers.

to Clara, Gaia, Marco, Michele, Silvia and the new comer

to Adriana and Gabriele

to Alessio and Elena

to my family: Rosario, Virginia and Alberto

to Sara, Alessandro and Filippo

to Giovanna and Marco

Foreword

This is a state-of-the- art monograph on the European Bonds markets, its infrastructure and the main trends that can be observed. The book is witty, well-written and accessible for an intelligent audience that is interested in the state and development of European Bond Markets. The authors are internationally recognized academic experts in this field and are also familiar with the daily practice of European Bonds.

The book can be used by those who want to acquire the necessary knowledge and insights to be able to start working with European Bonds. At the same time, the book is a rich source of references for all those who are already working with these bonds: Traders, brokers, investors, supervisory authorities are just a few elements of a long list of practitioners that can benefit from this excellent book.

As a bonus, the book give a range of insights and reflections on recent developments. This is a valuable input for the debate on the structure and development of European Bond Markets.

In brief: this is a highly recommended book!

Jaap Spronk
Academic Dean MBA Programmes and
Professor of Financial Management Science
Rotterdam School of Management
Erasmus University

Preface

This book was written with the express aim of providing an overview of the Euro denominated Bond Market since the creation of the EURO area. It represents the exceptional collaboration of a group of scholars who have taught and studied the features and the functioning of financial markets for many years. The six authors who collaborated have all carried out extensive research in the field of asset and derivative pricing, optimization techniques and trading, or risk management strategies.

The role and the development of bond securities and their markets have become crucial in the European economic context to understand the variously used risk management strategies. This book aims to provide a complete overview of the principal features of the Euro bond markets, its developments, criticisms and potential.

All the chapters were specifically developed for this book and grew out of the analysis of large sets of data provided by individual governments and reported by the European Central Bank and the Bank of International Settlements.

Readership

This book is written for Master's level students who are taking courses in the economics or the financial markets of the Euro area. The need for a book like this stems from the belief that European students need to become familiar with the different features in the bond market of each, and every, European country. The book may be used as the sole text for a course on Euro bond markets or as one of several if other management aspects are included. Many pertinent figures and tables are presented and discussed, illustrating the composition and evolution of European debt. This book will help students and scholars wishing to obtain an overview of the entire Euro area, not just their own country. We additionally hope the book will be of interest to anyone working in the manufacturing, finance and service sectors — the backbone of the corporate debt markets — as well as those working in the public sector who want to better understand the Euro bond market and its related risks. We believe the in depth description of its features and dynamics can help those trying to develop new strategies for managing public or private debt.

Contents Overview

The main body of this book is divided into eight chapters, each containing a glossary and bibliography.

Chapter 1 describes the building blocks of the Euro-denominated bond market. We review the history and development of the market in Europe since its creation, we describe the main features of the various bond types. An overview of both government and corporate bonds is provided. A description of the events leading to the 2008 financial crisis and the various reactions and proposals to solve it are discussed. In the Appendix a detailed review of the five main European bond markets is also given.

Chapter 2 describes the infrastructure needed for the Euro bond market to function, from issuance procedures to the clearing mechanisms. The role of the electronic market and the post-trade infrastructure and the clearing and settlement process are described. In addition to the current market infrastructure the chapter discusses the constantly evolving regulations and other initiatives for a safe and efficient clearing and settlement marketplace.

Chapter 3 describes the evolution of the Government bond markets, highlighting the role of bond spread dynamics in assessing specific country risk. An in-depth analysis of country risk during the period 2008-2012 and a discussion of various Central Bank strategies enrich the entire chapter .The various Euro area country financial risk premiums to the German Bund are also presented.

Chapter 4 focuses on the Corporate bond market, its evolution and the arrival of the Euro bond indices. The most recent Moodys global corporate analysis is critically reviewed.

Chapter 5 analyses the Credit Rating Agencies and their effect on bond markets. It presents a rating taxonomy, the regulation of Credit Rating Agencies and recent changes to the current regulation. A brief description of the criteria and models used to assign a rating to a Corporate, or an instrument, is provided.

Chapter 6 discusses the important process of securitization, the rationale behind it, its evolution and recent developments in the Euro area.

Chapter 7 covers the various structured products of bond markets, including Covered Bonds, Inflation-Linked Bonds and Bond Exchange Traded Funds. Their features and recent developments in the Euro area presented. An example of constructing a better diversified portfolio by using Euro structured products compared to the use of simple Euro bond portfolios is presented.

Chapter 8 analyses the role of Credit Derivative instruments in the Euro area. Their features, structure and pricing issues are analysed. The Credit Default Swap spread market development over the last decade is critically reviewed. An example of how to extract single and joint default probabilities from their market quotes is also provided.

Background Knowledge

It would be inaccurate to say that this book does not pre-suppose any knowledge on the part of the reader, but it is true that it does not pre-suppose too much. A basic knowledge of financial markets, instruments and their drivers (equities, bonds, interest rates, etc..) is certainly essential. A degree of analytical preparedness as well as some familiarity with logs and exponents, compounding, present value computations, basic statistics and probability will also help. But beyond this not much is required and this book can be considered largely self-contained.

Exceptional Contribution

We are particularly grateful to Vittorio Moriggia who took a significant lead in driving the entire format and style of the book.

M. Bertocchi
University of Bergamo
R. L. D'Ecclesia
"Sapienza" University of Rome
Birkbeck University of London
ESCP Europe London campus

Acknowledgments

We cannot begin to thank all of the people who made writing this book so enjoyable. We are especially grateful to Bill Ziemba, professor of Finance at BCU for 40 years, for encouraging us to write it. His enthusiasm and confidence in our knowledge strongly contributed to our final version. We are also grateful to David Stack for his patience in reading the book and helping us to revise it. We also thank our families for giving up the many hours we spent working on the book. We dedicate the book to them. We hope the next generation will make better choices for their future by understanding the world we live in.

We acknowledge the grants from University of Bergamo. Rosella Giacometti and Sergio Ortobelli acknowledge the MIUR PRIN MISURA Project, 2013-2015, for financial support.

the authors

Author Biographies

Marida Bertocchi is professor of applied mathematics in economics and finance at the University of Bergamo. She taught numerous courses at the Universities of Bergamo, Urbino and Milan, including basic and advanced calculus, portfolio theory, advanced mathematical finance, stochastic optimization and parallel processing. Bertocchi has been dean of the Faculty of Economics and Business Administration and Director of the Department of Mathematics, Statistics, Computer Science and Applications at the University of Bergamo. She is the scientific coordinator of the PhD program in Economics, Applied Mathematics and Operational Research. She is author of numerous publications on bond portfolio management, and economic and financial applications. She was referee and reviewer in the EEC Vth and VIth framework. She has been responsible for many grants from national and international sources as well as from private firms.

Giorgio Consigli is associate professor of applied mathematics in economics and finance at the University of Bergamo. He has A PhD in Mathematics from the University of Essex (UK), a Diploma in Economics of Financial intermediaries and a Honours degree in Economics from the University of Rome La Sapienza. He worked afterwards as Vice President responsible for quantitative analysis at UBM, the Investment Bank of the UniCredit banking group. From 2006 to 2012 he's been visiting Professor at the University of Svizzera Italiana in Lugano (CH), currently he is at Cass Business School, London. Since August 2007 he is elective member of the International Committee on Stochastic Programming (COSP). In 2011 he has been appointed Fellow of the Institute of Mathematics and it's Applications (FIMA, UK). He has an active research in the areas of stochastic optimization, financial modelling, dynamic portfolio selection and has coordinated several financially-related projects with national and international industry partners as well as scientific research projects in Italy and Europe. He has published in several international journals. He is Associate Editor of the IMA Journal of Management Mathematics (O.U.P.), the International Journal of Financial Engineering and Risk Management (Interscience) and Quantitative Finance Letters (Taylor and Francis), Advisory Editor of OR Spectrum (Springer).

Rita Laura D'Ecclesia is professor of Quantitative Methods and Finance at Sapienza University of Rome. She is also visiting professor at Birkbeck University of London. Rita has a Ba. Hon. in statistics from Sapienza University and a Ph.D in Finance from Bergamo University. She is Director of the PhD program in International Finance and Economics (Doctoral School in Economics) at Sapienza and Director of the International Summer School on Risk Measurement and Control. She is also president of the Euro Working Group for Commodities and Financial Modelling and associate editor of several Journals. She teaches courses at undergraduate, Graduate and PhD levels in Quantitative Methods, Asset Pricing and Finance. Her research topics are related to Financial Modeling, Risk Management, Optimization techniques and Commodity markets pricing and modelling.

Rosella Giacometti is associate professor at the University of Bergamo, where she teaches Credit and Operational risks, Mathematical finance and Statistics for Financial Markets. She worked for Cambridge Econometric as European Analyst and collaborated with many banks on teaching and consultancy activities. She has a PhD in 'Mathematics applied to the analysis of Financial Markets' from the University of Brescia (Italy), an MSc in Statistics and Operational Research from Essex University (UK), and a first degree in Computer Science from the University of Milan (Italy). Her research interests are pricing of financial products, portfolio management, credit and operational risk.

Vittorio Moriggia is associate professor in Computer Science for Finance and in MATLAB for Finance at the University of Bergamo. He holds a Ph.D. in 'Computational Methods for Financial and Economic Forecasting and Decisions' from the University of Bergamo. He taught Mathematic Models for Financial Markets, Financial Engineering, Computer Science both at the University of Bergamo and in professional courses granted by public and private institutions. He implemented several models in different languages for research and production. He is author of various papers and books on Stochastic Programming models applied to Finance and on Computer Science. His research and teaching interests are in the areas of Financial Derivatives, Logical Analysis of Data, Programming Languages and Stochastic Programming.

Sergio Ortobelli Lozza is an associate professor in Mathematical Finance at the University of Bergamo. He is also visiting Professor at VSB TU Ostrava Department of Finance, Czech Republic. He holds a Ph.D. in 'Computational Methods for Financial and Economic Forecasting and Decisions' from the University of Bergamo. He taught numerous courses at the Universities of Bergamo, Calabria and Milan, including basic and advanced calculus, measure theory, stochastic processes, portfolio theory, and advanced mathematical finance. His research, published in various academic journals in mathematics and finance, focuses on the application of probability theory and operational research to portfolio theory, risk management, and option theory.

Contents

List of Figures

List of Tables

Chapter 1

The Bond Market in Europe

(*Marida Bertocchi, Rita L. D'Ecclesia*)

1.1 Introduction

The word Eurobond was originally created by Julius Strauss. The first Eurobond was issued in 1963 by the Italian motorway network "Autostrade". It was a ten years straight bond of USD 15 million underwritten by an international syndicate, the London bankers S. G. Warburg and listed on the Luxenbourg Stock Exchange. The term Eurobond has been used to define different instruments. Originally, the term was used to describe foreign currency denominated bonds. This means that the bond is issued by an individual country Central Bank in a foreign currency. Multinational companies and national governments, including governments of developing countries, use Eurobonds to raise capital in international markets. Eurobonds are issued by multinational corporations; for example, an Italian company may issue a USD eurobond in Germany for investors living in European countries. In this context, the term has nothing to do with the Euro, and the prefix "Euro" is used more generally for deposits made in a different currency and managed by the local Central Bank [Gallant (1988); Abaffy et al. (1988)]. Most Eurobonds are now owned in electronic rather than physical form. The bonds are held and traded within one of the clearing systems (Euroclear and Clearstream being the most common). Coupons are paid electronically via the clearing systems to the holder of the Eurobond (or their nominee account).

In recent times, the term Euro bond (or Euro-denominated bond) has been used for bonds that are issued in one of the European Union (EU) member states according to the European membership. In Fig. 1.1 a description of the European countries and their use of the Euro currency is provided.

Fig. 1.1   Map of European countries.

- the medium grey represents the common currency Euro area made of 17 countries (Austria, Belgium, Cyprus, Estonia, Finland, France, Germany, Greece, Ireland, Italy, Luxembourg, Malta, the Netherlands, Portugal, Slovakia, Slovenia, and Spain);
- the light grey represents the EU members that do not use the Euro yet (Sweden, Latvia, Lithuania, Poland, Bulgaria, the Czech Republic, Romania, Hungary);
- the dark grey represents the two Euro countries with an option to leave the EU (United Kingdom and Denmark).

Note, Kosovo and Montenegro (the black ones) are not EU members but they accept Euro currency.

The European Union Bond (EUB) nowadays would be a securitized bond, backed by the European Central Bank (ECB), and guaranteed by the European countries, which is still a highly debated project aimed to foster a real monetary union. See Section 1.7 in this Chapter for more insights.

1.2   History and Development

The Euro bond market has grown impressively since 2000. The importance of the Euro as an investment currency has made the market for Euro-denominated securities more attractive for investors and issuers. This market is better integrated and more liquid and provides a larger selection of innovative products, such as Index-Linked bonds, real-time bond indices, Fixed Income Exchange Traded Funds, Credit Derivatives and other Structured Products. The development of a relatively vast and yet homogenous financial market in the Euro area has attracted international investors, especially institutional investors, such as pension funds, insurance companies and banks. In 2000 the outstanding volume of Euro denominated debt was around €6.6 billion and reached €14.8 billion by the end of 2012 as shown in Table 1.1. The appeal of European bond markets for international investors has been further enhanced by reducing information asymmetry and improving transparency together with increased liquidity and declining transaction costs. In the last twelve years a large increase in private issuers of Euro-denominated bonds further contributed to the large growth of the market. The outstanding amounts of Euro-denominated debt securities by different issuers from 2000 to 2012 is reported in Fig. 1.2.

Euro Governments and Central Banks, classified as General Government, represent the largest issuers in the market, see Fig. 1.3. However, General Governments have shown a constant reduction in their outstanding volume during the decade, with an average yearly reduction rate of 8%, while Monetary and Financial Institutions have reported an average growth rate equal to 5% and Corporate companies a steady yearly increase at an average rate over the decade equal to 16%.

At the beginning of the European Monetary Union (EMU) in 2000, corporate bonds represented only 9.6% of outstanding bonds. By the end of 2003 they had grown to 14% and by 2012 reached 23% (see Table 1.1), largely due to the growing uncertainty experienced by sovereign government bond markets. In the last five years the corporate bond markets have continued to grow and develop although recent market volatility has slowed the growth.

Frequent efforts have been made to move towards an effective integration of European financial services. The Financial Services Action Plan (FSAP) was adopted by the European Commission in 1999 and endorsed by the Lisbon European Council in March 2000. It represents the most ambitious initiative to foster the integration of capital markets and to strive for a

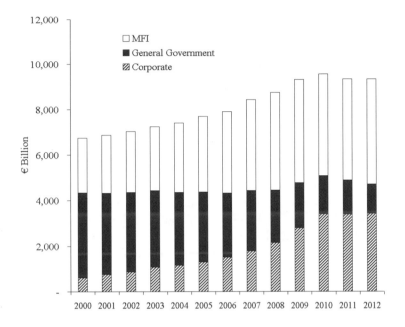

Fig. 1.2   Euro-denominated debt by issuers.

single market for financial services in the EU, [European Central Bank
(2004)]. The degree of integration of Euro bonds is still low and in the last
5 years, after the 2008 financial crisis, many differences between the bond
market across the various Euro countries emerged. At present investors
show different perception of the financial credibility and stability of the
various Euro countries, [Lojsch et al. (2011)].

1.3   The Main Features of Euro Bonds

The introduction of the Euro currency created one of the world's biggest
markets for bond issuance. According to Bank of International Settlements
(BIS) data, the European bond market ranks third (USD 14 trillion) after
the United States (USD 26 trillion) and Japan (USD 15 trillion), and the
three together account for almost 80% of world bonds outstanding today.
Although the market may be comparable in size to the US or Japanese
markets, both the sheer number of issuers and differences in issuer creditworthiness distinguish the Euro area bond market from its competitors.

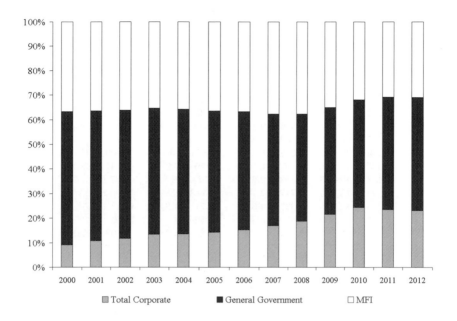

Fig. 1.3 Share of Euro-denominated debt by issuers.

The outstanding volumes of domestic debt securities for the entire Euro area amount to about half that of the US market volume. However, national debt markets are of different sizes: 63% of the entire debt market is made up by Italy (20%), France (25%) and Germany (18%), Spain and the Netherlands represent another 27%, while Austria, Poland, Portugal, Greece, and Ireland and the others account for the remaining 10% of the sovereign issues outstanding, as reported in Fig. 1.4.

In Table 1.1 the dynamic of Euro denominated outstanding debt securities, in billions of Euro, by issuer is reported.

The European bond market can be broadly categorised into three bond market sectors: General Government, Corporate and Monetary Financial Institutions. Within each market sector bonds with different credit ratings, coupon rates, maturities, yields and other features appear.

The volume of Euro debt securities more than doubled in the last decade from €6.6 trillion to €14.9 trillion. The impressive growth, however, can be noticed in the Euro Corporate debt volumes which grew from €636 billion to €3.5 trillion, showing an average annual growth of 17% for the 6 years up to 2007, surging in 2008 and 2009 when it grew by 20% annually.

Table 1.1   Euro 17 domestic debt outstanding.

year	total debt	Government	Corporate	MFI
2000	6,607	3,545 (53.7%)	636 (9.6%)	2,425(36.7%)
2001	7,054	3,674 (52.1%)	812 (11.5%)	2,569(36.4%)
2002	7,472	3,855 (51.6%)	931 (12.5%)	2,684 (35.9%)
2003	8,040	4,067 (50.6%)	1,121 (13.9%)	2,853 (35.5%)
2004	8,635	4,303 (49.8%)	1,200 (13.9%)	3,131 (36.3%)
2005	9,226	4,502 (48.8%)	1,380 (15%)	3,344 (36.2%)
2006	9,890	4,632 (46.8%)	1,591 (16%)	3,688(37.1%)
2007	10,803	4,771(44.2%)	1,929 (17.9%)	4,104 (38%)
2008	12,096	5,153 (42.6%)	2,556 (21%)	4,387 (36.3%)
2009	13,650	5,747 (42.1%)	3,413 (25%)	4,490 (32.9%)
2010	14,118	6,337 (44.8%)	3,471 (24.6%)	4,311 (30.5%)
2011	14,690	6,650 (45.3%)	3,459 (23.6%)	4,591 (31.3%)
2012	14,871	6,814 (45.8%)	3,449 (23.2%)	4,608 (31%)

After 2009 the amount of corporate debt volume grew at a slower pace. In 2000 54% of the total outstanding volume was represented by Government debt while the Corporate debt represented only the 9.6% and the MFIs the 36%. By 2011 the percentage of Government debt had declined to 45% while Corporate had risen to 24% and MFIs to 31%, see Fig. 1.3. In the last decade European market investors have shown increased interests in corporate debt securities with respect to the traditional Government securities, providing liquidity to the corporate sectors.

Fiscal performance has had a significant impact on the issuance activity of the Euro area governments. As a consequence, the borrowing requirements of Euro area countries have increased. For example, the borrowing of each of the biggest debt issuers, Italy, Germany and France, was equal to the outstanding debt volume of the seven "small" Euro area countries combined.

Governments represent the largest issuers in the Euro area. Governments issue bonds to borrow money to cover the gap between the amount they receive in taxes and the amount they spend, to re-fund existing debt and/or to raise capital. Government bonds are usually considered the highest quality bonds in the market because they are backed by central governments (not the case for emerging market bonds where defaults can represent a serious risk). Within the Central Government bond sector, the Sub-Sovereign bond sector is defined as any level of government below the national or central government, which includes regions, provinces,

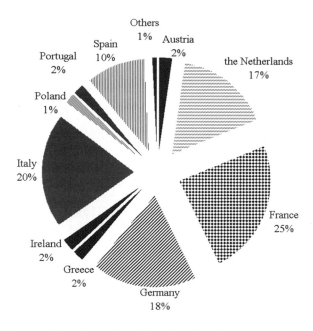

Fig. 1.4   Euro-denominated bond market by country in 2011.

states, municipalities. In Europe, the Sub-Sovereign bond market is primarily dominated by agencies and supranational institutions such as the World Bank, Kreditanstalt für Wiederaufbau (KfW) and the European Investment Bank (EIB). The market for Sub-Sovereign bonds in Europe has less individual participation than in the US; individual investors in the US municipal bond market enjoy significant tax advantages for their investments. As European countries have increasingly become a single market, the growth of the Sub-Sovereign bond market has been significant as well. It represents in 2012 9% of the general government outstanding volume (3% in 2001), from a €99 billion notional in 2001 to €609 billion in 2012. Growth in the number of Sub-Sovereign entities issuing debt has been related to changes in the structure and function of government entities below the national or sovereign level. Re-examination and reorganisation of sources of revenue for Sub-Sovereign entities and access to capital for new infrastructure are important in Europe. The European Union continues to expand and develop rules on which categories of Sub-Sovereign government borrowing are included in the national debt ceilings and which are excluded. Sub-Sovereign participation in the bond markets is expanding because local governments need to finance day to day operations of public services and capital infrastructure investments (i.e roads, hospitals, bridges, reservoirs) and the central governments have debt ceiling limits. In addition, a decentralization process is ongoing in most European countries. Government and Sub-Sovereign bond markets exist side by side and serve as independent sources of financing for the national or central government and local governments.

The second largest Euro-denominated bond market is the Monetary and Financial Institution (MFI) whose issuances grew from €2.4 trillion in 2000 (37% of total outstanding) to €4.6 trillion in 2012 (31% of total outstanding). The MFI represents the credit institutions (6,180 institutions in the Euro area in 2012) and financial institutions (1,088 money market fund institutions in 2012). They issue Bonds, Asset-Backed Securities and other collateralized Mortgage Debt Obligations enriching the set of debt securities suitable for different kind of investors. Collateralized debt has been one of the fastest developing investment vehicle in the last decade based on the idea that credit can be advanced on the basis of which collateral, security, or compensation a borrower can use to repay the loan in the case of default. The collateral or security can come from one or more sources such as mortgages, loans, bonds/debt or asset-backed securities. Collateralized debt instrument is therefore a kind of promissory note backed by collateral, security or other compensation in the event of a default by a borrower. The subject is further discussed in the following Chapters.

The corporate bond market sector is the sector which has reported the most impressive growth. Nearly 23% of outstanding bonds globally are corporate bonds. In Europe the corporate bond markets has been shown a steady increase even if the recent high market volatility has caused some decline. The assessment of corporate credit quality requires the collection, on a regular basis, of a substantial set of reliable data. It is impressive that the non banking sector has taken this responsibility on board. There are two categories of corporate bonds for investors: investment-grade bonds and speculative-grade (also known as high-yield and sub-investment grade). Investment-grade bonds are characterized by high credit quality, speculative-grade bonds are issued by corporations that are perceived to have a lower level of credit quality compared to more highly rated, investment-grade corporate issues. Speculative-grade refers to the fact that originally banks were not allowed to invest in bonds classified as speculative because rated by the credit rating agencies. A detailed description of the corporate bond market dynamics and its features is provided in Chapter 4.

Structured Debt Securities The large increase in corporate debt securities issuance is mainly due to the role of structured debt. Many different types of products are "structured" to some extent. "Structuring" usually refers to any type of obligation that is not a simple secured or unsecured government or corporate obligation. Although these types of transactions are usually issued through Special Purpose Vehicles (SPVs), this is not always the case. Covered bonds are a type of debt issued by banks that are fully collateralised by residential or commercial mortgage loans or by loans to public sector institutions. They typically have the highest credit ratings and most, but not all, have AAA ratings. The bonds offer an additional protection to the holders than traditional Asset-Backed Securities because in addition to looking at the collateral pool as an ultimate source of repayment, the issuing bank is also liable for repayment, although in some cases the rating of the covered bonds is based more on the collateral than on the rating of the bank. If the issuing bank is downgraded, then the covered bond may be downgraded but this depends on the specific situation. Covered bonds are the second largest segment of the European bond market after Treasury securities. Germany, whose creation of Covered bonds dates back to the 18th century, leads issuance in the European covered bond market. Twenty four other European countries issue Covered bonds to finance their mortgage markets and the most significant is Denmark's Realkreditobligationer which has a 16% market share; France's Obligations Foncières are 7%; Spain's Cedulas Hipotecarias are 9% and Sweden's Säkerställda Obligationers 5%.

Yet another type of structured product refers to the packaging or repackaging of bonds together with various types of interest rate swaps and/or credit derivatives which allow changes in interest and principal payment streams according to the investor's preference. For example, a Government bond could be placed into a SPV, a subsidiary company entity, which is used to isolate financial risk. The fixed rate on that Government bond can be converted to a floating rate– or alternatively to a rate based on changes in a specific fixed income instrument, or even an equity index. These types of structured products can be either reissued out of an SPV, or directly issued by a bank or other institution. In some cases, these products are also called "structured credit" if they involve products with some type of corporate or asset-related credit risks. These structured products are further discussed in the reminders of the book.

1.4   Government Bonds

In the past public issuers in the Euro area benefited from a quasi-monopoly situation but this has changed. The presence of corporate and credit institutions as issuers of debt securities creates a more competitive environment with a wider selection of instruments on offer. However, competition exists not only between Euro area countries but also in the top-rated non-sovereign market segment. In their function as basic investment products for institutional investors or central bank reserves European government bonds compete with US Treasuries. The sovereign issuance segment is still the most important segment of the bond market in the EU representing in September 2012 46% of the total Euro-denominated debt, at €6.8 trillion. The main features which distinguish sovereigns from other securities are: the size of the market, the creditworthiness of the borrowers, the availability of a wide range of maturities, the fungibility of issues facilitating trading, the high liquidity (particularly of recently issued securities), open market activity and lending facilities, the existence of a well-developed Repo and derivatives market and the coexistence of benchmark yield curves.

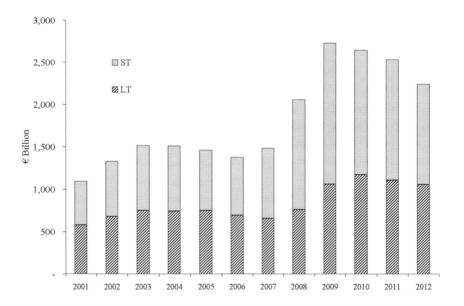

Fig. 1.5   Gross government bond issues by maturity (Short Term and Long Term).

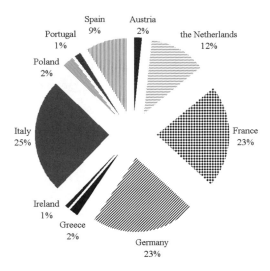

Fig. 1.6   Government debt in the Euro area.

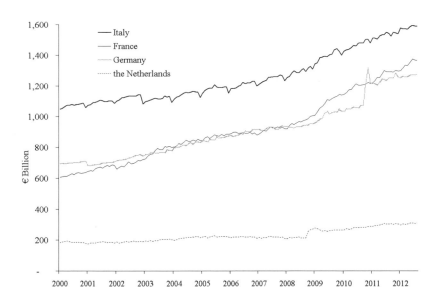

Fig. 1.7   Total outstanding Government securities in Italy, France, Germany and the Netherlands.

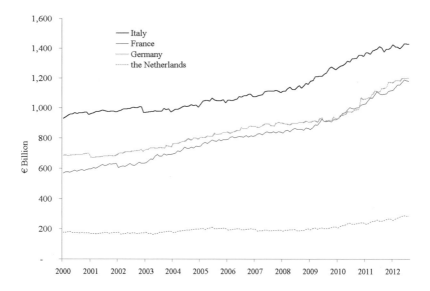

Fig. 1.8   Outstanding Long Term Government debt by country.

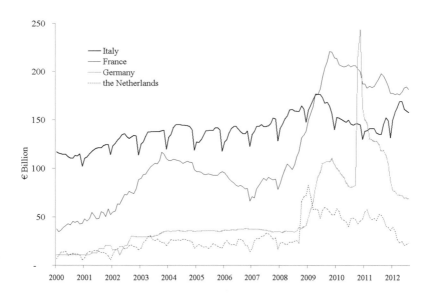

Fig. 1.9   Outstanding Short Term Government debt by country.

The size of the Government bond markets The European Government bond market in 2011, according to BIS ranks third (USD 7.7 trillion) after the United States (USD 12.9 trillion) and Japan (USD 12.88 trillion), the three markets together account for 79% of the outstanding world government bonds.

The distribution of Government bonds by country has changed over the years. In 2011 the main bonds issuers Italy (25%), France (23%), Germany (23%) and the Netherlands (12%), together represent 83% of the entire Government bonds market, as shown in Fig. 1.6. This contrasts with Italy representing 32% of the total European outstanding Government debt and France and Germany respectively 19% and 20% in 2001. The total amount of Euro-denominated Central Government securities in the Euro area almost doubled from €3.5 trillion in 2000 to €6.2 trillion in 2011.

The largest increase in issues occurred from 2007 to 2009, when new gross issuance of Government bonds again almost doubled from €1.5 trillion to €2.7 trillion in two years (see Fig. 1.5). Since then, a slight contraction has occurred. Over the period 2001-2012 the largest issuers of Government securities have been Italy, France, Germany and the Netherlands, see Fig. 1.7. The majority of the new issues had long maturities (53% of the total issued securities), even if from 2007 European Governments increased their issuance of Short Term maturity, as it is shown in Fig. 1.5.

Unlike Long Term debt (see Fig. 1.8), Short Term outstanding debt has shown an unstable pattern over the last five years. Countries like Germany, France, Italy and the Netherlands at the beginning of 2007 showed steady increasing trend in outstanding Short Term debt up to December 2009, this trend changed after 2009 and has been highly volatile since then, as shown in Fig. 1.9. Just two months before the Greek bailout, Germany raised short term issuance from €88 billion to €215 billion in October 2010 which was an enormous one-time change in German debt structure. For the next eight months the outstanding volume of short term securities was kept at these unprecedented levels (over the period 2000-2009 the average total outstanding volume of German Government securities increased from €900 billion to €1.3 trillion). This was thought to be a policy shift adopted by the German Central Bank to raise liquidity to support German banks, by offsetting the upcoming liquidity constraints coming from non-performing borrowers of other European Member States. By the beginning of 2012 the outstanding amount of short term securities for all European countries seemed to have returned to the average levels observed before 2007.

Bond yields of Euro area countries   From the beginning of the EMU
in 1999 the various European government bond yields tracked each others
nicely. Since the start of the 2008 financial crisis, the government bond
yields have diverged dramatically as shown in Fig. 1.10.

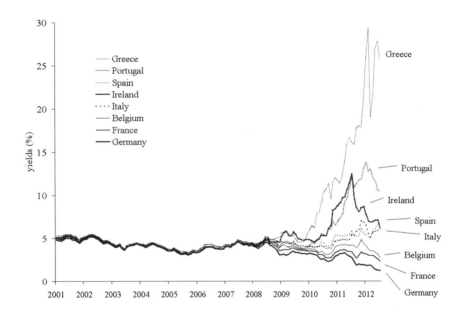

Fig. 1.10   Euro-denominated 10-year yields by country.

Among the three largest European bond markets, German bond yields
for long term maturities have shown least volatility ranging from 1.24 to
5.14 percent with an average over the 2000-2011 period of 3.78. Nowadays,
Germany is perceived by the market as the *last to default* country, its
Government bond as the liquid and safe asset and its Government bond
yield as "the European risk-free rate".

All Government bond yields are therefore bench-marked to the German
Government bond yield, generating what is often used as the measure of a
country's credit risk, the spread between one Euro Country's bond yields
and the German 10-year bund.

Prior to the EMU, yield differentials between Euro area government
bonds were determined by four main factors: expectations of exchange-rate
fluctuations, different tax treatment of bonds issued by different countries,

Table 1.2   Euro area Debt-to-GDP ratios.

Countries	2000	2001	2002	2003	2004	2005	2006	2007	2008	2009	2010	2011
Euro area	**55.8**	**55.7**	**55.1**	**55.6**	**55.8**	**55.24**	**53.63**	**51.67**	**55.02**	**64.12**	**70.22**	**75.46**
Greece	103.4	103.7	101.7	97.4	98.6	100	106.1	107.4	112.9	129.7	148.3	170.6
Italy	108.5	108.2	105.1	103.9	103.4	105.7	106.3	103.3	106.1	116.4	119.2	120.7
Portugal	50.7	53.8	56.8	59.4	61.9	67.7	69.4	68.4	71.7	83.2	93.5	108.1
Ireland	35.1	35.2	32	30.7	29.5	27.3	24.6	25.1	44.5	64.9	92.2	106.4
Belgium	107.8	106.5	103.4	98.4	94	92	88	84	89.2	95.7	95.5	97.8
France	57.3	56.9	58.8	62.9	64.9	66.4	63.7	64.2	68.2	79.2	82.3	86
Germany	60.2	59.1	60.7	64.4	66.2	68.5	68	65.2	66.8	74.5	82.5	80.5
Austria	66.2	66.8	66.2	65.3	64.7	64.2	62.3	60.2	63.8	69.2	72	72.4
Cyprus	59.6	61.2	65.1	69.7	70.9	69.4	64.7	58.8	48.9	58.5	61.3	71.1
Malta	54.9	60.5	59.1	67.6	71.7	69.7	64	61.9	62	67.6	68.3	70.9
Spain	59.4	55.6	52.6	48.8	46.3	43.2	39.7	36.3	40.2	53.9	61.5	69.3
the Netherlands	53.8	50.7	50.5	52	52.4	51.8	47.4	45.3	58.5	60.8	63.1	65.5
Finland	43.8	42.5	41.5	44.5	44.4	41.7	39.6	35.2	33.9	43.5	48.6	49
Slovenia	26.3	26.5	27.8	27.2	27.3	26.7	26.4	23.1	22	35	38.6	46.9
Slovakia	50.3	48.9	43.4	42.4	41.5	34.2	30.5	29.6	27.9	35.6	41	43.3
Luxembourg	6.2	6.3	6.3	6.1	6.3	6.1	6.7	6.7	14.4	15.3	19.2	18.3
Estonia	5.1	4.8	5.7	5.6	5	4.6	4.4	3.7	4.5	7.2	6.7	6.1

credit risk and liquidity. With the introduction of the Euro, currency related premia were eliminated by the irrevocable fixing of legacy currency
pairs. Good progress was made in harmonizing national tax treatments, as
we will see later on. Yield differentials today are mainly attributed to both
the credit premium and the liquidity of the market.

At present, the lowest yielding Government security in the 10-year segment is the German Bunds, with a long term rate of 1.24 and a short term
of 0.13%.

On average the European countries which have issued Government
bonds with high yields are those who reported large Debt-to-GDP ratios
as shown in Table 1.2. The goal for each European country should be to
keep the Debt-to-GDP ratio lower than a theoretical safe 60% level, which
was possible for most countries prior up to 2007, with the only exceptions
being Italy and Greece who showed triple digit ratios for the entire period.
Starting in 2007 the Debt-to-GDP ratios worsened for most countries with
Portugal, Italy, Ireland and Greece (the PIIG's) exceeding 100% the Debt-
to-GDP ratios in 2011 and Spain fast approaching the high double digit
area after its €100 billion bailout. It is clear that beyond certain thresholds of indebtedness it becomes virtually impossible for any EU country to
refinance itself in the market at a reasonable rate.

Some argue that if Member States were to follow similarly restrictive
policies as Germany, they would enjoy similar borrowing conditions. However, this is not true if we look at the various countries long term government
bond yields.

Figure 1.11 shows that in small Member States like Austria and the
Netherlands, (where debt-to-GDP ratios have remained below German levels and therefore do not present high economic instability), the Governments still had to pay a premium over Germany during most of the first
Euro-decade. These yield differentials are the generic or natural premia for
small illiquid markets.

Today, the Greek and Irish Governments pay three to four times more
to borrow money than Germany. The observable yield spreads of Euro area
sovereigns in 2000 were 14 to 41 basis points (bps) over German Bunds. In
2003, it varied between -3 and 15 bps and remained volatile through 2007.
For instance in November of 2004 the yields of 10-year S&P AAA-rated
government bonds in Austria, Belgium, France, Germany, the Netherlands,
Portugal and Spain were nearly identical. Finland was at a premium of
8 bps, followed by Ireland with a premium of 13 bps, Italy (having been
downgraded to AA) of 15 bps and Greece had an A rating and the highest

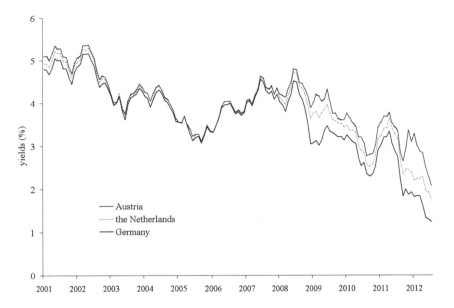

Fig. 1.11   Bond yields of Austria, the Netherlands and Germany.

premium of 16 bps. The bond yield spreads over the Bund for southern Euro countries were to subsequently show unprecedented stress: Spain's bond yield spread ranged from 15 bps on January 2008 to 555 bps on July 2012, while Greece went from 37 bps to 2,458 bps and Italy from 37 bps to 476 in the same period. From January 2008 to December 2012, all Euro area countries experienced a steady bond yield spread of double digits to the bund. The fractured nature of European debt markets during the recent financial crisis has not helped the long term investment and the economic growth. In addition job creation and international competitiveness have also proceeded at a slow pace. European markets are now less liquid than US and Japanese markets and this leads inevitably to structurally higher interest rates. Long term investors, like pension funds, have greater difficulty to find instruments which match their long term needs, and the debt issued in peripheral markets is not easily absorbed.

Fiscal integration   Good progress has been made on taxation differences within the Euro area. The EU decided to draw up a consolidating legislative framework to overcome existing differences in the effective taxation of savings income in the form of interest payments: the Council Directive 2003/48/EC of June 3, 2003 on the taxation of savings income in the form of interest payments. The Directive came into force on July 1, 2005, with the provision that agreements were also in place for certain third countries (Switzerland, Andorra, Liechtenstein, Monaco and San Marino) to ensure that equivalent measures are applied in those countries. Furthermore, a long transitional exemption was granted to Austria, Belgium and Luxembourg, allowing them to replace the required centralized exchange of information with a withholding tax.

Comparing different Euro area bonds The diversity of national legislative and regulatory frameworks together with a large variety of investment and debt management instruments made it difficult to establish a single market. Each country may freely structure and issue debt instruments. However, because of their placement focus for debt within the EU, the trend is for Governments to coordinate more than collaborate. One example of this is the adoption of a similar coupon calculation convention. Bilateral and multilateral contracts have also been developed and one forum for such contracts is the Economic and Financial Committee, the so called Working Group of EU Government Bonds and Bills, often referred to as the Brouhns Group, also.

Government bond markets focus on larger issuances with the aim of improving liquidity of the various instruments. National debt managers have been launching benchmark bonds of €5 billion, or more, in order to be eligible for trading on the EuroMTS electronic trading platform. 80% of total bonds outstanding are Bonds of €20 billion notional, while small bonds of up to €0.5 billion have all but disappeared and bonds up to €5 billion have a residual market share of only 4% of bonds outstanding. Smaller countries in particular are trying to increase the notional of existing bonds rather than issue new debt to obtain market liquidity (fungible issues). Certain countries have also arranged programmes to buy back or redeem bonds primarily in order to increase the liquidity of on-the-run issues and use this to replace or retire old illiquid bonds.

The maturity spectrum up to ten years is relatively homogenous in terms of the share of sovereign issuers. More interesting in terms of fragmentation is the long-term spectrum, where no single maturity is offered by the six largest Euro area sovereign issuers. This is due to the different size of each country's debt requirements. Only big countries are readily able to serve the whole maturity spectrum.

The coupon structure itself has not shown significant changes: 65% of Government bonds are fixed rate coupons, 35% offer floating rate note securities, EU Governments which have not joined the Euro currency, such as the United Kingdom and Sweden, are more likely to issue Index-Linked Bonds. The French Treasury, for example, started issuing bonds linked to the French inflation index in 1998, Greece and Italy in 2003 and Germany in 2006. Another niche is the "TEC-10" issued by France, with a quarterly coupon linked to an average of all French government backed notes adjusted to a constant 10-year maturity equivalence. These bonds were first issued in 1996. At the moment the Index-Linked Bond segment accounts for a small percentage of the bond market in most countries. In France it represents more than 12% and in Italy roughly 10%, as it is reported in the Danish Central Bank Bullettin [Danish Central Bank (2011)].

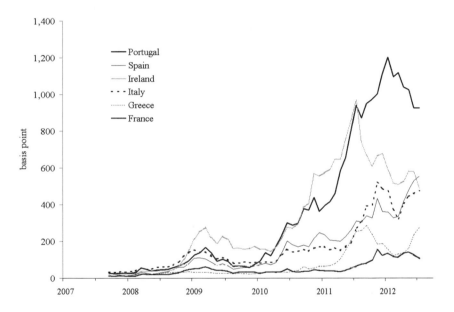

Fig. 1.12   Spread for selected Euro area countries after the 2008 financial crisis.

A brief description of the main features of the largest European government bond markets is reported in the Appendix to this Chapter.

1.5   Corporate Bonds

According to Merrill Lynch, individual European investors are less likely to be involved directly in the individual corporate bond market, compared to the U.S.. They are more inclined to invest in funds comprised of group of corporate bonds and other investment vehicles given a lack of familiarity with risk as it applies to individual corporate names. A change in individual investor preferences is ongoing and the corporate bond markets have been increasingly popular in the Euro area.

Most retail investors buy corporate bonds through a public offer. A company that makes a public offer will issue a prospectus and investors apply directly to buy bonds. The prospectus explains the key features and risks of the investment: it gives information about certain indicators that can help to assess the risks, describes the timing of interest payments and conditions around them.

Corporate bonds can pay fixed or floating rate, coupons are normally paid every three months. Some issuers include an option allowing them to adjust the payment frequency on a cumulative basis. This means that, if the issuer cannot pay the promised interest on the scheduled date, he may pay an accumulated amount including interest on the next scheduled payment date.

Companies with a solid historical financial performance of strong earnings, profitability and cash flows, are much better placed to meet their financial obligations. This is commonly reflected in their official rating made by specialized Credit Rating Agencies, whose principal role is described in Chap. 5.

The soundness of a company is usually measured by its ability to cover interest payments on money it borrows. According to standard budget analysis three common ratios are:

- Earnings Before Interest, Tax, Depreciation and Amortisation (EBITDA) divided by net interest expenses;
- Earnings Before Interest and Tax (EBIT) divided by net interest expenses;
- Gearing Ratio, which measures total liabilities divided by shareholder equity.

Regardless of which ratio is used, it is important that the company's earnings comfortably exceed net interest expenses and that the Gearing ratio does not exceed some threshold values.

Other credit indicators that are usually considered are:

- defaults on any current or previous debt obligations, or breaching the loans conditions (loan covenants);

- debt maturity profile, i.e the company has a significant amount of debt that will be maturing soon, and which may need to be rolled over.

When a company becomes insolvent, its assets may have to be liquidated, with the proceeds being distributed to everyone who has a stake in the company. This means all the creditors (including bond holders) and shareholders. There are two factors that determine how likely you are to get your money back:

- whether the corporate bonds are secured or unsecured;
- the ranking of the investor in the list of creditors.

Corporate bonds are exposed to the following risks:

- **Credit risk**: the risk that the issuer may not be able to pay back the money, interest rates or entire nominal value, to the investors.
- **Interest rate risk**: it affects the market value of the bonds in case the investor wants to sell the bond before maturity. For example, if interest rates go up, the market value of corporate bonds will generally go down (this means you may get less money than what you initially paid for your bonds when selling them on the secondary market).
- **Liquidity risk**: to be unable to sell your bonds at any time at the desired price.
- **Prepayment (or early redemption) risk**: the issuer may redeem the bonds before maturity if interest rates fall and the market price goes up. If this happens, you will be paid the face value of the bonds (you may have paid more for them or they may be worth more on the secondary market).

The performance of the European corporate bond markets has been evolving rapidly in the last decade. Spreads of corporate bond yields over Government bond yields were at exceptionally low levels at the end of 2003 having peaked in the autumn of 2001 or early 2002. Quantitative assessment of this phenomenon suggests that much of the low corporate spread level was attributable to historically low interest rate levels, encouraging companies to use this source of funding. So most of the largest European corporations in 2003 issued bonds with low default risk premia.

Corporate bonds are mainly a long term financing vehicle for European companies. In 2001 long term corporate bonds represented 83% of the total outstanding corporate volume, reaching 93% in 2012 as shown in Fig. 1.13.

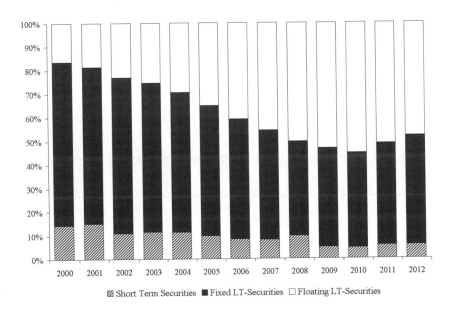

Fig. 1.13 Outstanding amount of corporate securities by maturity.

From the introduction of the Euro until 2008 a steadily increasing number of floating rate corporate bonds were issued. Long term floating rate notes were only 17% of the total long term outstanding volume in 2001 and reached 52% by December 2009. A slight reduction has occurred since then bringing floating rate issuance back to 42% of the entire outstanding volume, as of October 2012.

In the period between 2003 and 2008 there was both a broadening and deepening of the European corporate bond market, see Table 1.1, which is still ongoing since the financial crisis of 2008, this is due to the high interest rate available in the market for this type of bonds. Outstanding corporate securities in 2000 amounted to €600 billion and by 2012 had reached €3.4 trillion, an average annual growth rate of 16%. The largest increase, some 30%, occurred between 2008 and 2009, showing how corporations experiencing financial distress increased their funding by using the private debt markets.

Corporate debt by maturity   Most corporate bonds are issued with long maturity (minimum 10 years, maximum 30), as shown in Fig. 1.14. Long Term debt instruments after 2008 have become the main financing tool for European corporations.

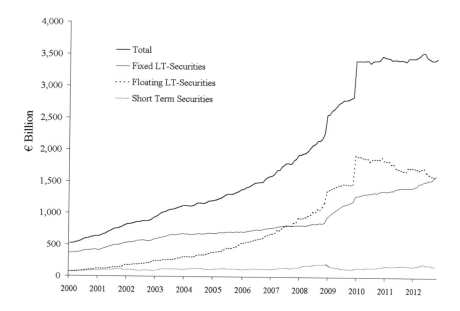

Fig. 1.14   Outstanding amount of corporate debt for the Euro area by maturity.

The type of Long Term bond issued by corporations has changed over the decade with an increasing role played by floating rate instruments. At the beginning of the EMU 84% of the corporate Long Term securities where issued with fixed coupon, this share has been slowly reducing up to represent in 2012 only the 50%, as it is shown in Fig. 1.13.

The changing interest rates and the large uncertainty dominating the economic context in the last five years has required corporations to issue more attractive instruments to guarantee they would be placed on the market.

Corporate debt by country   Italy (9%), France (16%), Spain (13%) and the Netherlands (21%) have the largest corporate bond markets representing over 56% of the entire Euro area corporate debt markets in 2012, as shown in Figure 1.15.

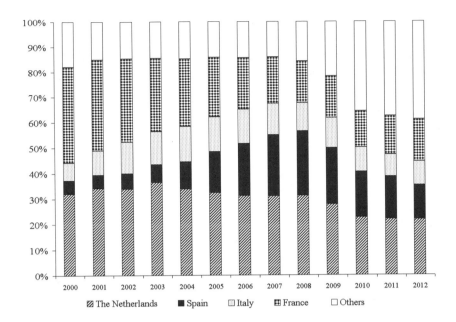

Fig. 1.15   Outstanding share of corporate debt by country.

In 2000 these four countries held 80% of the entire outstanding volume, showing how smaller Euro area countries had been increasing their share of corporate debt issuance over the decade. The Netherlands and Spain have been the largest issuers of corporate debt over the entire period starting respectively, from €180 billion and €27 billion and reaching €756 billion and €448 billion, as shown in Fig. 1.16 and Fig. 1.17. Spain increased at a monthly average rate of 2% over the period 2000-2009 to sharply invert this trend after February 2011 reporting a constant monthly reduction equal to 1% over the last 18 months as a result of the difficult economic conditions occurring in Spain. The Netherlands corporations have been issuing bonds at a steady pace up to December 2008 reaching an outstanding amount of €700 billion, starting on December 2009 the outstanding corporate debt did not change much and fluctuated around €750 billion. Unlike The Netherlands and Spain, French corporations showed different behavior. Until the occurrence of the financial crisis a steady monthly average increase of 1% occurred, however after December 2008 French corporations did not show a change in the trend and over the last 12 months a steady increase equal to 5%, occurred. French corporations, as a consequence of the financial

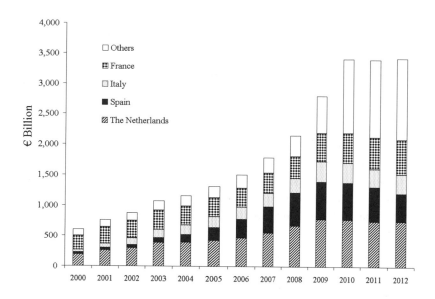

Fig. 1.16   Oustanding amount of corporate debt by country.

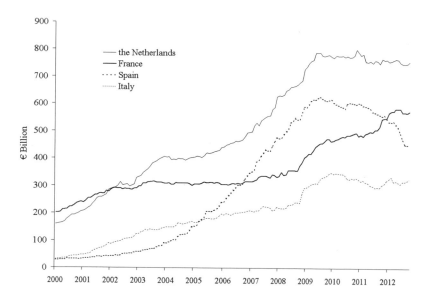

Fig. 1.17   Oustanding amount of corporate debt for four European countries.

crisis, needed to increase their financing issuing more bonds and therefore increasing the outstanding corporate debt. Italian corporate debt has shown a constant positive trend with a monthly average increase of 2% up to December 2009, a slight reduction during the heart of the sovereign debt crisis in 2010, and then an upward trend again in the last 10 months.

France and the Netherlands, were the largest issuers of corporate bonds in 2000, with 38% and 31% respectively. In particular, France corporations by 2012 represented only 16% of European corporate debt outstanding, while the total outstanding volume had grown from €200 billion to almost €600 billion. Dutch corporate debt declined to 20% of the entire European corporate debt in the same period. Having grown rapidly from 2003-2007, Italy and Spain reduced their borrowing starting from 2008.

1.6   The 2008 Financial Crisis

The Euro area sovereign debt crisis intensified in 2010 and 2011. In the first half of 2010 massive sell-offs occurred in Greek government bonds with CDS spreads on Greek bonds jumping above 1,000 basis points. These tensions brought the European public authorities to intervene with a number of measures aimed to reduce distress in financial markets. In particular the European Financial Stability Facility (EFSF) was launched by the EU ministers providing as a start €440 billion to support Euro area Governments which were having difficulties in accessing public debt markets. After 2010 bond yields for two of the largest debtors, Italy and Spain, rose sharply and continued to drift upwards for the second half of that year. Towards the end of 2011, yields on some of the other highest-rated Euro area Government bonds, including Austria, Belgium and France, also increased, widening relative to Germany's yields. Several factors contributed to this sharp rise:

- First, official lenders, who were considering a second support ECB package for Greece, demanded private sector involvement in reducing Greece's debt burden as a condition for additional loans. This raised uncertainty among bondholders regarding their treatment in any future Euro area support program.
- Second, economic growth in the Euro area was beginning to falter, making it harder for local governments to strengthen their financial positions in the near term.
- Third, the downgrade of the United States by one rating agency heightened investor focus on fiscal sustainability.

In Portugal, Ireland and Greece, official support programmes prescribed substantial fiscal tightening that required deficit cuts of several percentage points of GDP. In the second half of 2011, Euro area banks reduced their overseas financing by 4% in Africa and the Middle East, 20% in Asia and the Pacific, 13% in emerging Europe and 9% in Latin America and the Caribbean. Reductions were especially sharp for loans with high risk weights, such as leveraged loans or project finance, and for loans that often required dollar funding, such as aircraft or ship leases and trade finance. In this context other forms of financing were introduced for the Euro area, in some cases, this included loans from non European international lenders. For example, some Australian, Japanese and UK banks which already had a focus on Emerging Asia increased their lending in Europe. Local domestic lenders also boosted credit, in Latin America, and less so in Emerging Europe, where Western European banks continue to have a large market share. In addition, some large corporate borrowers turned to the bond markets, where gross issuance increased by almost 30% in the final quarter of 2011, alone.

In October 2011 and again in February 2012, the Euro area leaders agreed on further measures designed to prevent the collapse of Member State economies. This included an agreement whereby banks would accept a 53.5% write-off of Greek debt owed to private creditors, increasing the EFSF to about €1 trillion, and requiring European banks to achieve a dramatic increase in capital requirements which was set to 9% (before September 2009 banks could hold as little as 2% common equity against risky assets). To restore confidence in Europe, EU leaders also agreed to create a European Fiscal Compact requiring the commitment of each participating country to introduce a balanced budget amendment aimed to reduce their Debt-to-GDP ratio. While sovereign debt has risen substantially in only a few Euro countries, it has become a perceived problem for the entire area. The three countries most affected, Portugal, Ireland and Greece, collectively account for only 6% of the Euro area's gross domestic product (GDP), the high instability in these countries greatly affected the dynamics of the Euro/Dollar exchange rate during 2011, which averaged 1.40 with a minimum of 1.31 and a maximum of 1.45.

The Euro area crisis was inevitable, as there remains a structural contradiction within the Euro system. Countries are allowed to follow a similar fiscal path, but they do not have a common treasury to enforce it. That is, countries with the same monetary system have freedom with their own fiscal policies, taxation and expenditure. Even though there is some agreements on monetary policy through the European Central Bank, countries may or may not choose to follow it. This feature brought the so called "fiscal free-riding" of peripheral economies, especially Greece, since it was hard to hold national financial institutions to any panEuropean standard. This lead to failure in the complete prevention of contagion of other areas, and it remains virtually impossible for the Euro area to respond quickly to any problem, [Anand et al. (2012)].

Membership of the Euro area established a single monetary policy, individual member states were no longer able to act independently, they were prevented from printing money in order to pay creditors and ease their default risk. By printing money a country's currency is devalued relative to its (Euro area) trading partners, making its exports cheaper, in principle leading to an improved balance of trade, increased GDP and higher tax revenues in nominal terms. However, countries which hold assets in a currency which has devalued also suffer losses. For example by the end of 2011, the GBP/Euro exchange rate fell by 25% and an inflation of 5% was reported in UK, as a consequence investors holding assets in GBP, lost approximately 30% in repayment ability.

Prior to the crisis it was assumed by both regulators and banks that sovereign debt issued in the Euro area was safe. Banks had substantial holdings of bonds from weaker economies such as Greece which offered a small premium and were supposedly just as sound. As the crisis developed it became obvious that in particular for Greece, and possibly for other countries, bonds offered substantially more risk than had been assumed. The lack of information about the risk of European sovereign debt caused a conflict of interest for banks that were earning substantial sums from underwriting the bonds.

The bond yields of southern countries as Portugal, Italy, Greece and Spain increased more than expected and their spread widened respect to the German bund. The reduced creditworthiness of these countries was marked by a large increase in Credit Default Swap (CDS) trading volumes over the last four years. CDS market and quotes are actually considered a reliable measure of the market price of credit risks, providing the market perception of credit stability of a company or a country. In the last four years sovereign CDS quotes of riskier countries reached unprecedented levels. A detailed description of the sovereign CDS market and its features is provided in Chapter 7.

Investors now have increased concern about the ability of policy makers to quickly contain any crisis. Since Euro currency countries have fewer monetary policy choices, strong solutions require pan-European cooperation. The European Central Bank has an inflation control mandate but not an employment mandate, while the U.S. Federal Reserve has a dual mandate. The 2008 crisis appears to be as much political as economic, and on a day-to-day basis, the Euro area is less supported by an institutional apparatus. Heavy bank withdrawals have occurred in weaker Euro area states such as Greece and Spain. In June of 2012 the Euro/Dollar exchange rate hit a new low level as high net-worth individuals moved assets out of the Euro area. Closer integration of European banking remains one of the goals of political leaders. The EMU is at a crossroad, member countries must choose:

(1) to keep the current structure of the Euro area which could lead to its eventual disintegration, or
(2) to become more integrated.

The structural faults of the EMU are no longer academic but real. Reforms are usually initiated as a reaction to Crisis and it is rarely a surprise that preventive measures were not already in place. Now that the current Crisis is real, the EMU again scrambles to put together a new road-map for Crisis Reaction and Prevention.

In the short run the goal is to stop the deterioration in Greece and Spain and to limit contagion to other countries. It is also important to resume economic growth. Long-term growth depends on structural reforms and greater productivity but these take time to achieve. A long-term solution must also include greater fiscal discipline as prescribed under the rules of the EMU: low deficits and low public debt. The main reform must come from a fiscal union between the Member countries. A fiscal union would pool the risk to public finances across the members. However, for that to happen there would also need to be appropriate checks and balances on taxation and spending at the Union level. That means that the EU and the EMU, in particular, must advance toward deeper political union. A central authority must become responsible for allocating an increased portion of the tax burdens and the revenue.

1.7 The European Union Bond

The 2010 sovereign debt crisis in the Euro area has raised interest among academics, politicians and many financial experts to design a European

Union Bond (EUB) backed by the ECB, which could play a key role in the financial and poltical integration of the European Union and help over-indebted countries to lower their Debt-to-GDP ratios to provide a more sustainable cost of funding.

The project needs to be well planned starting from an economic and institutional layout. Several generically defined types of EUBs have been presented and discussed in the recent years. Only one of these has been implemented so far: the Stability Bond (SBs), others have been proposed but not implemented as the Union Bond (UBs), the Project Bond (PB), the Blue Bond (BB), the Euro Bond (EBs) and the recent debated European Redemption Fund (ERF).

These long-term European public debt securities were proposed by the European Commission President Jacque Delors in the White Paper for Growth, Competitiveness and Employment of 1993. UBs would have been guaranteed by the European Community budget to finance investments in big pan-European infrastructure projects, whose proceeds would have gone to the promoters of those projects (public sector bodies, privately held companies) burdened by interest payments. This proposal has often been picked up on, recently also by the European Parliament. A limited variant of the UBs are Project Bonds (PBs) supported by the current EU president, José Manuel Barroso and by the European Commission in 2010 to carry out single European infrastructure projects with public financing. PBs would be issued by private subjects but guaranteed by the Community budget and by the EIB. Some have already been issued by the EIB and the Marguerite Fund,[1] active since 2008 with its core sponsors being the French, German, Italian, Polish and Spanish Deposits, Loan Fund or similar bodies and the EIB.

The Stability Bond (SBs) was introduced in August 2010 and man-aged by the EFSF (European Financial Stability Facility). They are an important novelty even if how they operate is limited to defensive rescue measures. Up to €440 billion of committed capital was available to issue securities to be used for conditional loans for Euro area Member States in financial difficulties. The shares of the capital of the Fund are proportion-ate to the size of Member States in the ECB. Germany therefore guarantees 27%, France 20%, Italy almost 18%, a total of 65%, of the EMU.

---

[1]The 2020 European Fund for Energy, Climate Change and Infrastructure, is a fund lunched by Europe' leading public financial Institutions.

This Fund has issued just €13 billion of SBs loans to Portugal and Ireland up to June 2012. A subsequent broadening of the scope of the Fund, including amendments in July 2012, increased the guaranteed capital to €780 billion and conferred extra powers onto the EFSF. In particular, the Fund will be able to buy public debt on the primary and secondary markets of over indebted Member States which are undergoing financial restructuring. The broadening of the scope is subject to the ratification of the States that are shareholders of the Fund. For now the Fund can just issue loans. From October 8, 2012 the EFSF has been replaced by the European Stabilization Mechanism (ESM) a permanent crisis resolution mechanism for the countries of the Euro area signed on February 2 2012 by an intergovernmental treaty. The ESM replaces the exiting EFSF, the maturing EFSF bill will be financed via long term funding from the EFSF or temporarily through the proceeds of ESM bills. The European Stability Mechanism's (ESM) aim is to preserve the financial stability of Europe's Economic and Monetary Union by providing financial assistance to Euro area Member States in difficulty. The ESM is authorized to issue bonds or other debt instruments in the market to raise those funds needed to provide loans to countries who need them, intervene in the primary and secondary debt markets, act on the basis of a precautionary programme and finance re-capitalizations of financial institutions through loans to Governments, including non-programme countries. All financial assistance to Member States is linked to appropriate conditionality. The shareholders of the ESM are the 17 Euro area Member States. It has a total subscribed capital of €700 billion which comprises €80 billion in paid-in capital and €620 billion in committed callable capital. The ESM's effective lending capacity is €500 billion On January 8 2013 the ESM launched its short term funding program with a three-month bill auction. The action was met with strong demand attracting over €6,2 billion in bids of which over €3,1 billion were non-competitive.

The Blue Bond was proposed by Delpla and Wizsacker in 2010 (Bruegel Policy Brief 2010/03) and it provides an incentive-driven tool. Under this project homogenous Government debt would be broken down into two tranches: a senior ("blue") tranche which is assumed to be 60% of GDP; and a junior ("red") tranche for any additional debt above that threshold. In the case of a partial default, the red tranche will be impacted first and the blue tranche will only be affected by that part of the default (if any) that is not absorbed by the junior tranche. In other words, any Government funds used to service and repay Government debt will always first be used to satisfy the claims of the Blue Bond holders. As a result, the blue tranche will be less risky than status quo debt, and the red tranche will be more risky, leading to a differentiation in interest rates. This rate differentiation is reinforced by liquidity effects. With the Blue Bond project, all the countries participating in the Blue Bond would pool and merge their blue tranches, creating a Government bond market similar in size, liquidity and quality to the US Treasury T-bill market. Due to this gain in liquidity, the cost of borrowing would be further reduced for the blue tranche. By contrast, the liquidity of the red tranche would be substantially less than the liquidity of the homogeneous national bonds. This reduced liquidity is expected to further increase borrowing costs for Red debt. Additional risk considerations are usually mentioned when talking about the Blue Bonds: First the Blue debt includes several liabilities to create a triple A-rated asset. Second, from an investor's perspective, joint and several liabilities will further reduce the risk of the asset because default risks tend not to be perfectly correlated. Therefore, the Blue debt cost of borrowing in the Euro area should be lower. Finally, defaulting on the entire Red tranche would be less disruptive, because in this eventuality, the borrowing capacity in the senior tranche would not be destroyed. From an investor's perspective, the expectation of a less disruptive default on the junior tranche increases the risk of default, thereby calling for an additional risk premium (see Jochimsen and Konrad, 2006). Tightened European supervision of banks and Rating Agencies would need to ensure that the financial sector does not become vulnerable to a default of Red debt by fiscally less-robust sectors.

The European Redemption Fund (ERF) is emerging as one of the most credible options recently under discussion. This would secure market access to indebted countries at a reasonable and sustainable funding cost, while at the same time forcing them to engage into an irrevocable consolidation of their public finances. The ERF, first proposed by the German Council of Economic Experts on November 2011 (although the original version dates back to 2010) is set up in order to receive the portion of debt exceeding the 60% ceiling Debt-to-GDP ratio from each Euro area country members. Including Greece, Ireland and Portugal, the ERF could amount to a total €2.7 trillion. Italy, Germany and France altogether would account for 76% of funds transferred, with Italy keeping the lion's share.

However, given that Ireland, Greece and Portugal are already under the EFSF and ESM protection scheme, they could be excluded from the ERF, which would take the ERF size to a maximum of €2.3 trillion. Alternatively, the ERF could be open to all EU 17 members with EFSF and ESM funding capacities merged into the ERF. By offloading the excess current debt, all Euro area Members have a unique opportunity to be fully compliant with the Maastricht criteria, i.e. with the Fiscal Compact. The aggregate funding cost benefit for European countries would be in the region of 70 bps of GDP, according to [Guglielmi and Tchibozo (2012)].

The European Union Bonds (EUBs) has been proposed by and discussed in the EU Parliament. The basic idea is to introduce a European Financial Fund (EFF) that issues EUBs having the following four characteristics.

(1) EMU member States should give capital to the EFF in proportion to their stakes in the ECB.

(2) The capital would be backed by actual gold reserves of the European System of Central Banks, the largest in the world with some 350 million ounces, worth around €450 billion. To place gold as collateral, the bylaws of the ESCB and of the ECB would have to be amended (with an impact on European Treaties, but not on the Central Banks Gold Agreements that deal with gold sales). These institutions could therefore become shareholders of the EFF as they are the ones conferring assets.

(3) Assuming the capital paid up to the EFF is of €1 trillion, each EMU Member State will have to contribute other assets such as bonds and shares assessed at real market values and not at overvalued book values. These contributions should eliminate German fears of having to pay for other States debt. Each country would have to confer the EFF a predefined amount of Euros, of which a part in ounces of gold and the rest in other assets. It would be important that each country in addition to gold, confer shares of companies belonging to homogeneous sectors in energy, telecommunication and transportation. The EFF with €1 trillion of paid up capital could issue EUBs with a leverage of €3 trillion and a 10 year (and larger) duration at an interest rate of 3% possibly variable rate after a certain period of time.

(4) There could be further guarantees with legal commitments from EMU Member States. The €90 billion of annual interest charges, to date equal to some 1% of GDP of the EMU, would be payable with the profits from the equity conferred to the EFF, part of the VAT of EMU Member States and with interests. The EFF should divide in two parts the €3 trillion raised with EUBs. In order to bring the average Debt-to-GDP ratios of the EMU from the current 85% to 60%, the EFF could pay back €2.3 trillion of State bonds from EMU Member States.

The remaining €700 billion of this issue would go to investments in large European projects aimed at unifying and helping pan-European companies in the energy, telecommunications and transportation sector. The EFF would become a shareholder to grow.

There are several advantages for the EUB issuance. First, the EFF would represent a stabilizing factor in managing individual State Treasury bonds to hold on to reducing speculation. Second, to have a unified market of large-scale and raising funds at lower average interest rates compared to those that Member States national bonds can obtain. Third, higher liquidity deriving from sovereign Funds may find a market with the real collateral attracting. In this way, EUBs can really become competitive when compared with US Treasury bonds, in which China wishes to reduce its exposure. Fourth, the EFF has to have a precise structure and corporate governance system (that could in part be taken from the EFSF and the ESM), including voting rights of EFF members, which, even though subject to their share in the capital, should be reviewed periodically in order to take into consideration by how much single States exceed the 60% Debt-to-GDP threshold. In this way, the different States would be pushed to bring down their debt-to-GDP ratio. Markets would happily gorge on bonds backed by the full faith and credit of the Euro area. Euro bonds would cut borrowing costs for the European Unions to large troubled members. And it would spare German and other taxpayers from the EU's solvent northern countries from having to fund yet another bailout of a southern member state. Nineteen years of experience with the Maastricht Treaty, which created both the EU and the Euro, has shown convincingly that the set limit of the Debt-to-GDP ratio= 60% are unenforceable. Countries with the power to flaunt the limits will do so whenever it is politically expedient. The question is not what to do when debt gets near its limit, however high or low. It is how to prevent debt from getting near that limit in the first place, except in very extreme and unusual circumstances. To prevent debt from reaching the limit we need fiscal rules. A fiscal rule is any pre-specified mechanism that constrains spending or the budget deficit. According to a study by the International Monetary Fund ([International Monetary Fund (2012)]), 81 countries around the world use different fiscal rules. If too vague, a rule is merely ornamental. If too restrictive, such as one requiring a constitutional amendment to force a balanced budget, for example, the rule could create rather than solve problems. Euro Bonds combined with fiscal rules may save the EMU.

Appendix 1.A. The Major European Bond Markets

Bunds: Rebenchmark   The German bond market is comprised of Bubills (less than one year maturity), Schaetze (two years maturity), Bobls (five years maturity) and Bunds (ten to thirty years maturities).

Today there are more than 30 Bunds traded on the secondary market, accounting for roughly half of the outstanding German Government securities, the remainder being the other above mentioned type of bonds. In 2011, the total outstanding volume of all Government securities reached over €1,607 billion. According to Finance Agency of Federal Republic of Germany data, the outstanding volume of Bunds, Schaetze and Bobls accounts for about 75.9% of the total, while Bubills account for 4.7%, inflation linked securities for 17.1% and other instruments for about 2.3%.

10-year Bunds are the flagship financial instrument in the secondary market. They are characterized by fixed interest and principal due dates of January 4th, July 4th and, from 2010, on September 4th of each year; redemption is at par and interest is calculated on an actual/365 or actual/366 basis; they are not redeemable prematurely and not callable by the issuer. Since 2010 on the primary market, three new 10-year Bunds are issued every year, each of which is reopened two to three times and reaches peak issue volumes of up to 27 billion Euro. Thirty-year bonds are usually issued twice a year, with one new issue roughly every two years. Ten and thirty (or more)-year Bunds represent the long end of the German Government yield curve. In 2011 ten and thirty-year Bunds account respectively for 18% and over 3%, adding to a total of more than 21% of the annual issuance volume in 2011.

With original maturities of five years, Bobls cover the middle maturity segment of the German Government yield curve. German Bobls previously auctioned twice a year, they are now auctioned in January, April and September of each year. The series issued in 2011 have been of roughly up to €150 billion, they represent about 17% of the 2011 annual issuance calendar.

There are generally eleven series available to investors in the secondary market, with some reaching a total volume in circulation of €20 billion at their peak. In July 2012, the volume in circulation averaged 221 billion Euro. The interest is paid annually and is calculated on an actual/365 or actual/366 basis, redemption is at par; interest and redemptions dates are in February (since 2010), April and October; they are not redeemable prematurely and not callable by the issuer.

With a maturity of two years, Federal Treasury notes (Schaetze) are the shortest-dated capital market instruments issued by the Federal Government and one of the most liquid class of German Government securities. They account for about 12% of the Government's outstanding debt portfolio in 2011. In the primary market there are four new issues each year, each with a volume of about €18 billion in the following month through one or two reopenings. Schaetze represent about 24% of the annual issuance calendar in 2011. There are usually eight Schaetze in circulation in the secondary market. They pay annually interest calculated on an actual/365 or actual/366 basis; redemption is at par; they are not redeemable prematurely and not callable by the issuer.

Bubills are the Bund's money market securities. They are zero coupon bonds with coupon paid as discount on the par value calculated on an actual/360 basis. New issues come in maturities of six and twelve months. Bubills account for about 5% percent of its total debt portfolio in 2011. On January 8 2012, for the first time since the creation of the Euro, at a six month Bubill sale a negative yield was paid. A total of €3.9 million at an average yield of -0.0122%. In the primary market the monthly issues of six-months Bubills have an initial volume of €5 billion. Also monthly new twelve-months Bubills with an initial volume of €3 billion are issued. These when having a remaining time to maturity of nine months are reopened monthly by €2 billion. In December 2011 there was no reopening of a twelve-months Bubill scheduled. The share of Bubills in the issuance calendar 2011 accounts for about 38%. In the secondary market, the volume of individual Bubills in circulation reaches up to €9 billion Euros. Redemption is at par; they are not redeemable prematurely and not callable by the issuer; the par value/denomination 0.01 Euro.

As of July 2012 there are currently five inflation-linked German Government securities in circulation: two 5-year Federal note and three 10-year Federal bonds. These new financing instruments in 2012 account for over 4% of the Federal Government's debt portfolio and their outstanding volume is €50.5 billion. The issuer's long-term aim is to build up a full curve of real-yield German Government securities. Similarly to the issuance patterns for nominal-yield securities, the strategy in the inflation-linked market is for initial placements in benchmark volumes to be followed by smaller reopenings. The Federal Government also operates on secondary market to support market liquidity in these securities. The Federal Government's issued this first index-linked security in 2006 due to the longer-term expectation of a reduction in interest costs. It was also aimed at broadening the investor base, increasing financing flexibility, and extending the choice of securities offered to investors. Based on prevailing market conditions the Bund will continue the development of its index-linked segment with a quarterly issuance volume in the range of 2 to 3 billion Euros. The timing of new issues is dependent on market conditions and are therefore announced separately to the issuance calendars. Issues in the primary market are placed chiefly by auction.

A comparison of the turnover in real-yield and nominal German Government securities demonstrates that liquidity in inflation-linked instruments has risen continuously since they were first issued. The trading volume during the first half year of 2011 was about €130.5 billion. With the current outstanding volume of inflation linked securities the Bund has a comfortable market depth with sufficient flexibility also in terms of support for secondary market activities.

The German Government meets most of its borrowing requirements through single issues in the primary market. Smaller contributions to its funding are made by the sale of German Government securities in the secondary market that stems from the portions set aside in the auctions as well as some permanent issues distributed to retail customers. The single issues that the Bundesbank plans for the following calendar year are announced at the end of the each year and are placed exclusively by auction. In exceptional cases the German Federal Government uses a banking syndicate to place special funding tools in the primary market. Only members of the Bund Issuance Auction Group can participate in the auctions.

Figure 1.A.1 illustrates composition of debt from 2000 to July 2012.

French Government bonds The composition of French Government debt includes three categories of standardized Government securities: OATs, BTANs and BTFs. These securities, whose nominal value is one Euro, are distinguished by their maturity on issue.

Obligations Assimilables du Trésor (OATs, or Fungible Treasury Bonds) are the Government's long term debt instruments with maturities from seven to fifty years. There are fixed rate and index-linked OATs. Most OATs are fixed-rate bonds redeemable at par on maturity. The floating-rate bonds (TEC 10 OATs) are pegged to the constant 10 year maturity rate) and inflation-indexed bonds (OATi) in relation to the French consumer price index. OATs are auctioned on the first Thursday of each month. Accrued interest is calculated annually on the "exact number of days" basis (ACT/ACT). OATs' principal and coupons are paid on the 25th of the

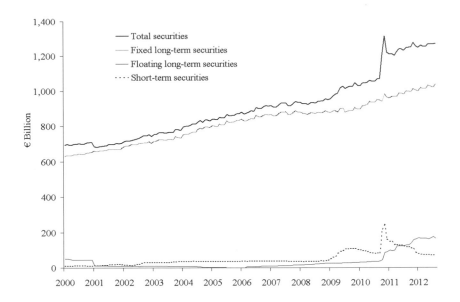

Fig. 1.A.1   Euro-denominated debt securities by maturity: Germany.

month. In October 2001 the State issued an OAT indexed on the Euro
area price index (OATEi). These issues were part of the reduced cost
Governement security management scheme.

Bons du Trésor à intérêts ANnuels (BTANs or negotiable fixed-rate
medium-term Treasury notes with annual interest) represent medium-term
Government debt. On issue, their maturity is either two or five years.
They are auctioned on the third Thursday of each month as part of a semi-
annual calendar published in advance. The Treasury issues at least one line
of BTAN with a maturity of either 2 or 5 years. BTANs are denominated
in units of one Euro. Accrued interest is calculated on the "exact number
of daysexact number of days" basis (ACT/ACT). BTANs principal and
coupons are paid on the 12th of the month.

Bons du Trésor à taux Fixe et à intérêts précomptés (BTFs or negotiable
fixed-rate discount Treasury bills) are the Government's cash management
instruments. They are used to cover short-term fluctuations in the Government's cash position (less than one year), mainly due to differences between
the flows of revenues and expenses and to the schedule of the debt amortization. On issue, BTFs have a maturity of less than one year. They are
auctioned every Monday as part of a quarterly calendar, which specifies
the maturity of the BTFs to be auctioned. Every week, one BTF with a

maturity of 3 months is issued. As applicable, this issue is complemented by semi-annual or annual BTFs. Certain BTFs with maturities from 4 to 7 weeks may be issued outside the calendar if needed for cash management requirements.

The Government debt outstanding in 2011 was of 1,313 billion Euros of which 888 in OATs, 247 in BTANs and 178 in BTFs. Figure 1.A.2 illustrates composition of debt from 2000 to July 2012.

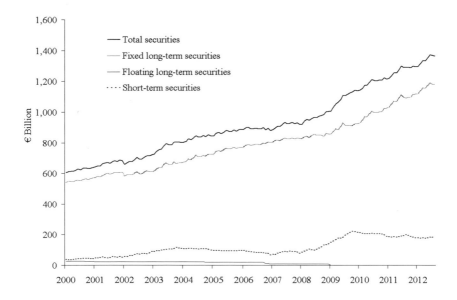

Fig. 1.A.2   Euro-denominated debt securities by maturity: France.

Spanish Government bonds   Spanish Government bonds include Letras del Tesoro (less than 1 year maturity), Bonos y Obligaciones del Estado (3,5, 10, 15, 30 years maturities), Fondtesoros (three types of mutual funds). Letras del Tesoro are the money market instruments for the Spanish Government, they are short term bills issued at a discount for a minimum of 1,000 Euro, are issued with maturities of 6 months, 12 months and 18 months. All interest is paid at maturity and it is computed on an actual/360 basis. Bonos and Obligaciones del Estado (so called Government bonds) are Treasury bills with exactly the same features except for different maturities. The Treasury currently issues bonos with 3 and 5 year maturities and obligaciones with maturities of ten, fifteen and thirty years.

These bonds pay annual coupons. Some Government bond issues are also strippable, that is, the coupons and principal can be separated and traded separately.

The Spanish Treasury issues also Fondtesoros. Fondtesoros are mutual funds that hold most of their assets in Treasury bonds. There are three kinds of Fondtesoros with the main difference among them being the investment policy they are required to follow. Fondtesoros do not distribute returns from the portfolio but reinvest them in the fund itself and are open to all individual investors who can meet the minimum entry investment which may be no more than 300 Euro. Investors can withdraw all or part of their holdings any time they wish by filling out a redemption order to the fund manager which must meet the request within 72 hours. Fees for Fondtesoros are protected by agreement.

There are different tax implications to Spanish Government bonds depending on whether you are resident or non-resident.

At the end of 2011 the total gross debt accounts for €592 billion of which 91 in Letras del tesoro, 148 in medium term Bonos y Obligationes del Estado, 343 in long term Bonos y Obligationes del Estado, 1.2 in other securities. Figure 1.A.3 illustrates composition of debt from 2000 to July 2012.

Italian Government bonds   Italian Government Bonds are issued by the Ministry of the Economy and Finance. There are five different types of Government bonds: Buono Ordinario del Tesoro (BOT less than 1 year maturity), Certificati del tesoro Zero Coupon (CTZ, 2 years maturity), Buoni Poliennali del Tesoro (BTP, 3-30 years maturities), Buoni Poliennali del Tesoro BTP€i note (inflation linked securities), Certificati di Credito del Tesoro (CCT, floating rate notes, 7 years maturity). They are held by both individual investors and institutional investors. In the average portfolio among their holdings, individual Italian households hold about 19% of Italian Government bonds. Tax rates on these bonds for Italians are 12,50%, but foreign holders may be tax exempt.

BOTs are zero coupon bonds with maturities up to 365 days. Standard maturities for these bonds, expressed in days, are three, six and twelve months. The minimum denomination is €1,000. These bonds are sold at discount, with the tax for individual investors taken at the time of purchase.

CTZs, like BOTs, are zero coupon bonds with 24 months maturity, issued with a deep discount and the minimum nominal denomination is €1,000 reedemed at par.

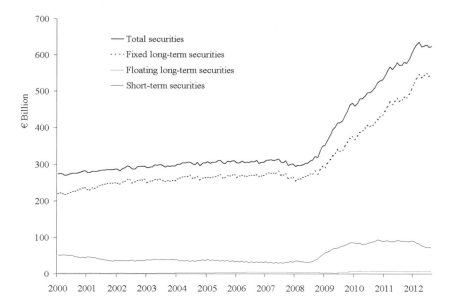

Fig. 1.A.3   Euro-denominated debt securities by maturity: Spain.

BTPs are Italian Treasury bonds, issued with maturities of three, five, ten, fifteen and thirty years. These are straight bonds with semi-annual coupon interest payments with principal repaid at maturity. BTPs have a minimum denomination of 1000 Euro. Some BTP issues are "strippable", that is the principal and the coupons can be separated and the income streams separated as well to meet different investor needs.

Italian Treasury Bonds indexed to Euro-zone inflation are named BTP€i notes. These bonds are issued in maturities of i= five, ten, fifteen and thirty years. They provide investors with steady return in real terms, in terms of purchasing power by providing protection against increases in inflation in the Euro-zone. Individual Italian investors can buy or sell BTP€i notes on the MOT (Mercato Telematico delle Obbligazioni e dei Titoli di Stato), or regulated market for retail investors, for a minimum amount of 1,000 Euro. Principal of the notes and their coupons, payable semi annually, take into account rates of inflation in the Euro-zone as measured by the Eurostat Harmonised Index of Consumer Prices (HICP), excluding tobacco. At the notes' maturity, holders of these bonds are compensated for any loss in purchasing power that has occurred over the term of the notes.

For investors that want a bond with a feature that allows the coupons to adjust to market rates, Italian Government issues CCTs which are Treasury

Certificates, floating rate securities that have a 7 years maturity. Interest is paid with semi annual coupons indexed to the yield of 6 months BOT Treasury bill yield. The difference between nominal value and the issue price accounts for the yield.

Figure 1.A.4 illustrates composition of debt from 2000 to July 2012.

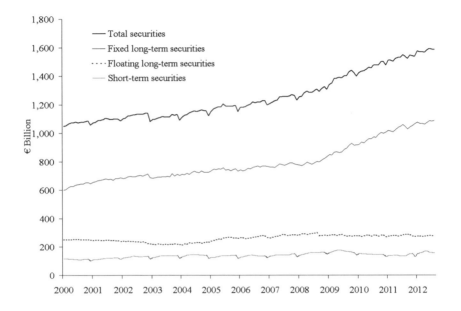

Fig. 1.A.4   Euro-denominated debt securities by maturity: Italy.

The Netherlands Government bonds   Dutch Government bonds include DTC (less than 1 year maturity), DSL (3 to 40 years maturity) and perpetual bonds.

DTC are T-bills issued at discount. This implies issuance at less than 100% of the bill's nominal value, which is redeemed at the end of its maturity. Redemption of T-bills takes place on average 3, 6, 9 or 12 or 24 months after issuance, but maturities in between are possible as well. DTC issues are announced in the quarterly calendar and in press releases. Auctions are held on the first and third Monday of each month. Each auction consists of multiple programs, i.e. maturities. The DSTA uses the Bloomberg Auction System for the auctions.

DSLs cover longer maturities (3, 20, 40) than DTCs. These bonds pay annual coupons and cover maturities up to 40 years.

There are also perpetual bonds with an interest rate of 2.5% paid with half year frequency.

Figure 1.A.5 illustrates composition of debt from 2000 to July 2012.

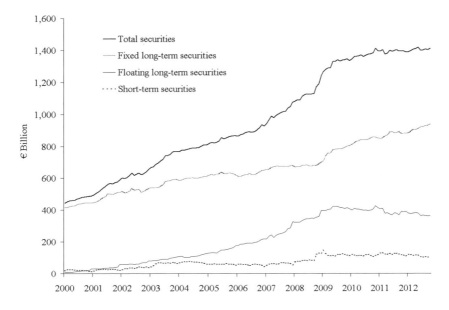

Fig. 1.A.5   Euro-denominated debt securities by maturity: the Netherlands.

The maturity spectrum up to ten years is relatively homogenous in terms of the share of sovereign issuers.   The long-term spectrum varies

Table 1.A.1   Euro area Governement bonds characteristics.

Countries	money market (up to 1 year)	short term bonds	medium term bonds	long term bonds	other type	Central Gov. debt end of 2011 (€ billion)
Germany	3,6,12	2	5	10,30	x	1,329
France	< 1 year	-	2-5	7-50	x	1,405
Spain	< 1 year	-	3,5	10,15,30	x	622
Italy	3,6,12	2	3,5	10,15,30	x	1,794
Finland	< 1 year	-	5-6	10-30	x	86
the Netherlands	< 1 year	2	3	10,20,40	x	353
Austria	< 1 year	-	3,7	10-40	x	198
Greece	1,3,6,12	-	3,5,7	15,20,30	x	n.a.
Portugal	3,6,12	2	3,5	10,15,20	x	181

among the various countries. Only 10-year maturity is offered by all of the six biggest Euro area sovereign issuers as it is shown in Table 1.A.1, which is illustrating the main figures characterising the more relevant Euro area Governement bonds issues. The sixth column refers to other type of issues like commercial paper, saving certificates, private loans, inflation-indexed bonds or variable coupon bonds or other type of bonds which may differ from country to country.

Glossary

BIS Bank of International Settlements

Blue bond A bond, that in case of a country default, will be firstly reimbursed. The blue tranche will correspond to debt up to 60% of GDP.

Collaterized debt Promissory note backed by collateral, security or other compensationin the event of a default by a borrower.

Corporate bond Bond issued by non financial corporation or financial corporation different from monetary financial institution.

Covered bonds Bonds issued by bank, fully collateralised by residential or commercial motgage loans or by loans by public sector institutions.

Credit risk The risk that a counterparty will not settle the full value of an obligation, neither when it becomes due, nor at any time therafter [European Central Bank (glossary)].

CDS Credit Default Swap: special structured derivative to transfer credit risk.

ECB European Central Bank.

EBIT Earning before interests and tax.

EBITDA Earning before interests, tax, depreciation and amortization.

EIB European Investment Bank.

EFF European Financial Fund, the issuer of the new European Union Bond.

EFSF European Financial Stability Facility: a limited liability company established by the Euro area Member States for the purpose of providing loans to Euro area countries in financial difficulties [European Central Bank (glossary)].

EMU European Monetary Union: the outcome of the process laid down in the Treaty establishing the European Community for harmonisation by EU Member States of economic and monetary policies and for introduction of the Euro [European Central Bank (glossary)].

ESCB European Systems of Central Banks, composed of the ECB and the EU national central banks.

ESM European Stability Mechanism: a permanent crisis resolution mechanism for the countries of the Euro area signed on February 2 2012 by an interGovernmental treaty.

Euro area The area encompassing the EU Member States whose currency is the Euro and in which a single monetary policy is conducted under the responsability of the Government Council of the ECB. It currently comprises17 European states: Austria, Belgium, Cyprus, Estonia, Finland, France, Germany, Greece, Ireland, Italy, Luxembourg, Malta, the Netherlands, Portugal, Slovakia, Slovenia, and Spain [European Central Bank (glossary)].

Eurobond Foreign currency denominated bond.

Euro bond (Euro-denominated bond) Bond issued in one of the European member states.

EuroMTS Electronic trading platform

European Redemption Fund It is the fund that could be set up to receive the portion of of the country debt exceeding the 60% ceiling Debt/GDP.

EU European Union.

European Union Bond (EUB) Securitized bond backed by European Central Bank (ECB).

Eurosystem The central banking system of the Euro area.

FSAP Financial Services Action Plans: plan for integration of European financial services.

GBP Great Britain Pound.

General Government A sector defined in ESA 95 as comprising entities that are engaged primarily in the production of non market goods and services. Included are central, regional and local Government authorities as well as social security funds. Excluded are Government-owened entities that conduct commercial operations, such as public enterprises [European Central Bank (glossary)]

GDP Gross Domestic Product.

Interest rate risk The risk that affects the market value of corporate bond when the holder wants to sell it.

Investment-grade bond Bond characterized by high credit quality.

Liquidity risk The risk that the holder of corporate bond faces when he want to sell the bond at a desired price.

Member States A country that is a member of the European Union.

MFI Monetary Financial Institutions: Financial institutions which together form the money-issuing sector of the Euro area; these include the Eurosystem, resident credit institutions (as defined in the EU law) and money market funds, [European Central Bank (glossary)].

Monetary Financial Institution Financial institutions which form the money-issuing sector of Euro zone. Include the Eurosystem, resident credit institutions and money market funds [European Central Bank (glossary)].

Prepayment risk The risk that the issuer may reedem the bond before its maturity.

Speculative-grade bond Bond characterized by low credit quality.

SPV Special Purpose Vehicle: a subsidiary company entity which is used by banks to isolate financial risk.

Sovereign Government Bond Bond issued by central Government.

Sub-Sovereign bond Bond issued by any level of Government below the central Government, which include regions, provinces, municipalities.

References

Afonso, A., Furceri, D., Gomes, P. (2011). Sovereign Credit Ratings and Financial Markets Linkages. Application to European Data, *European Central Bank*, Working Paper Series, **1347**.

Anand, M. R., Gupta, G. L., Dash, R. (2012). The Euro Zone Crisis Its Dimensions and Implications, *REPEC*, Working Paper **4764**, `http://ideas.repec.org/p/ess/wpaper/id4764.html`.

Abaffy, J., Bertocchi, M., Dupačová, J., Giacometti, R., Hušková, M., Moriggia, V. (2003). A Non Parametric Model for Analysis of the Euro Bond Market, *Journal of Economic Dynamics & Control*, **27**, pp. 113–1131.

Budina, N., Kinda, T., Schaechter, A., Weber, A. (2012). Fiscal Transparency, Accountability, and Risk, *International Monetary Fund*, WP/12/273/, November.

Danish Central Bank (2011) Inflation-linked bonds, Ch. 10, in Danish Government Borrowing and Debt, pp. 89–99.

European Central Bank (2004) The Euro Bond Market Study, December.

European Central Bank (2008). Recommendations of the Governing Council of the European Central Bank on the pricing of recapitalisations, November 20.

European Central Bank (2012). Corporate indebtedness in the Euro area, Monthly Bullettin, February, pp. 87–103.

European Central Bank (glossary). All glossary entries, http://www.ecb.int/home/glossary/html/glossg.en.html.

Gallant, P. (2004). *The Eurobond Market Study* (Woodhead-Faulkner Ltd).

Glockler, G. (2009). Euro Area Governance and the Financial Crisis: New Quality or Flash-in-the-pan?, Little, R. Ed., *After the crisis: A new socio-economic settlement for the EU*, Policy Network, London.

Guglielmi, A., Tchibozo, A. (2012). European Banks. *Medio Banca Securities Report*, July 25.

Lojsch, D. H., Rodriguez-Vives, M., Slavik, M. (2011). The Size and Composition of Government Debt in the Euro Area, *European Central Bank*, Occasional Paper Series, **132**, October.

Quaglia, L., Eastwood, R. and Holmes, P. (2009). The Financial Turmoil and EU Policy Cooperation in 2008, *Journal of Common Market Studies*, **47**, pp. 63–87.

Salines, M., Glöckler, G., Truchlewski, Z., del Favero, P. (2011). Beyond the Economics of the Euro. Analysing the Institutional Evolution of EMU 1999-2010, *European Central Bank*, Working Paper Series, **127**.

Chapter 2

The Market Infrastructure

(*Marida Bertocchi, Rita L. D'Ecclesia*)

2.1 Introduction

The pubic sector's role in the financing process is to provide an efficient infrastructure for bond markets guaranteeing an active participation of the private sector. We need to understand the main features and developments of

- the retail markets;
- the electronic markets;
- the clearing and security settlement systems;
- the role of custodians.

The first includes the issuance modality-auction, the underwriting procedure and the captive or mandatory transactions; the second takes into account the bidding modality (remote electronic vs. physical, open vs. primary dealer); while the third deals with the delivery and settlement system (whether a book entry or scriptless settlement exists) [ECB (2004)].

In the context of promoting competition and efficiency in the Euro-denominated bond market the role of custodians - the purchasers and providers of custody services - became a crucial element. Custody is offered by a variety of institutions, as brokers, commercial banks and investment banks, which have developed specialized services that cater to different customer segments.

The creation of an efficient financial infrastructure in Europe required the integration of local and fragmented Member States markets. The most important barriers were represented by inefficiencies in the clearing and

settlement systems. To get an efficient pan-european clearing and settlement system for the EU the various Member States had to intervene
on the divergent technical requirements and market practices, differences
in national tax procedures and differences relating to legal certainty. In
2004 the Commission issued a communication on "Clearing and Settlement
in the European Union- The Way Forward [COM (2004)]" which established three high-level groups to deal with the removal of the market, legal
and fiscal barriers to post-trading: The Clearing and Settlement Advisory
and Monitoring Experts Group (CESAME)[1], the Legal Certainty Group
(LCG)[2] and the Fiscal Compliance Group (FISCO)[3] So after 2004 legislative progress took place to remove these barriers and the Markets in
Financial Instruments Directive (MiFID) was implemented, [COM (2005)].
The Legal Certainty Group provided advices on harmonising legislation
which led to the issuance of the Recommendation on Simplified Withholding Tax Relief Procedures [COM (2009)]. The EC, in close cooperation with
Member States, gave the guidelines to make it easier for investors resident
in one Member State to claim entitlements to relief from withholding tax
on securities income (mainly dividends and interest) received from another
Member State.

2.2   The Retail Markets

Euro-denominated Government bonds are issued mainly through the Primary Issuance Auction, in some countries banks and registered dealers may
also underwrite the issuance. Almost all retail markets use an electronic
platform, so the number of intermediaries operating in markets located in
other countries of the EU have increased after the introduction of the Euro.
However, as most regulated retail markets are multi-product ones, in the
sense that bonds, equities and other securities are listed on the same market, it is not possible to assume that this increase, strictly speaking, is due
to the integration of the bond market. The Exchanges and other trading
platforms are the most visible part of Europe's market infrastructure even
if not all securities are necessarily traded on a trading platform (and are

---

[1]http://ec.europa.eu/internal_market/financial-markets/clearing/cesame/
index_en.htm.
[2]http:
//ec.europa.eu/internal_market/financial-markets/clearing/certainty_en.htm.
[3]http:
//ec.europa.eu/internal_market/financial-markets/clearing/compliance_en.htm.

defined instead as over-the-counter or OTC), and there are a host of complex infrastructures that sit behind the exchanges usually beyond the public's view.

In the corporate Euro bond market retailers have been playing a key role. Since 2008 high stock volatility, weak housing markets, low deposit rates and economic uncertainty caused European retail investors to buy bonds directly, many for the first time. Retail investors include ordinary small investments in bond funds and wealthy individuals buying large amounts of bonds through their private banking brokers. This last kind of investors are new in Europe causing large number of bids coming from a collection of small private banks, some of whom not known to the syndicate desk. Retail investment directly into bonds was relatively common in both Asia and the US, with syndicate banks collecting large orders from retail bank networks and private banks and it had a large increase also in Europe after 2009. At present retail investors provide tremendous support to the market, both primary and secondary with a large increase of deals denominated in 1,000 notes rather than the more typical 50,000 size. A research by the Royal Bank of Scotland has reported that deals denominated in notes worth 1,000 each, rather than the 50,000 size, typically outperform in the secondary market because of the retail bid. However, issuing 1,000-denominated notes makes more work for the issuers who, to meet regulations, have to provide more information because of the likely retail interest.

The financial crisis moved the attention to the role of post-trade infrastructure to the financial markets. This infrastructure has to take into account the trade being made on an exchange and an investor receiving their securities.

2.3 The Electronic Markets

Developments in wholesale markets have been substantial over the last decade. At the end of 1998, most wholesale markets in the European Union were telephone based, with the exception of MTS in Italy and HDAT in Greece. This situation has been reversed as the consequence of a combination of factors. The much broader Euro-denominated market, compared with those of legacy currencies, has led to an increase in the number of parties in almost every segment, and intensified competition within each category. The advantages of telephone trading, such as ex ante knowledge of one's counterparty or the ability to conduct a transaction without it being disclosed to the rest of the market, has been largely reduced. At the same time, the efficiency that can be provided by technological innovation has caused increased competition which led to increased demand.

The Investment Services Directive (ISD), published in 1993, allows authorized intermediaries established in any Member State of the European Union to operate in any other Member State.

For electronic regulated markets, financial intermediaries operate without opening a branch in the country where the market is located. The share of public bonds held by "domestic" investors (investors resident in the same Euro area Member State as the issuer) have declined since the introduction of the Euro. The share held by non-residents as a whole (including non-Euro area residents) has accordingly increased. Where data is available (in particular in Spain and Belgium) it appears that these shifts are largely attributable to purchases by investors from other Euro area countries. Anecdotal evidence provided by institutional investors confirms this trend towards diversification.

The Euro-denominated bond secondary market has been characterized by the growing use of multilateral electronic trading systems, related to their benefits in terms of lower costs, higher liquidity, transparency and easier cross-border trading. While the trend towards more widespread use of technology in the bond market has been reinforced by the introduction of the Euro, this is not a consequence of the single currency per se. Several different patterns of development of wholesale markets have been witnessed in the Euro area. At the end of 2000, the MTS group consisted of 5 national MTS markets (Italy, the Netherlands, France, Belgium and Portugal) as well as the London-based EuroMTS. MTS started out in the late 1990s as Europe's first market mandated to do electronic government bond trading. It remains the dominant platform for many of the market's largest dealer-brokers to trade among themselves, but its technology has begun to lag that of newer technology. MTS supports the full chain of pre-trade, trade execution and post-trade capabilities across cash and repo markets, and also provides independent benchmark market data and comprehensive fixed income indices. Various counterparties use MTS's platforms every day providing high liquidity to the various markets. In 2012 MTS provides the following platforms:

- the MTS Cash, which is the leading electronic market for dealers of fixed income rates products;

- the MTS Repo, an order driven market for electronic transaction of repo agreements and buy/sellbacks;
- the MTS BondVision, the European multi-dealer-to-client electronic market for trading bonds;
- the MTS Credit: the electronic market for non-government bonds;
- the MTS Data Real-time tradable prices for European government, quasi-government and covered bonds;
- MTS Indices: the benchmark for European fixed income - tradable, real-time and independent indices.

In 2012 the European government bond trading market started to trade on a high speed platform. Specific trading technology companies will allow customers to trade euro and non-euro denominated bonds of 17 countries on MTS, which is controlled by the London Stock Exchange and also owned by a group of banks. The penetration of high-frequency trading into fixed income markets has been slowed by large differences between bid and offer prices, higher costs of connectivity and differences in technology. The European Market Infrastructure Regulation (EMIR), is likely to profoundly change the fixed-income market by requiring central clearing and open access to OTC interest rate products.

2.4 The Clearing and Settlement System

Several central counterparty clearing houses already exist in the Euro area and a number of mergers and alliances are currently under consideration or being implemented. Economies of scale and network externalities seem to favour a high degree of concentration. A group of major global investment banks has therefore expressed support for the idea that Europe should only have one central counterparty clearing house, which would be a multi-currency and multi-product (equities, bonds, derivatives and commodities) service.

The Clearing is managed by Central Counterparties (CCPs) which acts as the buyer to the seller and the seller to the buyer, representing so a guarantor of the deal against a default by either party. The CCP absorb the systemic risk and represent a tool to strengthen the financial system.

The settlement of the securities is provided by Central Securities Depositories (CSDs). They are mainly responsible for the transfer of the securities from the seller to the buyer by debiting and crediting their respective electronic accounts in a process known as "Delivery vs. Payment" (DvP). This process is essential for efficiency, eliminating risk from the transaction, and providing proof of ownership.

A recent new infrastructure is represented by the Trade Repositories (TRs), they centrally collect and maintain the records of derivative contracts.

Regulators, CCPs and other market participants will rely on the data maintained by these entities which may also offer associated services such as trade matching, trade confirmation, and portfolio reconciliation or compression.

The Governing Council considers crucial the settlement systems and the securities clearing. For this purpose

(1) The Eurosystem has an interest in central counterparty clearing and considers that it is essential to establish, in co-operation with the other relevant authorities, effective risk management standards.
(2) The natural geographical scope for any domestic market infrastructure (including central counterparty clearing) for securities and derivatives denominated in Euro is the Euro area. Given the potential systemic importance of securities clearing and settlement systems, this infrastructure should be located within the Euro area.
(3) The process of consolidation of central counterparty clearing infrastructure should be driven by the private sector, unless there are clear signs of market failures.
(4) Whatever the final architecture, it is essential that access to facilities for trading, clearing and settlement should not be unfairly impeded. This policy of open and fair access should ensure the safety, legal soundness and efficiency of securities clearing and settlement systems, guarantee a level playing-field, and avoid excessive fragmentation of market liquidity.
(5) The Eurosystem supports co-operation between providers of central counterparty clearing services at a global level and should be involved in monitoring global multi-currencies transactions.

2.4.1 *Post trading costs*

Clearing and Settlement is characterised by tight margins so low costs are critical to achieving efficiency and accessibility. The Commission has published various analysis of the post trading costs in the Euro financial markets over the last decade. Each study tries to measure the impacts of integrating the EU's financial markets from different angles. The last report published in 2011 highlights that:

- Indicative analysis of the value chain conducted in 2011 for funds on their holding and transacting costs shows the distribution as 3 basis points (bp) for safekeeping (to custodians), 11.7bp in commissions (to brokers), and 0.3bp for clearing and settlement (to custodians). This translates as 71% for the broker; 4.5% for the trading platforms; 1% for the CCP; 22% for the custodians and 1.5% for the CSD.
- The prices and costs of using infrastructures have come down between 2009 and 2011.
- Average trade sizes have fallen with the effect of increasing the number of transactions needed to complete the trade.
- The costs of using intermediaries have fallen.
- Investors' portfolios are concentrated in their domestic markets, however, the way in which transactions in securities across borders are traded, cleared, and settled suggests that markets are becoming more integrated.
- The costs of doing a cross-border transaction has fallen, however they have not fallen as fast as domestically and are therefore still proportionately more expensive.

In 2006 the Commission introduced an industry-led Code of Conduct which fostered the harmonisation of Europe's clearing and settlement systems. Few initiatives were introduced:

- **CCBM2** The Collateral Central Bank Management Model aims to make the whole process of mobilising securities to obtain credit at any central bank in the Eurosystem much more fluid and in real time. The abolishment of the repatriation rule (the previous CCBM relied on bonds to be repatriated to the country of issuance each time they were needed to be mobilised. Due to different local rules and services, the costs to the users remained high and while it did not bring the full benefits that it had been expected to bring to the use of collateral in the euro area on a similar basis the use of cash, it was still widely used by counterparties) as well as the introduction of triparty services that are already widely used in bilateral collateralisation transactions in the wholesale markets makes access to and movement of collateral more flexible.

- **Target2** The launch of the Euro currency in 2000 created an urgent need to build a Euro Real Time Gross Settlement (RTGS) system. The short timeframe forced the choice of keeping the 25 existing national systems while interconnecting them using a Eurosystem platform that was called Target. The Eurosystem's central and commercial banks started to work together on a new "Single Shared Platform" called Target2. It is a core component for Euro clearing and settlement secured consolidation and delivers payments facilities to the banking industry as a real time consolidated overview of Euro flows and liquidity. The Target2 system is based on the widely accepted and internationally used SWIFT FIN and XML standards, so it is fully interoperable with other systems and functions. It is open to 700 European direct participants and gives access to more than 4,000 worldwide banks. Even though the relations between the commercial and the central banks remain local, Target2 benefits from a well harmonised contractual framework and a unique set of specifications and rules which makes its uses simple and easy.

- **Target2 Securities** (T2S) In parallel to the Commission's work, the ECB announced plans in 2006 to create a single technical platform, which could settle virtually all securities transactions in Europe. The platform will be operated by the Eurosystem and will provide commoditised and harmonised Delivery versus Payment (DvP) settlement services in Euros as well as other European currencies. T2S will address many of the existing barriers to cross-border securities processing in Europe and it will create a de facto domestic market for the settlement of European securities thanks to a single platform and harmonised services and prices for all participating CSDs. The impact of T2S on harmonisation will be both direct and indirect. Direct, because the development of the platform itself will force harmonisation to take place in those areas related to the core settlement process, and indirect, because T2S can be expected to trigger a virtuous cycle whereby the harmonisation of core processes will create both pressure and incentives to harmonise further aspects such as safekeeping and custody. In terms of its direct impact, T2S will foster harmonisation by replacing current divergent national practices with a single solution. A common settlement platform for European CSDs has the advantage that it involves going from standards agreed on paper to the definition of common processes which will become market practice. In early 2011, a Harmonisation Steering Group (HSG), composed of senior level representatives from the industry and public sector, including the EU Commission, was established in order to support the T2S Advisory Group in formulating and monitoring the T2S harmonisation agenda.

- The MiFID. In 2007 the Markets in Financial Instruments Directive (MiFID) was introduced across the EU. By removing the concentration rules at national exchanges, MiFID had a revolutionary effect in the equities arena. Incumbent exchanges found themselves challenged by new entrants called Multilateral Trading Facilities (MTFs). MTFs enabled competition at the clearing level by employing new entrant CCPs. These new CCPs had pan-European coverage, and were also able to price more competitively and be more innovative than the incumbent CCPs. The combined pricing power of the new MTFs and CCPs was so effective that incumbent exchanges and CCPs lost considerable market share and had to review their pricing models as well as their technology. The lowering of exchange and clearing costs has benefited market participants significantly. UK and Swiss regulators have approved the arrangements between LCH Clearnet and EuroCCP if one CCP fails. This could act as the basis for more interoperable links between exchanges and clearinghouses in these jurisdictions. Falling fees have challenged the profitability of the business models of exchanges and CCPs. There has been some compensation as the number of transactions has gone up considerably since MiFID was introduced because trade sizes have reduced as high frequency trading has increased.

2.4.2 *The current market infrastructure*

The market infrastructures for the equities cash, fixed income markets and derivatives have evolved in Europe pre- and post-MiFID and the Code of Conduct. The Market structures have changed particularly on the level of trading and in the creation of interoperable links between CCPs. The fixed income market in Europe, as described in Chapter 1, is composed of two sectors the government bond market and the corporate bond market, each with its domestic and international component. Each Member State domestic market is supported by domestic infrastructure, (CSDs), which is in the process of adapting to the Eurozone; T2S is a key development here. The international markets based in Europe have long been served by the International Central Securities Depositories (ICSDs), with increasingly efficient links between them. Much government bond trading and most corporate bond trading takes place on a bilateral basis, rather than on multilateral electronic platforms, as does government bond repobusiness (mainly in short term dates). Automated trading is becoming more widespread. The fixed income markets are not independent of other markets; developments in derivatives will influence the shape of the fixed income markets and the infrastructure that serves them. Participants in the market include banks, insurance companies and pension funds, as well as a range of investment managers managing money for a wide variety of funds. In addition to the market for debt securities, fixed income include an important market for secured financing, referred to as the 'repo' (for repurchase) market. Securities are sold subject to an agreement to repurchase them, providing the seller with temporary cash liquidity; the difference between the sale and purchase prices represents a rate of return to the lender. Participants in this market make very specific demands of the market infrastructure which are increasingly being met, but more remains to be done. Fixed income securities, principally, but not only, government bonds, are widely used in the financial system to provide security against the failure by a market participant to perform its obligations ('collateral'). Members of clearing houses (or CCPs) post collateral to the clearing house; banks post collateral to each other in the interbank market; and there are other examples. Collateral needs to move promptly without risk between participants; large sums of money and tight deadlines are involved. The European market infrastructure, with its mixture of domestic and international systems, is not well adapted to this task. Private sector initiatives, such as tri-party repo, have mitigated some difficulties; but considerable legal and operational problems remain. Day-to-day bond settlement is supported by CSDs in national markets. In international markets, in addition, the ICSDs provide a settlement service in domestic bonds for their clients. The chief role of the ICSDs is twofold: first, to settle transactions in the securities for which they act as a CSD (international bonds); and secondly, in providing settlement across systems/borders in various currencies (principally Euro, US Dollar and Sterling). The 'bridge' between the ICSDs permits interoperability between various users in different settlement locations. While this has helped straightforward transactions to settle in a relatively efficient manner, the market for collateral does not yet have a robust and efficient pan-European infrastructure. The ability to transfer collateral cross-border/cross-system needs to be brought up to the same level of efficiency as the transfer of collateral within the same settlement system in order to support an efficient European capital market. A wide range of market participants are affected by the shortcomings of the repo market infrastructure, including investors who make bonds available for repo trades, investors who finance their bond operations in part with borrowed money and the banks and other intermediaries that facilitate this business. The necessary reforms will also have the wider benefit of providing an efficient settlement platform for less demanding users of the market, who are not involved in repo business. Further efficiency gains could arise from continuing to modernise and improve (i) links between CSDs and ICSDs and (ii) the 'bridge' link between the ICSDs. The case for urgent action is reinforced by the wider regulatory reform programme. Initiatives to make banks safer and more liquid, and to encourage banks to lend to other financial institutions on a secured rather than an unsecured basis, for example the reforms of Basle 3/CRD IV for liquidity buffers, demands high quality collateral to support a wide range of financing operations. Given the increasing role of secured financing for payment or collateralisation of all financial market activities, the repo business is often time-critical. While an increasing proportion of repo business is centrally cleared or cleared on a tri-party basis, bilateral settlement remains important, particularly between intermediaries and end investors.

2.5   The Role of Custodians

Custody is provided primarily by brokers, commercial banks, investment banks and other authorized institutions. They developed specialized services directed to different customer segments. Banks were the natural providers of physical safekeeping services as they would usually already have strong vaults for the holding of cash and other valuables taken for deposit, cf. [Benjamin and Yates (2003)]. The scope of their services is

- **settlement**: when securities are bought or sold, the custodian takes care of the delivery and receipt of securities against the agreed amount of cash. This is basically the exchange of securities against funds;
- **asset services**: to ensure that the investor receives what he is entitled to, holding securities in an investor's portfolio attracts benefits, rights and obligations. These services usually fall into several broad categories: collection of dividends interest; corporate actions such as rights issues, re-denominations or corporate reorganizations; payment and/or reclaim of tax; voting at shareholders' meetings by proxy. A custodian plays the role of information intermediary.

Custodian banks have developed economies of scale to provide services to their customers at a price that is less than what the customer would spend, and probably faster and with less operational errors than if the customer were to do the same work itself. In each market, there are usually a number of local custodian banks that provide custody services. When banks provide custody services in multiple markets through one service agreement with customers, they are called global custodian banks.

2.5.1   *The Central Securities Depositories*

In order not to favour any specific custodian bank Central Securities Depositories (CSDs) were set up as market utilities serving all market participants to immobilize the securities certificates for the whole market and to eliminate the physical movements. Nowadays securities exist in physical and electronic form. They are transferred from one holder to another in CSDs by book entry settlement between securities account holders, which are commonly called members or participants. In markets where securities were legally required to be in paper form, enabling legislation needed to be passed to recognize ownership of securities in electronic form and change of legal title via book-entry settlement. As a general rule, one issue of a security is immobilized in one CSD only, as it is the most efficient arrangement. In some markets, investors were given the option to hold physical certificates if they wished, in other markets the entire issue was held by the CSD in electronic form only. The first immobilization of securities in central institutions to facilitate settlement without physical deliveries happened at the end of the 19th century in Germany; these institutions were called Kassenvereine. The CSD in France, the Caisse Centrale de Dépôts et de Virements des Titres (CCDVT), was established in 1942. The majority of the other European CSDs were established in the 1960s onwards. The establishment of CREST in 1996 in the UK finally completed the immobilisation of securities in all the European Union (EU) Member States prior to enlargement in 2004. Investors in some markets, however, still have the option to hold physical securities if they prefer, [Chan et al. (2007)].

The constitution and range of CSD services has become highly diverse in European Member states, but they do share some key common features. They are central service providers established with a common objective, which is to provide the definitive record of ownership and subsequent transfer of title and through immobilisation of securities to facilitate the central settlement of securities without the movement of physical certificates. CSDs are systemically important infrastructures in modern securities markets. They perform crucial services that allow at a minimum the registration, safekeeping, settlement of securities in exchange for cash and efficient processing of securities transactions in financial markets. While securities markets traditionally relied on the physical exchange of paper, CSDs now assume a critical role to guarantee a safe and efficient transfer of securities that exist to a large extent only in book entry form. They have now become a central point of reference for an entire market. Furthermore, being located at the end of the post-trading process, CSDs witness all the settlement fails occurring during the settlement period. They are therefore a key element of any policy of settlement discipline. Given the systemic importance of CSDs and their strategic position at the end of the post-trading process, there is a strong need for an appropriate regulatory framework for CSDs.

The initiative is an important part of the Commission's agenda to enhance the safety and soundness of the financial system. Together with the proposal for a Regulation on OTC derivatives, CCPs and TRs adopted by the European Commission on 15th September 2010 and the Markets in Financial Instruments Directive (MiFID, currently under review), EMIR will form a framework in which systemically important securities infrastructures (trading venues, central counterparties, trade repositories and central securities depositories) are subject to common rules on a European level. The particular importance of CSDs, as the cornerstones of any efficient settlement system, has progressively led to their supervision by national central banks and securities market authorities, which pay considerable attention to the prevention of systemic risk. Supervisors generally require CSDs to manage operational risks with robust mitigation measures and to avoid taking credit risks. Furthermore, where dematerialization was implemented on a broad scale or mandatory basis, CSD activities have been defined and strongly regulated in their role as central safekeepers of dematerialized securities and operators of securities settlement systems.

The immobilization or dematerialization of physical securities in CSDs should, in theory, eliminate the need for any investor to use custodians or brokers to safekeep physical securities. Under immobilization or dematerialization, safekeeping is reduced to a reconciliation activity, whereby the custodian's task is to ensure that its holdings at the CSD are equivalent at all times to the amount of securities owned by its customers. Yet investors continue to use custodians, for several reasons

- Ineligibility: some investors and market participants are not eligible to become a member of the CSD. Some CSDs only want members that are regulated, financially sound, have robust operational capabilities, and have the ability to continuously invest in technology that ensures straight-through processing. These membership criteria are primarily designed to minimize the probability of disruption to a CSD's smooth functioning.
- Intermediation solution: even when investors and market participants could be a direct member of the CSD, they might still decide to buy the services of a custodian with economies of scale and expertise in the procedures of the CSD, market practices and the management of securities holders' rights and entitlements. Intermediation enables a market participant to change fixed overheads into variable costs.

Glossary

CESAME Clearing and Settlement Advisory and Monitoring Experts Group.

CCP Central Counterparty Clearing house: a guarantor of the deal against a default by either party.

CCBM2 Collateral Central Bank Management Model.

CCDVT Caisse Centrale de Dépôts et de Virements des Titres.

CREST Central Securities Depositories for the UK.

CRDIV Capital Requirement Directive IV.

CSD Central Securities Depository.

DvP Delivery versus Payment.

EMIR European Market Infrastracture Regulation.

FISCO Fiscal Compliance Group.

HDAT Hellenic Electronic Market.

HSG Harmonization Steering Group.

ICSD International Central Securities Depository.

ISD Investment Services Directive.

LCG Legal Certainty Group.

MiFID Markets in Financial Instruments Directive.

MTF Multilateral Trading Facilities.

MTS Electronic Market for Securities Trading.

Repo market Market for repurchase agreement.

RTGS Real Time Gross Settlement system.

Target2 "Single Shared Platform" for Euro clearing and settlement secured consolidation and delivers payments facilities to the banking industry.

TRs Trade Repositories, collector of derivative contracts.

T2S Target 2 Securities.

References

Bank for International Settlements (2007). Quarterly Review, March.

Benjamin, J., Yates, M. (2003). *The law of global custody: Legal risk management in securities investment and collateral*, second edition (Butterworths).

Chan, D., Fontan, F., Rosati, S., Russo, D. (2007). The security custody industry, *European Central Bank*, Occasional Paper Series, **68**.

European Central Bank (2004). The Euro Bond Market Study.

European Central Bank (2006). Business continuity oversight expectations for systemically important payment systems (SIPS), June.

COM (2004). Clearing and Settlement in the European Union – The way forward, COM/2004/0312 final, 52004DC0312, *Communication from the Commission to the Council and the European Parliament* (EUR-Lex, Access to European Union law), http://eur-lex.europa.eu/LexUriServ/LexUriServ.do?uri=CELEX:52004DC0312:EN:HTML

COM (2005). Resolution on the Proposal for a Directive of The European Parliament and of the Council of amending Directive 2004/39/EC on markets in financial instruments, as regards certain deadlines, COM(2005)0253, 52005AP0498, *Commission of the European Communities* (EUR-Lex, Access to European Union law), http://eur-lex.europa.eu/LexUriServ/site/en/com/2005/com2005_0253en01.pdf.

COM (2009). Commission Recommendation of 19.10.2009 on withholding tax relief
procedures, COM(2009)7924, http://ec.europa.eu/internal_market/financial-markets/docs/compliance/booklet-simplified_en.pdf.

Russo, D., Rosati, S., Papathanassiou, C., Caviglia, G. (2008). Prudential and oversight requirements for securities settlement: A comparison of CPSS-IOSCO Recommendations with other regulatory regimes, *European Central Bank*, Occasional Paper Series.

Chapter 3

Government Bond Markets

(*Giorgio Consigli*)

3.1 Introduction

Individual European countries have been listing Eurobonds before the introduction of the Euro as the legal currency within the *European Monetary Union* (EMU). Sovereign liabilities were denominated in convertible currencies, primarily USD, and the market size and liquidity was strictly linked to the growth of foreign deposits in the International banking system. Sovereign issuers from Latin America and Central Eastern European Countries had largely used foreign denominated liabilities in USD. The Euro sovereign fixed-income market, from now on and for our purposes the *sovereign bond market*, includes Euro denominated bonds specifically issued and traded since the introduction of the Euro by sovereign borrowers belonging to the Euro area. As we write and over the last two years the sovereign bond market is undergoing a prolonged crisis in various member countries of the EU, whose government bonds show higher yields, and the increasing risk of a few countries is threatening the stability of the currency, [Abad et al. (2009)]. In August 2012 National and International policy makers started a difficult discussion on the establishment, within the Euro area, of a European Stability Mechanism whose explicit aim will be to help Member States with heavy financial and economic problems, likely to affect the very existence of the common currency.

3.2   The Euro Sovereign Bond Market Evolution

Looking at the sovereign debt markets of the Euro area over the past two decades, we can distinguish three main periods; prior to 1999, 1999 to 2008, 2008 to present. The *first*, before 1999, in which the National Monetary Authorities and Governments acted in order to converge towards the German interest rate term structure. The introduction of the Euro in 1999 eased the convergence in the secondary markets of Member States sovereign bond yields. A lack of currency risk together with inflation reduction represent the main sources of stabilization for government bond yields. The common currency and the market of interest-rate securities had to operate in order to foster the convergence between Member States as clearly stated in the 1992 Maastricht treaty, which defined a set of macroeconomic convergence criteria:

(1) Price stability;
(2) Sustainability of public finances (through limits on government borrowing and national debt);
(3) Exchange-rate stability (through participation in the Exchange Rate Mechanism (ERM II));
(4) Long-term interest rate convergence (as indirect signal of economic convergence).

The *second*, ranging from the introduction of the Euro in 1999 to the collapse of Lehman Brothers in September 2008, when government bond yields remained at moderate levels and did not differ much from country to country. During this period the differences between the Euro-economies remained relevant in terms of public finances. The spreads of ten-year government bond yields vis-à-vis German Bunds during this period reach a maximum of about 70 basis points (bps) with an average spread of around 15 bps.

Taking only Euro economies into account it can be easily observed that while the first and fourth criteria have been satisfied, Member States have faced considerable difficulties in satisfying the second criterion.

The absence throughout these years of positive credit spreads on sovereign paper reflected the lack of uncertainty regarding the eventual convergence to equilibrium of Member States. Market expectations were altered dramatically by the September 2008 Lehman Brothers default.

Table 3.1 Government deficit/surplus and Debt-to-GDP ratio for selected countries at the end of 2008.

Country	deficit to GDP	debt to GDP
Austria	-0.9	63.8
Belgium	-1.1	89.2
Finland	+4.3	33.9
France	-3.3	68.2
Greece	-9.8	112.9
Ireland	-7.3	44.5
Italy	-2.7	106.1
Portugal	-3.6	71.7
Spain	-4.5	40.2
the Netherlands	+0.5	58.5

The *third*, after the autumn 2008 until today, when a sudden re-pricing of sovereign credit risk took place and is still ongoing. Government bond yields started to diverge. During the last months of 2012, an unprecedented effort by the ECB in terms of *moral suasion* and the agreement between the Greek government and private creditors reduced market volatility but spread levels remain high for several core EU borrowers such as Italy and Spain.

We analyze the drivers of such a dramatic change of perspective and try to examine the economic outlook in the Euro area. It is worth noting that policy makers and researchers are currently reconsidering several well-established assumptions, dramatically contradicted by the crisis. We refer to the European Central Bank (www.ecb.int) and the EU (europa.eu) websites for a comprehensive set of references on these topics.

The impact of ECB interventions in the sovereign bond market and, conversely, the role of market premiums as signals of forthcoming market turbulence forcing the monetary authority to ease their monetary stance, characterize the recent history of the Euro bond market as a whole. A set of relevant factors which are crucial for fixed income investors in the Euro area:

- Country risk, which affects EU interest rates, sovereign credit spreads and overall financial stability;
- ECB monetary policy, sovereign spreads and economic recovery;
- fixed-income markets and financial risk premia.

3.3 Country Risk

Despite persistent differences in macroeconomic fundamentals of the various countries during the first period, market participants, demonstrated an undifferentiated pricing of government debt securities. The first part of the last decade coincides with the *Great Moderation* period [Stock and Watson (2002)] which experienced with significant success by monetary authorities in their fight against inflation.

Several factors determine sovereign bond yields. The systemic relevance of any credit event affecting a sovereign issuer and the interest of monetary authorities to prevent financial instabilities are key to the analysis. We distinguish between shared and country-specific risk factors.

Among shared factors: the ECB monetary policy, the risk premia in the bond market and global economic uncertainty, [Pericoli and Taboga (2009)]. Economic uncertainty lead to a cooperative effort by international monetary and financial authorities to prevent a systemic crisis and bond yields have discounted the degree of cooperation between the authorities during the crisis. Among country-specific factors we recall idiosyncratic default and liquidity risk variations and the effectiveness of country-specific economic policies (relative to possibly different policy aims).

During the second period, the differences between the countries' public debts were reconciled by the general confidence of EU leaders and financial players in the possibility to comply with EU budget constraints. The global financial crisis that started in 2007 in the US and then spread globally, which lead to a dramatic worsening of liquidity and solvency conditions in the international banking system and to the Lehman Brothers default, is behind the observed dramatic change of market expectations. Following Lehman Brothers default in September 2008, other EU government bond yields start diverging from German bond yields. The divergence affected not only sovereign bonds issued by the *critical* so-called PIIGS countries (Portugal, Ireland, Italy, Greece and Spain) but also bonds issued by virtuous (in terms of public finance) sovereign countries such as Austria, Finland and the Netherlands. Roughly one year after, on October 16, 2009, the Greek Prime Minister George Papandreou in his first parliamentary speech disclosed the country' severe fiscal problems and immediately after on November 5, 2009 the Greek government revealed a revised budget deficit of 12.7% of GDP for 2009, which was double the previous estimate. Over the 2009-2012 period, supra-national and ECB interventions aimed primarily at reducing individual countries' risk exposure and neutralizing contagion effects. Financial markets have been mostly left free to determine sovereign bond prices with the ECB only marginally supporting bond prices in the secondary markets.

The evolution of 10-year government credit spreads for Spain, Portugal, Italy, Ireland and Greece with respect to Germany is shown in Figure 3.1.

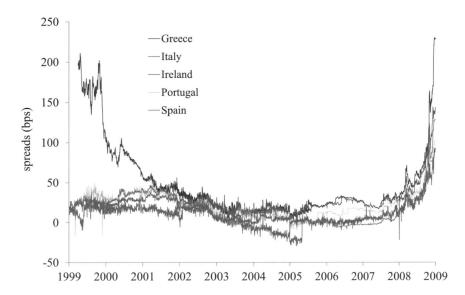

Fig. 3.1   Selected sovereign bond spreads with respect to the 10-year German yield by country.

During the 2001–2008 period, the co-movement of sovereign yields was perfect and 10-year bond yields were positively and perfectly correlated, close to German bond yields. After 2008, an increase in sovereign spreads occurred putting several questions on the agenda of global investors and policy makers. Was the previous spread alignment justified? Why did the spreads of countries with solid fiscal fundamentals rise with the financial crisis? After adjusting for outliers, is the current condition of divergent government spreads natural and consistent with monetary stability in the Euro area?

We try to provide some insights analyzing some key variables:

- the Euro rates term structure, which reflects borrowing default-free conditions in the Euro area. The dynamic of Euro rates term structure is reported in Figure 3.2.

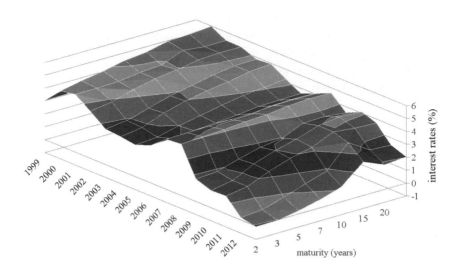

Fig. 3.2   EU interest rates term structure.

- the 5Y-CDS quotes for all EU sovereign issuers and for the European banking sector, as reported in Figure 3.3, [Fontana and Scheicher (2010)]
- a global stress indicator, the Financial Distress Index (FDI), introduced by the ECB in a recent study [Schwaab (2011)] whose dynamic is reported in Figure 3.4.

The three variables show increasing systemic risk, a worsening of default expectations by markets and a smooth easing of monetary conditions in the EU economy since 2008.

The third period is characterized by the sudden and persistent divergence of government spreads as witnessed by figure 3.5.

During 2009, while spreads on Greek, Irish and Portuguese bonds start increasing, short term yields on safe government bonds such as Bunds, decreased significantly reaching 0 at the beginning of 2012. On January 10, 2012, *German yields went south of zero. Investors agreed to pay the German government for the privilege of lending it money. In that auction, Germany sold €3.9 billion ($4.96 billion) of six-month bills that had an average yield of negative 0.0122%, the first time on record that yields at a*

Fig. 3.3   5-year CDS prices on Sovereign and Banking sector liabilities, average estimate.

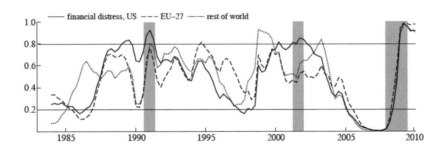

Fig. 3.4   Financial Distress Indicators, from [Schwaab (2011)]. Reproduced after the kind permission of Dr. M. Schwaab and co-authors.

German debt auction moved into negative territory. This means that unlike most other short-term sovereign debt, in which investors expect to be repaid more than they lend, investors agreed to be paid slightly less. And they are willing to do that because they are so worried about the potential for big losses elsewhere. That is particularly the case in Europe, where sovereign-bond markets have been rocked by a years-long crisis. Switzerland and the Netherlands, also seen as relatively safe countries in which to invest, are

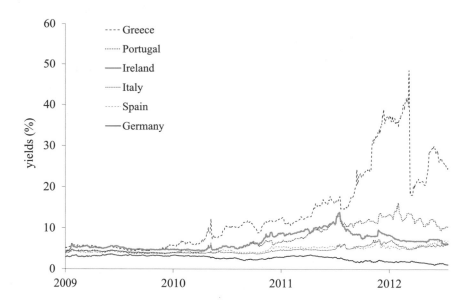

Fig. 3.5   Selected sovereign bond 10-year yields in the Euro area.

among the few that have sold debt with negative yields in recent months as commented the Wall Street journalists Phillips and Bartha.

At the same time the ECB was reducing reference interest rates through a sequence of interventions starting in December 2008 to 2.5%, then in January 2009 to 2%, and in May 2009, after other three interventions, to 1% official rate. A moderate tightening of market conditions occured after that bringing the rate to 1.5% in July 2011, turning to 1% again in December 2011 and then, in June 2012, reaching the historic low of 0.75%.

The unprecedented easing of the ECB rates and of the short term Euro rate, supported by a relatively slower reduction of 10 year and 30 year interest rates demonstrate the systemic degree of the 2008 crisis and aim to support market liquidity and facilitate the economic credit cycle at times of growing difficulties in the overall banking system. The worsening financial stability of the various European countries can be also shown analyzing the *Credit Default Swap* (CDS) spreads, in this period. A detailed description of CDS market is given in Chapter 8.

The average CDS rates on Banking liabilities were already rapidly increasing by the end of 2007, following the signs of a banking crisis emerging from the US, see Figure 3.3. At that time sovereign bonds were still regarded as safe investments. The situation changed dramatically in October

2008 when default premiums on sovereign securities increased to 200 basis points in one week. From then through the end of 2011, sovereign CDS spreads were in line with spreads on banking liabilities.

In Figure 3.4, where we see long-term dynamic of financial distress at the global level [Schwaab (2011)], the positive effects of the Euro on financial stability in the period 1999-2008 is immediately evident as well as the rapid and significant increase of instability and aggregate risk after 2008. Periods of economic recession coincide with the grey areas, and the 80-th and 20-th percentiles of the Financial Distress Index frequency distribution are used to discriminate between periods of financial exuberance and financial distress in the financial sector. The chart makes it easier to understand the degree of global financial stability underlying sovereign bond yields dynamics. From Figures 3.1 and 3.5 it is evident that positive and high correlation between sovereign yields in the Euro area holds during periods of low financial distress. Conversely, their divergence is associated with periods of high financial distress, as measured by ECB FDI. The divergence of spreads after 2008 is based on the global uncertainty affecting market expectations and the growing awareness by investors of the unlikely recovery

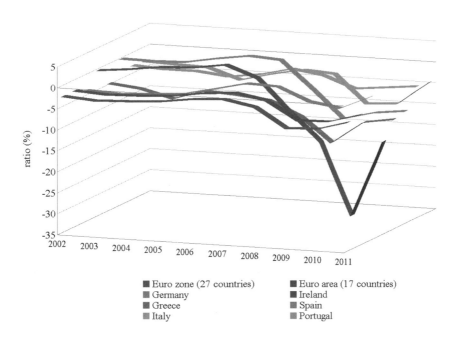

Fig. 3.6   EU Countries deficit/GDP ratios.

of economic and fiscal equilibria within the EU area within any short term horizon.

The 2008 turning point came after several years of financial stability and positive market outlook. The period however witnessed a lack of effective public balance control, required by the EMU treaty. Indeed public deficits and deficit to GDP ratios didn't converge to common policy targets and the diversified budget conditions turned out to be one of the driving factors of growing turbulence in the sovereign bond market over the last four years.

Figure 3.6 shows average deficits to GDP ratios for the EU countries, the EU17 and the six countries. We note the deterioration of deficits over the last five years as well as the progressive worsening of the EU17 economies and the emerging heavy budget disequilibrium for Greece. Sovereign spreads as shown above reflect only partially the country fiscal conditions.

3.4 Bond Spread Dynamics Country-specific Risk

After 2008, sovereign spreads start fluctuating freely: market movements in this phase resemble a fixed exchange rate mechanism which becomes unsustainable, resulting in a sudden divergence of key economic indicators. Financial risk increased globally affecting interest-rate securities in general and sovereign securities in particular. The 10-year spread between the German government-guaranteed KfW (Kreditanstalt fur Wiederaufbau) bond and the German sovereign bond, both carrying the same default risk, became the driver of spread movements on liabilities issued by *virtuous* Countries. During the financial crisis, the German Bund seems to have benefited from the safe haven status, which has historically characterized US Treasuries, the Swiss franc, the Japanese Yen and gold. Before 2008 agents' strategies for Euro government bonds assumed no default risk and were based on arbitrage opportunities and convergence trades along the Euro curve. After 2008, portfolio diversification and speculative strategies occurred in the sovereign bond market. Focusing on the period after the Lehman Brothers default, we can see from Figure 3.5 that until the Greek Prime Minister declaration in October 2009 sovereign spreads decoupled but remained within a relatively tight spread corridor of roughly 150 bps. After October 2009, Greek sovereign yields started diverging dramatically while the other sovereign yields diverged moderately until May 2010. At this point the entire Euro government bond market entered the current crisis.

By August 2012, Greek bonds carried an extremely high default premium and sovereign spreads remained high for Spanish, Italian and Irish goverment bonds in the secondary market. As of today no policy maker envisages a return of borrowing conditions for sovereign issuers to pre-2008 levels. Indeed sovereign spreads fluctuations above the reference 10 year German bund yield are regarded by many as consistent with todays monetary Union and the diverse conditions of public finance among Euro-countries.

The country specific risk factors discounted by investors in the sovereign bond market are associated with

- political risk: as the Greek experience after the 2009 declaration, and the Italian crisis at the end of 2011 have shown, ineffective policy making combined with unstable political scenarios is immediately translated into an inability to pursue safe economic policies and lead to sudden fluctuations of a country's credit stability. A stable political scenario is regarded as a necessary, not sufficient condition for bond yields reduction.
- macroeconomic risk: sovereign bond spreads reflect the economic perspectives, in particular, during negative economic phases. When general macroeconomic conditions deteriorate, sovereign yields are expected to express increasing premiums in anticipation of a foreseeable increasing State budget deficit. As such macroeconomic risk is strictly related to the fiscal condition of the State budget: this is an additional policy tool which, following Maastricht constraints, can be used only by a limited number of countries as of today. Most of the sovereign borrowers who were in financial trouble in 2011 and 2012 were suffering from an inability to undertake expansive fiscal policies.
- credit and default risk: credit events include rating revisions on sovereign issuers and default announcements, [Afonso (2011)]. The latter have not been observed yet but default probabilities expressed by bond prices have been steadily growing for several borrowers. Country downgrading has been reported several times over the last three years and credit spreads have been closely following those announcements.
- liquidity risk: a lack of market liquidity has generated two combined effects. Borrowers over the past two to three years suffered from a lack of market investors and only specific securities have attracted the residual investment power.

Macroeconomic risk and sovereign credit risk are clearly related and in general an improving economic outlook relative to EU peers translates into additional Government borrowing capabilities and reduced credit spreads. Persistent public deficits and high debt-to-GDP ratios, because of the EU fiscal constraints which do not allow expansive fiscal policies, reduce both the likelihood of a positive economic upturn and the deterioration of the Sovereign borrowing costs, related to the increasing risk premiuns demanded by fixed-income investors. Almost all the Countries in economic trouble (Italy, Spain, Portugal, Greece) were in this condition for the last few years. In the absence of internal compensatory fiscal adjustments to promote economic recovery, a positive impact on the market is expected to be brought about by a supra-national guarantee or European "relief" Fund created by EU Countries to support National bailouts and financial efforts. It is worth noting however that the resources to be channeled into the Fund by Member States are meant to inhibit the collapse of the EU rather than represent new resources for investment and development.

Over the last six months the sovereign bond market has probably suffered the deepest crisis of his short history. In June 2012 10-year Greek sovereign bonds were providing on average a 26% yield, Portugeese bonds a 10%, while Spain, Italy, Ireland, Slovenia provided yields 5% above the average European rate. All other sovereign borrowers issued long term bonds at around 2% rate. No issuer however faced the same risk premium in the primary market. Germany 10-year Bunds were issued at the beginning of June at 1.3% interest rate.

3.5   Fixed-income Markets and Financial Risk Premia

The dramatic increase of credit spreads not only in Greece, but also in Italian, Spanish, Portuguese and Irish sovereign securities over 2011-2012 occurred across almost all maturity buckets. Specifically for Italian and Spanish securities, given their relevance in global bond markets, a *moral hazard* issue has been widely recognized by analysts to justify unprecendented credit spread increases. The impact of persistent speculative strategies in sovereign bond markets between November 2011 and May 2012, mainly in short-term debt, has been significant.

The 10-year National benchmark bonds, as of August 24, 2012, in the MTS market, the largest electronic market for Euro area Government securities, are in Table 3.2.

Italy had a 10-year BTP issued in June 2012 with a 5.5% fixed coupon which traded 437 bps above the German Bund. Among major EU

Table 3.2   MTS 10 year benchmark yields for Sovereign issuers in the Eurozone, August 24, 2012.

Issuer	closing yield %	spread wrt Bund (bps)	previous yield %	change
Germany Bund 4 Jul 2022 1,75%	1.36	-	1.33	0.03
Belgium fix rate 28 Mar 2022 4,00%	2.52	117	2.37	0.15
France fix 25 April 2022 3%	2.08	72	2.05	0.03
Italy Treas 1.9.2022 5.5%	5.73	437	5.77	-0.04
Spain Govt 31 Jan 2022 5.85%	6.42	506	6.46	-0.04
Finland 15 April 2021 3.5%	1.54	18	1.51	0.03
Austria 20 Apr 2022 3.65%	2.00	64	1.94	0.06
Denmark 15 Nov 2021 3%	1.08	-28	1.05	0.02
the Netherlands 15 Jul 2022 2.25%	1.76	40	1.73	0.03
Slovenia 18 Jan 2021 4.375%	6.86	550	6.86	0.00
Ireland 18 Oct 2020 5%	6.26	490	6.03	0.23
Czech Rep. 29 Sep 2021 3.85%	2.18	82	2.20	-0.02
Hungary 24 Jun 2022 7%	7.50	614	7.50	0.00
Portugal 15 April 2021 3.85%	9.71	835	9.63	0.08

borrowers a relevant risk premium is required on Spanish bonds (506 bps), while smaller borrowers such as Ireland and Portugal showed a spread over the Bund equal to 490 bps and 835 bps, respectively. The table does not display current conditions in the Greek debt which is presently (September 2012) frozen awaiting future developments at diplomatic levels within the EU.

Table 3.2 shows that as of today financial investors are differentiating their positions across sovereign securities and employing diversified fixed-income strategies when compared to pre-2008 levels. It is interesting to analyze the recent bond yield dynamics of Germany, Spain and Italy. As of today Germany represents the key player in the Euro market. Spain and Italy have been targeted by portfolio managers and investors with heavy and prolonged market selling. It is of further interest to reconsider the dynamics of the 10 to 2 year and 5 to 2 year interest rate spreads to analyse how market expectations have evolved and whether cross-over strategies along the curves might have actually been beneficial to fixed income portfolios within the Euro zone.

Figures 3.7 and 3.8 show further evidence of the stability of the German sovereign yield curve characterised through the 2009-2012 period by low short-term rates and decreasing 10 year and 5 year versus 2 year rate differentials. The 3 month rate as mentioned converges over this period to an unprecedented zero value, consistent with ECB monetary policy.

The dynamic of the Italian and Spanish sovereign yield curves, has been quite different from the German one with high short term rates and very volatile 5 and 10-year yields. Quite interestingly the spreads are highly

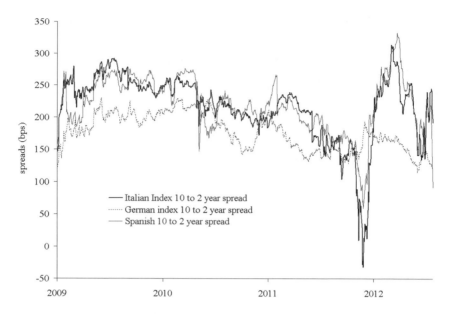

Fig. 3.7   Selected 10 to 2-year sovereign spreads in the Euro bond market.

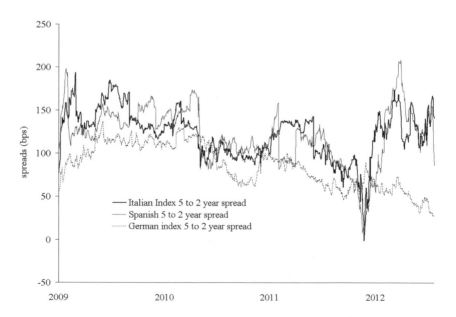

Fig. 3.8   Selected 5 to 2-year sovereign bond spreads.

correlated throughout the period and by the end of 2011, across the political crises suffered by both Countries, short term yields jumped upwards reflecting a sudden increase of market risk premiums. On November 26, 2011 the 2 year BTP reached its historical maximum yield to maturity of 7.61% due to the deepening political crisis in Italy. The election of a new Government restored market stability and led to a record reduction in the 2 year yield of more than 3% in a month. However the fixed income markets still showed high volatility for most of 2011. In 2012 speculative strategies have exploited the spread between German and Italian or Spanish sovereign yields. The Italian and Spanish bond market during the severe 2011-2012 crisis have shown co-movements of both their respective yield curves and their slopes.

The key elements of the sovereign debt crisis experienced by the Euro area over the last three years have been, [De Santis (2012)]:

- diversified risk pricing across Sovereign bonds for different maturities;
- persistence of a common, nondiversifiable, risk premium component due to global uncertainty and a lack of effective cooperative exit-strategies (from the current severe crisis) between National governments;
- relevant macroeconomic risks specifically in those Countries of the Eurozone characterized by extremely weak credit cycles and heavily constrained fiscal manoeuvres: most Governments, whose liabilities are currently discounting high risk premia, are inhibited by external EU rules from pursuing expansionary fiscal policies to stimulate economic growth;
- growing dependence of selected sovereign spread movements on, often simultaneous, rating revisions and negative watches reported by the S&P, Moodys and Fitch Agencies.

After the period of stability brought about by the convergence to the Euro which lasted until 2008, in the last two years markets have started to discount different default premia on several Sovereign securities which are not caused by relevant idiosyncratic risk factors. Thanks to the ECB policy easing in the Euro area the sovereign market has preserved a sufficient degree of overall liquidity and the current key role in the recovery of stable market perspectives can be attributed to the reversal of the negative economic outlook in several core EU Countries. The final establishment of an effective ESM should facilitate the removal of a speculative moral-hazard effect in the Euro bond market.

3.6   Sovereign Risk and ECB Policy

Growing systemic risk and the remarkable effort to rebalance high Debt-to-GDP ratios by several EU countries have enormously increased the importance of ECB monetary interventions in the Euro area. Market participants expectations and their confidence in the stability of the currency are crucial to a change in the sovereign bond market scenario as well. It is important to analyse the widely discussed role played by the ECB in the stabilization of the sovereign bond market. Between 2011 and 2012 the support given by the ECB to the European banking system amounted to roughly €1 trillion. In addition through the so-called *bond buying* program channelled by the *European Financial Stability Facility* (EFSF), the central bank has intervened in both the Italian and Spanish sovereign bond primary markets.

We consider three channels through which government bond markets affect the transmission of monetary policy:

- Government bonds as essentially risk-free instruments, provide a transmission channel for current and expected policy rate revisions resulting in shifts in the government bond yield curve. Changes in long-term bond yields are recognized to provide driving factors for banks' lending rates and corporate cost of capital, facilitating a smooth transmission of monetary policy. The post-2008 increase of sovereign yields volatility has deeply affected the proper functioning of the interest rate channel, jeoparadising an effective transmission of monetary policy signals to the real economy.

- Strong price declines of sovereign bonds cause losses in investors portfolio and a negative wealth with consequences on their wealth and consumptions causing economic recession. Under these circumstances monetary easing by the ECB may prove ineffective for economies like Italy and Spain where household portfolios are mainly concentrated in sovereign bonds. At the same time, the joint effect of monetary easing and sovereign spreads reduction will reinforce positive wealth effects in virtuous Countries, thereby consolidating yield differentials in the Euro area.

- Sovereign bonds historically represented a relevant source of collateral refinancing for the banking system and a core asset class in banks' balance sheets. The observed re-pricing of government debt since 2008 has had a direct negative impact on banks' riskiness with respect to the evolving Basle regulatory framework. The adoption of risk-based capitalization measures at a time of increasing sovereign spreads impedes resolving the crisis in the Euro area. On the one hand, rising sovereign credit risk affects banks' credit risk via their exposure to government debt. On the other, a fragile banking sector may increase the cost faced by governments. This can in turn become a major obstacle to granting loans to the real economy and an incentive to economic recovery.

Going back to figures 3.1 and 3.5, the Countries characterised by high risk premia on their sovereign debt also didn't benefit from the recent ECB monetary stance, confirming the poor functioning of the described monetary channels. The remarkable increase in sovereign yields across 2011-2012 and the persistent efforts of national authorities to restore economic confidence have so far not been able to cause a market reversal for troubled sovereign borrowers, calling indirectly for new types of intervention by the ECB. With the exception of Greece, we can identify some common factors underlying the vicious cycle faced by Italian and Spanish policy makers:

- increasing interest rates in the primary market and budget refinancing costs,
- lack of economic growth and severe public finance re-equilibrium policies,
- banking sector undercapitalization and insufficient credit flows to the economy,
- negative wealth effects on household portfolios and individual consumption.

The large risk premia for Italian and Spanish bonds are strongly related to the uncertainty affecting the speed and timing of an unsure economic recovery and the re-establishement of effective transmission channels for monetary policy. A lack of effective transmission of ECB policies combined with a lack of internal degree of freedoms due to fiscal constraints appear to be at the core of the markets current instability and high risk premia.

At the end of 2012, the persistant global uncertainty and a base rate at 0.75% brought the ECB to consider unprecedented measures to restore market confidence.

The options currently in place to reverse the sovereign debt crisis are as follows:

- The ECB has already cut interest rates to a record low, bought €211.5 billion of troubled Euro zone governments' bonds and has loosened its collateral rules. The main idea under consideration (in September 2012) was to re-activate the bond-buying programme for Spain and Italy in tandem with the Euro zone's rescue funds. Supporting Spain would entail a negotiated agreement stipulating fiscal targets and economic reform conditions. A depreciation of the euro's exchange rate is also likely to carry a positive effect for peripheral countries such as Portugal and Italy, which compete with China in sectors such as textiles, shoes and furniture. The Euro slipped from around $1.50 to just above the $1.20 level last seen when the sovereign debt crisis erupted in early 2010. Any move by the ECB to weaken the exchange rate would however jeopardise the relationship with the the the U.S. Federal Reserve and the Bank of Japan. The ECB confirmed the intention to be a market counterparty for troubled sovereign issuers, emulating the U.S. Federal Reserve and the Bank of England Quantitative Easing policies.

- The most radical option for the ECB would be to create money to buy debt across the Euro zone without sterilising the purchases. When the ECB did buy PIIGS bonds, a programme which had been suspended since March 2012, it insisted that for each extra Euro created, a Euro was withdrawn from circulation by taking in interest-bearing deposits from banks. Insiders say that if the ECB used such an operation to buy debt from all Euro area countries, there would be no accusations of financing individual governments. A risk of deflation could facilitate the ECB quantitative easing, and some policymakers think that in extremis the Bundesbank could go along with such a policy (so long as it did not involve buying government bonds).

We complete this analysis by considering two possible future scenarios ahead for the Euro sovereign bond market:

(1) The eventual return to the pre-2008 situation with sovereign bond yields closely reflecting the Euro benchmark curve dynamics and acting as a unique asset class.
(2) The current condition of diversified interest rates across Euro sovereign liabilities considered consistent with the normal functioning of the monetary union.

Prior to 2008, markets were accustomed to regard all sovereign liabilities in the Euro area as equally risk free and safe investments, essentially fungible with one another and no risk premia were considered. Rating Agencies and market experts all supported this condition, regarded as natural within

Table 3.3   Selected sovereign issuers rating revisions, Fitch August, 2012.

Sovereign	revision/assessment date	long term rating	outlook
France	16.12.2011	AAA	negative
	21.09.2000	AAA	stable
Germany	21.09.2000	AAA	stable
Greece	17.5.2012	CCC	
	13.3.2012	B	stable
	22.2.2012	C	
	13.7.2011	CCC	
	20.5.2011	B+	negative
	14.1.2011	BB+	negative
	9.4.2010	BBB	negative
Ireland	27.1.2012	BBB+	negative
	9.12.2010	BBB+	stable
	6.10.2010	A+	negative
Italy	27.1.2012	A	negative
	16.12.2011	A+	negative
	7.10.2011	A+	negative
	19.10.2006	AA	stable
Portugal	24.11.2011	BB+	negative
	1.4.2011	BBB	negative
	23.12.2010	A+	negative
	3.9.2009	AA	negative
Spain	7.12.2012	BBB	negative
	27.1.2012	A	negative
	16.12.2011	AA	negative
	7.10.2011	AA	negative
	4.3.2011	AA+	negative
	28.3.2010	AA+	stable

the monetary union. Indeed political instabilities, weak economic policies within EMU countries, diverging fiscal deficits, and so on, had no impact at all on sovereign bond prices. After 2008 everything changed and markets were left free to *speak* and in particular while we still have one Euro benchmark yield curve core Euro countries experience different borrowing conditions in the market and carry a quite dispersed credit risk assessment. In Table 3.3 we report the rating histories taken from Fitch at the end of August 2012 for a few selected sovereign borrowers in the Euro zone.

As of September 2012, rating outlooks remain uncertain and rather spread out across Countries. Leaving Greece aside, Spanish and Italian sovereign yields are still affecting the bond prices' volatility.

There is however a general consensus among EU policy makers that with the recovery of a positive economic outlook and effective adjustment policies by troubled country governments, EU sovereign spreads will start converging again and the pre-crisis condition will be recovered. Scenario 1 is still regarded as the natural scenario for government bonds traded within a currency union and driven by a unique monetary authority. The time it may take to return to such a state is uncertain however! Persistent divergence of public debt service costs, associated with structural bond yield differentials, is likely to jeopardise the currency stability. As of today scenario 1 can be regarded as a likely long-term scenario, while several factors contribute to look at Scenario 2 as the one which will characterize the next one to two years, with some positive effects as well.

Throughout 2013 we can expect the market to be primariliy driven by policy announcements and investors largely maintaining a short-term planning horizon. In this scenario, political accountability and strong National leadership appear key to the implementation of effective economic policies which may lead to more stable investment decisions and lower yields volatility, by restoring market confidence. The persistence of Country specific credit spreads within the government bond market appears desirable for two reasons: to allow the market to convey short and long term expectations for sovereign borrowing forward conditions and to provide a clear signal to policy makers of the likely effectiveness of their interventions.

Glossary

Bond Rating A grade given to bonds that indicates their credit quality. Private independent rating services such as Standard & Poor's, Moody's and Fitch provide these evaluations of a bond issuer's financial strength, or its the ability to pay a bond's principal and interest in a timely fashion.

Country risk The term is sometime used to indicate a collection of risks associated with investing in a foreign country. These risks include political risk, exchange rate risk, economic risk, sovereign risk and transfer risk, which is the risk of capital being locked up or frozen by government action.

Credit spread The spread between Treasury securities and non-Treasury securities that are identical in all respects except for quality rating. The difference between yields on treasuries and those on single A-rated industrial bonds. A company must offer a higher return on their bonds because their credit is worse than the government's.

Default premium The additional amount a borrower must pay to compensate the lender for assuming default risk. A default premium is generally paid by all companies or borrowers indirectly, through the rate at which they must repay their obligation.

Exchange Rate Mechanism An exchange rate mechanism is based on the concept of fixed currency exchange rate margins. However, there is variability of the currency exchange rates within the confines of the upper and lower end of the margins. This currency exchange rate mechanism is also commonly called a semi-pegged currency system.

FDI Financial Distress Indicator, introduced by ECB to compare distress in the different part of the world.

Monetary policy channels The process through which monetary policy decisions impact on an economy in general and the price level in particular is known as the monetary policy transmission mechanism. The individual links through which monetary policy impulses proceed are known as transmission channels.

Moral hazard In economic theory, a moral hazard is a situation where a party will have a tendency to take risks because the costs that could incur will not be felt by the party taking the risk. In other words, it is a tendency to be more willing to take a risk, knowing that the potential costs or burdens of taking such risk will be borne, in whole or in part, by others. A moral hazard may occur where the actions of one party may change to the detriment of another after a financial transaction has taken place.

Risk premium The return in excess of the risk-free rate of return that an investment is expected to yield. An asset's risk premium is a form of compensation for investors who tolerate the extra risk - compared to that of a risk-free asset - in a given investment.

References

Abad, P., Chuliá, H., Gómez-Puig, M. (2009). EMU and European Government Bond, *European Central Bank*, Working paper, **1079**, August.

Afonso, A., Furceri, D., Gomes, P. (2011). Sovereign credit ratings and financial markets linkages. Application to European data, *European central bank*, Working paper series, **1347**, June.

De Santis, R. A. (2012). The Euro area sovereign debt crisis. *European Central bank*, Working paper series, **1419**, February.

European Central Bank (2009). Financial integration in Europe, Report, February.

European Central Bank (2011). Annual Report 2010.

Fontana, A., Scheicher, M. (2010). An analysis of Euro area sovereign CDS and their relationship with government bonds, *European central bank*, Working paper series, **1271**, December.

Pericoli, M., Taboga, M. (2009). Bond risk premia, macroeconomic fundamentals and the exchange rate, *Bank of Italy*, Working paper, **699**, January.

Schwaab, M., Koopman, S. J., Lucas, A. (2011). Systemic risk diagnostics. Coincident indicators and early warning signals, *European central bank*, Working paper series, **1327**, April.

Stock, J., Watson, M. (2002). Has the business cycle changed and why?, *NBER Macroeconomics Annual*.

Chapter 4

The Corporate Bond Market

(Giorgio Consigli)

4.1 Introduction

The most significant change in Euro-area financial markets after the introduction of the Euro currency has been the growth of the corporate bond
market. Prior to the introduction of the Euro, the outstanding notional of
domestic debt securities issued in the Euro area by corporations was about
USD 200 billion. The US dollar was by far the most important currency
for non-financial corporations in international bond markets. About two
thirds of the total issued volume was denominated in US dollars. After
1999 the Euro became the most important currency for issuing bonds by
non-financial corporations. Approximately 45% of the total volume issued
has been denominated in Euro since its introduction. The notional of international debt securities was about $130 billion in 1998 for Euro firms
and $115 billion for non-Euro firms.

The monetary unification and elimination of foreign exchange risks created an integrated pan-European bond market that provided an important
alternative to traditional bank loans. In the late 1990s, the de-regulation
of important economic (e.g. telecommunication and energy) sectors led to
increased borrowing requirements by large corporations to finance investments and acquisitions. At the same time, bank loans became more expensive due to tighter regulation of European banks.

In the wake of the comprehensive liberalization of capital transactions
and the subsequent introduction of the single currency, the European financial system has thus experienced an unprecedented transformation, most
notably impacting the corporate bond market.

The corporate bond market amounts to 55% of the total Euro area GDP in early 2010, compared to only 6% in 1999. By comparison, US corporate bonds reached approximately 100% of the GDP in the first quarter of 2010 according to the BIS statistics.

4.2   Recent Evolution

The corporate bond market has experienced two distinct periods:

(1) a market expansion prior to the recent financial crisis;
(2) the *deleveraging* phenomenon observed in the EU and in the US after 2009 and during the last three years: the growth of corporate liabilities was heavily affected by the credit cycle deterioration, see [ECB (2012)].

Before 2009 the remarkable growth of the market of Euro-denominated corporate bonds has been determined by several, direct or indirect, factors. Among direct factors are:

- the introduction of the common currency at the beginning of the 1999;
- the parallel and unprecedented growth of the credit derivative market;
- the increasing relevance of Credit Rating Agencies (CRA) as providers of credit reports and studies;
- increased demand for liabilities by institutional investors.

The adoption of the Euro acted as a *one-time* elimination of currency risk within the Euro area for liability issuers and investors and had a positive impact on corporations' liability management *per se* enhancing significantly markets' integration within the currency area.

The increasing use of credit derivatives allowed an efficient risk transfer across market participants, providing investors with a tool to mitigate the risk embedded in corporate bonds, facilitating an expansion of the investment base.

CRA had been playing a significant role to determine not only the value but also the marketability of corporate liabilities.

Institutional investors, mainly pension funds and insurance companies, having long-term obligations, had to match their assets and liabilities, so, to a large extent, they became committed to investing in government and corporate bonds.

Indirect factors can be:

- the EU Stability and Growth Pact requiring that the governments of EU countries reduce government debt;
- a move away from equities by market participants, which was spurred by the decline in most European economies and bad experiences with Internet/IT type;
- a change in bank behavior. In the aftermath of the Internet bubble in 2000, banks tightened their lending policies to protect against corporate defaults. They became quite reluctant to provide corporate loans and instead preferred bonds.

The role played by increasing equity volatility and negative risk premiums during the first period being the key determinants of individual and institutional investors preference for fixed-income securities has been confirmed by several authors, see [Mehra (2008)]. Similarly during the second period the observed, to a certain extent regulatory-driven, risk aversion and pro-cyclical behaviour of financial intermediaries in the credit market has facilitated the interest of corporate borrowers for market liabilities. After 2009 corporations have been encouraged to decrease significantly the duration of their liabilities despite unprecedented low interest rates in the market, as shown in Fig. 4.1.

As shown in Fig. 4.2 the amount of bank loans as part of corporate financing has been growing steadily until 2008, after that a steady decrease occurred until the first quarter of 2010, [Bris (2011)]. Thanks to an aggressive ECB policy, bank loans started to increase again even if largely below expectations, during early 2011. At the same time the corporate bond market experienced an above-average growth.Non-financial corporate debt includes loans (excluding inter-company loans), debt securities issued by non-financial corporations and accessing own pension fund reserves of non-financial corporations.

The role played by market liabilities as economic drivers, and the sustainability of an increasing leverage from a market perspective can be assessed by looking at the corporate Debt-to-GDP ratio and the debt-to-financial assets ratio. The sharp increase in the Euro area of non-financial corporate debt, with a Debt-to-GDP ratio of 55% in the first quarter of 1999 and of 79% at the end of 2009, reflects a build-up of corporate debt over different phases. Prior to 2002 the non-financial corporate Debt-to GDP ratios increased due to the leverage of the dot.com phenomenon. After 2002

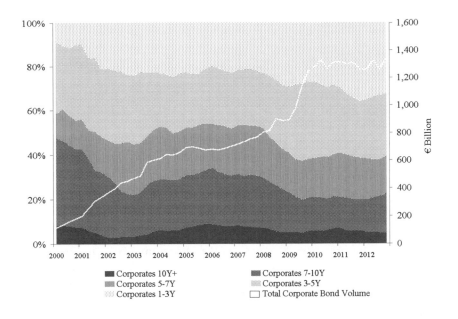

Fig. 4.1   European corporate bond market by duration (line in billions and area in %).

a period of stability and economic expansion followed, which started to deteriorate in 2006 to end in 2009 when the deleveraging period has started again within an overall negative economic cycle.

The various debt indicators for non-financial corporations over the entire decade results very heterogeneous in the Euro area, see Fig. 4.3. In Germany non-financial corporations have shown the lowest Debt-to-GDP ratio among the five largest Euro area countries since 2004. By contrast, in Spain the ratio was considerably above the Euro area level for most of the period under review. In all countries, non-financial corporations debt ratios started to decline in the second quarter of 2009, reflecting Euro area economic conditions.

The debt-to-financial assets ratio, see Fig. 4.4, is defined as loans, debt securities and insurance technical reserves (the non-financial corporations debt) to inter-company loans, shares and other securities, accounts receivables and short therm currency and deposits (the financial assets). The ratio provides a generic measure of the degree of leverage of the corporate sector and its increases denote the exposure to economic cycles, borrowing conditions and growing credit risk at aggregate level.

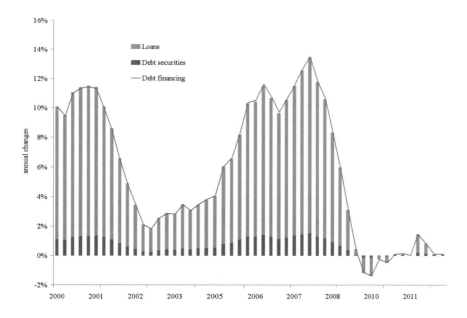

Fig. 4.2   Debt financing growth of non financial corporations in the Euro area.

Most of the debt ratios of Euro area non-financial corporations peaked in the course of 2009 and ease during 2011, when some stabilisation effects finally appeared. This reflects the impact of the business cycle and non-financial corporations efforts to deleverage in an environment of increased sensitivity towards credit risks. The rise in the debt-financial assets ratios was generally more moderate than that in the ratios of debt to economic activity. This shows that the rise in non-financial corporations indebtedness was backed to a large extent by an increase in assets, which can be used as collateral and allowed firms to take up more debt. At the same time, the rise in indebtedness relative to firm income raises concerns regarding corporate debt sustainability.

The strong decline in economic activity in 2008 and 2009 led to a fall in the demand for credit due to lower capital formation and less need for working capital and a decline in the accumulation of corporate market debt. This is also evident from the ongoing bank lending survey conducted by the European Central Bank [ECB (2012)] in which participating banks reported a decline after 2009 in net demand for enterprises loans.[1]

---

[1]See http://www.ecb.int/stats/money/surveys/lend/html/index.en.html.

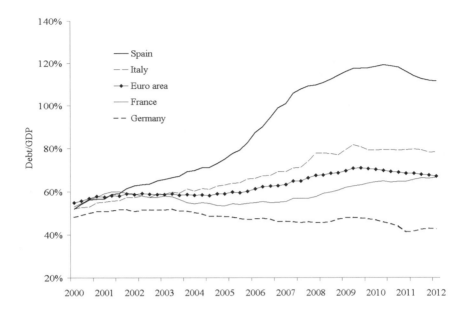

Fig. 4.3 Debt-to-GDP ratio of non financial corporations in selected Euro area countries.

Before the financial crisis, the increased firms debt levels received limited attention as the cost of financing was moderate. During the financial crisis banks did not have easy access to funding due to increased costs and to balance sheet concerns.

According to the ECB study on credit policies across the Euro area, a tightening of credit standards on loans to enterprises, primarily due to cost of funds and balance sheet constraints occurred. During the same period, a substantial proportion of banks reported a widening of margins on loans. Similarly the cost of debt securities financing (for non-financial corporations) rose in 2008 in the context of increasing market concerns about the creditworthiness of borrowers. As a reaction to such developments in bank lending and market-based debt financing, and to the cyclical decline in demand for external financing, firms have increased their efforts to deleverage to improve their creditworthiness.

Debt deleveraging by non-financial corporations can also be seen from developments in real debt financing growth and real GDP growth [Buchmann (2011)]. In 2008 and 2009 the real debt financing growth of non-financial corporations declined markedly and turned negative from the

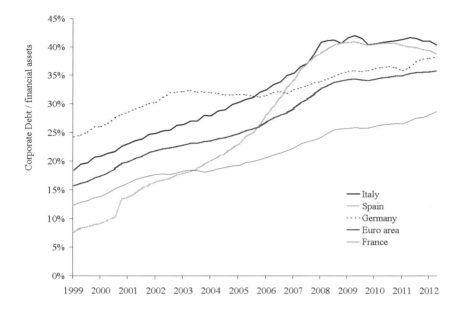

Fig. 4.4   Corporate debt to financial assets ratio in selected Euro area countries.

fourth quarter of 2009 until the first quarter of 2011. This was helped by the internal funds accumulated in the years before the crisis. From the third quarter of 2009 to the second quarter of 2010 non-financial corporations markedly increased their retained earnings. Corporate saving remained broadly stable in relation to GDP from that time until the second quarter of 2011. This led, in combination with declining capital formation, to the narrowing of the ratio of net lending (+)/net borrowing (−) to GDP, which even turned temporarily into a surplus (from the fourth quarter of 2009 to the fourth quarter of 2010).

Euro-denominated corporate bond market experienced few economic and financial cycles, which can be analyzed studying the Iboxx corporate bond total return indices.

4.3   Euro-corporate Bond Indices

Relying on slightly different information sets we analyse the return dynamics in the corporate bond market first over the 1999-2012 period, then more specifically focusing on the 2003-2012 period. The comparative analysis

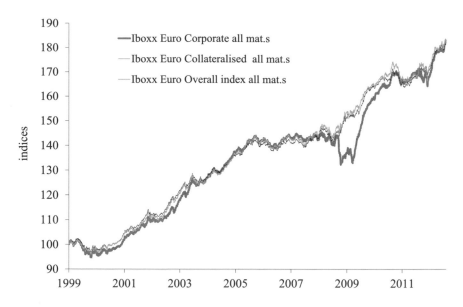

Fig. 4.5   Iboxx corporate bond indices.

helps clarifying the relationship between the corporate bond market and the global fixed income market. The following Markit Iboxx Euro total return indices (TRI) are considered:[2] the *Corporate TRI* (CORP) for all maturities (mat.s), the TRI *collateralized* (COLL) all mat.s, the overall TRI all mat.s (INT), the TRI *high yield* (HY) fixed rate, the TRI *covered* (COV) 1-10 year maturity. All indices in the Markit family include liquid bonds and are rebalanced monthly. The COLL index includes only corporate bonds with a collateral and thus with a protection relative to CORP. The cost of the collateral however, net of default events will reduce the expected return of the index. The growth of the corporate bond primary market, is reflected into the dynamics of the three indices CORP, COLL and INT shown in Fig. 4.5 at least up to mid-2007. During the Autumn of 2007, the market started showing an increasing volatility, resulting in a significant drop in September 2008 and eventually the recovery found by mid 2009. The recovery turned out to be sufficient to close the gap with the overall index and the collateralized around the end of 2010.

---

[2]Cf.   www.markit.com/en/products/data/indices/bond-indices/iboxx/benchmark-indices page.

Table 4.1 Distribution of European debt issuers by rating (year-end figures)

Rating	1985	1990	1995	2000	2005	2010
Aaa	59%	26%	11%	6%	5%	4%
Aa	12%	45%	34%	28%	22%	14%
A	22%	23%	42%	35%	33%	27%
Baa	2%	4%	7%	14%	18%	25%
Ba	2%	1%	3%	5%	8%	10%
B	23%	1%	3%	10%	10%	14%
Caa-C	0%	0%	0%	2%	3%	6%
Inv-grade	96%	98%	94%	82%	79%	70%
Spec-grade	4%	2%	6%	18%	21%	30%
No of issuers	49	231	543	1048	1365	1179

Two major points specifically associated with the last five years can be pointed out:

- the increasing role played within the corporate bond index by high-yield bonds;
- the overall reduction of the average durations reflecting the contraction of investors' planning horizons.

For the *first point*, as shown in Fig. 4.6, the evolution of the high-yield segment relative to the Euro corporate index is reported (the first is rebased to 100 at the beginning of January 2003). High yild bonds, in roughly four years, gains more than 70% (from 2003 to 2007) before falling back to a six-year low and then gaining 10% at the beginning of 2009. After May 2009 the market shows a remarkable rebound with an 80% total return between the second half of 2009 and the first quarter of 2010. Since the advent of the Euro, the market share of speculative-grade companies has increased constantly, as reported in Moody's 2011 report. From a long term perspective, without taking the debt currency into account, an increase from a 4% market share in 1985 to 30% market share in 2010 is shown in Table 4.1. After the introduction of the Euro the relative increase of the high yield segment has been more pronounced.

Speculative grade corporate securities after the 2009-2010 market recovery experienced a period of highly volatile dynamics due to the persisting weak economic conditions and the increase of corporate defaults registered in this period. The Iboxx bond indices market performance is primarily linked to the dynamics of the underlying risk factors. We refer to [Taboga

(2009); Aussenegg (2011)] for a discussion on the key drivers of corporate spreads. Here it is worth recalling that yields of investment-grade as well as speculative-grade corporate bonds are determined by the joint movement of the term structure of interest rates and the rating class by specific credit spreads. Individual securities may depend in addition on specific idyosincratic risk factors related to the overall economic sector, liquidity and other factors.

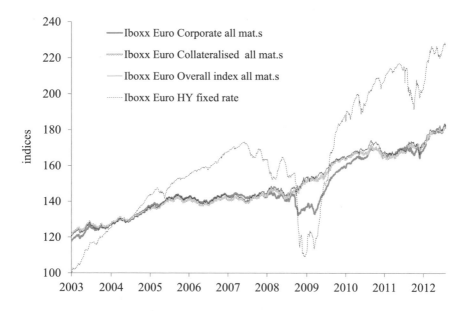

Fig. 4.6   Iboxx investment and speculative grade indices.

For the *second point* from above, the reduction in corporate debt, consider Table 4.2, with a particular focus on the most relevant corporate bond markets in the Euro area.

Within this market framework, Fig. 4.7 shows the behaviour of aggregate corporate credit spreads for different rating classes relative to government yields as computed from Barclays aggregate yield to redemption Indices.

The pronounced departure of speculative-grade from investment-grade yields during the 2007-2009 period reflects the increasing number of defaults in this market during the crisis.

Table 4.2   Average maturity (years) of corporate bond debt in selected Euro area countries.

Issuers Country	1999-2007	2008	2009	2010	2011
Germany	4.7	5.1	5.9	5.0	4.8
Spain	7.3	10.1	8.0	6.2	9.0
France	6.3	6.7	7.5	9.2	8.3
Italy	8.5	8.8	8.9	8.3	7.3
the Netherlands	7.6	9.7	8.3	8.6	8.7
Portugal	7.5	7.2	7.8	7.8	7.0

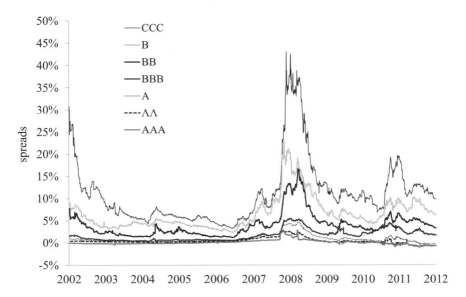

Fig. 4.7   Credit spreads by rating class (Barclays Euro Aggregate yield-to-redemption to Government index).

After June 2007 Euro denominated spreads for CCC securities never went back to the 2004-2007 levels and in the second half of 2011 up to 2012, speculative-grade spreads almost reached defaultable levels.

Credit spreads analysis by rating class can be further qualified by considering the current dynamics of short-term interest rates and the associated movement of the triple A class securities. Since 2007 interest rates in the Euro area have reached historically low levels and the ECB showing the expected negative correlation between credit spread and short-term interest rates.

At the same time systemic risk in the economy has increased (see the systemic stress indicator in Chap. 3) after 2007 and the AAA spread curve on short maturities increased showing a regime switch over the 2008-2009 period. The phenomenon is representative of an overall increase of default events in the corporate bond markets during the last three years. Due to increasing sovereign risk, in 2009, a period of negative AAA corporate spreads relative to Government yields is reported.

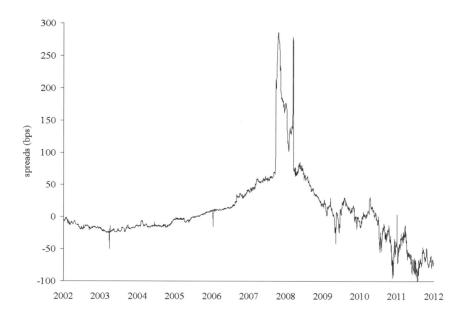

Fig. 4.8 AAA credit spread (Barclays Euro Aggregate AAA corporate yield-to-redemption to Government index).

The 1.5% floor on AAA corporate spreads observed since 2009, is also representative of an overall increase in default events in the corporate bond market over the last three to four years. At the same time it conveys the economic uncertainty of the Euro economy and a required market compensation for increasing systemic risk. Corporate bond yields are well known in finance and risk theory to be driven by several factors:

(1) the interest rates term structure dynamics which provide the fundamental pricing kernel in the economy and determines the lowest cost of borrowing across maturities at any point in time;

(2) the rating stability: within both investment-grade and speculative-grade sectors bond yields share a common risk factor specific to the class and then carry an idiosyncratic risk which may depend on the economic sector, the business climate, the geographic region and so forth;

(3) the default and recovery rate announcements by rating agencies and monetary or financial institutions;

(4) the corporate earnings and fundamentals across the economy and the specific sectors which largely determine market participants strategies and their investment choices;

(5) the bond's liquidity and the market phase.

Corporate bond spreads reflect the demand of risk premiums by market participants due to any of the above factors. The interdependence between rating announcements, specifically in case of rating downgrades, and spread movements has increased over time also in consideration of the growing frequency of company outlooks and *rating watches* published by rating agencies in recent years. Credit spread movements tend to anticipate public and private information sources and are influenced after they become available. As shown in the methodological note here below, the relationship between the default statistics published by rating agencies and the expected losses extracted from corporate bond yields is not straightforward, since default probabilities implied out from market prices differ from default statistics published by CRA.

4.3.1 *Bond indices and default probabilities*

Following the ongoing BIS revision of risk management rules across OECD countries, credit risk assessment is based over the canonical 1 year risk horizon on the estimation of expected and unexpected losses on the credit portfolio. It is sufficient here to focus on the concept of expected credit losses to clarify the dependence of corporate bond indices on credit spreads and default probabilities.

For the sake of simplicity let us consider the price of a discount risk-free bond, $p_{0,T}$ at time 0 for maturity T. Under continuous compounding, the current price of a bond paying €1 at T is determined by $p_{0,T} = 1 \cdot e^{-r_{0,T}T}$ where $r_{0,T}$ is the interest rate quoted on the money market. For default free securities, this is equivalent to $p_{0,T} = 1 \cdot e^{-r_{0,T}T} \cdot Q(\tau > T)$ where τ is a random time associated with a credit event (e.g. rating transition including defaults) and $Q(\tau > T)$ is the probability of observing such event after the maturity T. Intuitively for risk-free bonds we have that the survival probability $Q(\tau > T) = 1$. In presence of credit risk the survival probability is below 1. For corporate bonds, the price $v_{0,T}$ may be lower than the price of a risk-free bond $p_{0,T}$ traded at 0 with the same maturity T and $v_{0,T} = e^{-r_{0,T}T} \cdot [Q(\tau > T) + \beta Q(\tau \leq T)$. Here $Q(\tau \leq T)$ is the probability to observe a credit event before the maturity and β reflects the impact of such event on the corporate bond price, namely *Recovery Rate* (RR), the value of the bond recovered in case of a credit event. Bond market prices allow to estimate the default probability for each given RR and specific maturity. The expected loss from holding the risky corporate bond is then determined per unit bond by the product of the default probability and the complement to one of the recovery rate (e.g. loss-given-default). The probability to observe a default, $Q(\tau \leq T)$, conditional on survival up to t is also referred to as *default intensity* or *hazard rate*.

Credit spreads for different maturities are adopted by credit analysts as proxies for the default intensities, relying on the above simple relationships. Default intensities actually reported in the economic system may differ from the above market implied estimates, since they reflect other risk factors and typically depend on the market phase. In general credit spread quotes in the corporate bond market, particularly at an aggregate level (for all securities within a certain market area) reflect investment strategies and tend to anticipate the changes occurring in the rating assigned to each company by the CRA. It is important to distinguish between the ex-post defualt probabilities published published by CRA from the ex-ante implied probabilities derived by market prices.

4.4   Moody's 2011 Global Credit Report

The credit report published by Moody's at the end of 2011 provides important information for the analysis of rating assessment and default events from 1985 until 2011. It evaluates at a global level the consequences of the crisis of the last five years. Corporate bond spreads and prices are heavily affected by default news.

For the first time after two years of constant deterioration, the credit quality of Moody's-rated European debt issuers improved in 2010-011. The primary driver was the significant reduction of rating downgrades, which have been only 163 in 2010 while had been 516 in 2009. The upgrade-

Table 4.3   Issuer-weighted average RR, 1985-First half of 2011.

Security class	Europe	North America
Senior secured bonds	44.27%	52.68%
Senior unsecured bonds	28.99%	37.44%
Senior subordinated bonds	34.33%	30.43%
Subordinated bonds	31.21%	30.42%

to-downgrade ratio remains, however, low at 0.25 in 2010 and 0.33 in the first half of 2011. The European speculative-grade default rate has declined during 2010 and we expect it will stay relatively low after the 2009 peak. In the study Moody's provides a forecast for the 2012-2013 years, according to which default intensities are again expected to increase in both Europe and in the U.S. Default intensities published by CRA, related to historical information, are known to generally depend on the economic cycle and they barely reflect the implied credit risk information contained in market prices of Credit Default Swap (CDS) spreads.

Market returns in Fig. 4.6 are determined by the fluctuation of credit spreads which incorporate both default intensities and Recovery Rates. On average over the 1985-2011 period credit loss rates remain very low for investment grade borrowers and high for speculative grade borrowers.

After the 2008-2010 period, the credit loss estimates remained above 10% for Caa-C rated corporations. Table 4.3 shows the weighted average RR for different kind of bonds estimated using *post-default* prices.[3] The post-default recovery prices are adopted by financial intermediaries and credit institutions to assess the expected losses on their credit portfolios affecting their capital requirements and tolerance of risk.

During the last three to five years the increasing share of speculative-grade bonds within the corporate bond universe led to a reduction in historical RR both in Europe and in the US. At the same time the default intensity reached an unprecedented high of 11.2% in 2009. The annual default rate was determined in particular by a 2.6% default rate for Caa-C rated borrowers (both financial and non-financial firms). In 2009 the credit derivative market experience a liquidity reduction affecting credit risk hedging more and had a negative impact on bond prices, [Biais (2006)]. The figures in Table 4.3 provide a direct link between the bond and credit mar-

---

[3]Post-default prices are estimated using 30-day post-default bid prices on rated and unrated defaulted debt.

Table 4.4   Moody's 1-year default rate forecasts by economic sector

Industry	Europe	U.S.
Media: Advertising, printing and publishing	7.4%	2.0%
Services: Business	3.5%	1.7%
Telecommunications	1.8%	1.2%
Containers, packaging	1.5%	2.7%
Retail	0.9%	1.5%
Hotel, Leisure	0.6%	3%
Construction and building	0.4%	1.2%

kets. A reduction of corporate spreads to the pre-2008 state depends on the economic cycle rebound.

The sectors that have been mostly affected by the crisis are reported in Table 4.4 where a sample of the one-year default forecasts by Moody's is reported.

The affected sectors are cyclical sectors, whose business and profit generation is typically and heavily affected by negative economic cycles. The different default rates in Europe versus the US reflect the structure of the two economic areas. It must be said however that anti-cyclical sectors that should have benefited from the weak cycle did not actually do so. The non-cyclical are the ones that produce or distribute goods and services that should not be affected by a crisis: food, power, water and gas. Utilities are a classical example.

The dependence on the economic cycle will in general result into bond price dynamics tracking to a certain extent the economy. Non-cyclical sectors will instead be reflected into price dynamics which will not depend on the economic phase. Between 2009 and 2011 such stylized evidence also did not actually materialize and we have observed growing market volatility and very bad market performances also on non-cyclical or even anti-cyclical securities. In 2011, Moody's reports a reduction of defaults occurred and the emergence of rather weak but positive spread dynamics in several sectors, including utilities, real estate, renewable energy, which anticipate a possible positive market rebound and the end of an extended period of deleveraging.

Following the recent market experience and the challenge of well-established claims by credit analysts in global corporation, a set of evidences can be summarized on the relationship between the corporate bond market and the default and transition statistics published by Moody's. Namely:

- yield dynamics in the corporate bond market have been shown to depend primarily on foreseeable default intensities at times of negative economic cycles and widespread economic weakness, while liquidity risk and sector specific factors become more relevant in normal times;
- credit spreads are correctly interpreted as leading indicators of future corporate troubles, either resulting in default events or just in negative transitions towards lower grades. Recent market experience shows that default probabilities are increasingly associated to growing borrowing costs and increasing leverage;
- over the last five years corporate yields, not just speculative-grade, have suffered from a significant increase in global systemic risk, reflecting an increase of *non-diversifiable* risk;
- the historically high correlation existing between short-term spreads of different rating classes securities has been slightly reduced during the recent crisis, but remains consistent with the observed (increasing) downgrade-to-upgrade ratios published by Moodys (the one reported in the last five years);
- corporate spread volatility is heavily dependent on default forecasts and expectations on the economic cycle and appears correlated with market stocks volatility.

The current (Fall 2012) debate on the economic recovery in the Euro area has been linked to the necessary reduction of the public debt by several sovereign borrowers and specifically Spain and Italy as major bond issuers in the Euro market. As discussed in Chap. 3 this appears to be a condition for recovering a more efficient allocation of economic resources and, relevant to the topic discussed here, it is necessary to allow a reduction of corporate bond spreads. As of today the dynamics of the corporate bond market suffer from the underlying condition of relatively high systemic risk, which is primarily determined by the persistent sovereign debt crisis in the Euro area.

Glossary

CRA Credit Rating Agencies: companies that assign credit ratings for issuers of financial assets, often used to finance a type of debt.
Credit risk The risk of loss of principal or loss of a financial reward

stemming from a borrower's failure to repay a loan or otherwise meet a contractual obligation. Investors are compensated for assuming credit risk by way of interest payments from the borrower or issuer of a debt obligation. Credit risk is closely tied to the potential return of an investment, the most notable being that the yields on bonds correlate strongly to their perceived credit risk.

CDS Credit Default Swap: a derivative instrument able to transfer and hedge the default risk.

Default intensity The instantaneous rate of default is called the default intensity or, to borrow a word from insurance, the hazard rate.

High-yield bonds A high paying bond with a lower credit rating than investment-grade corporate bonds, Treasury bonds and municipal bonds. Because of the higher risk of default, these bonds pay a higher yield than investment grade bonds. Based on the two main credit rating agencies, high-yield bonds carry a rating below 'BBB' from S&P, and below 'Baa' from Moody's. Bonds with ratings at or above these levels are considered investment grade. Credit ratings can be as low as 'D' (currently in default), and most bonds with 'C' ratings or lower carry a high risk of default.

Loss Given Default The amount of funds that is lost by a bank or other financial institution when a borrower defaults on a loan. There are several methods for calculating the loss given default, but the most frequently used method compares actual total losses to the total potential exposure at the time of default.

Recovery Rate Amount recovered through foreclosure or bankruptcy procedures in event of a default, expressed as a percentage of face value.

Term structure of credit spreads The credit spread is the spread between Treasury securities and non-Treasury securities that are identical in all respects except for quality rating. Credit spreads across different maturities define a term structure of credit spreads. If constructed relying on credit-risky (namely corporate) bonds belonging to different rating classes, those are also referred to as credit curves (one for each rating class) in the corporate bond market.

Yield curve The relationship between yields on fixed income securities in the market and their maturity. Different contracts, from interbank contracts to swaps and fixed income securities of up to

30 years maybe used to define the current yield curve, which will provide the reference set of interest rates across the economy.

References

Aussenegg, W., Goetz, L., Jelic, R. (2011). Common factors in the performance of European corporate bonds – evidence before and after the crisis, *University of Vienna , Department of Finance and Corporate control*, Working Paper series, October.

Biais, B., Declerck, F., Dow, J., Portes, R., von Thadden, E-L. (2006). European corporate bond markets: transparency, liquidity, efficiency. *CEPR Research Report* (The Corporation of London, Centre for Economic Policy Research), May.

Bris, A., Koskinen, Y., Nilsson, M. (2011). The Euro and corporate financing, *Bank of Finland*, Research Discussion Papers, *6/2011*.

Buchmann, M. (2011). Corporate bond spreads and real activity in the Euro area, *European Central Bank*, Working paper series, **1286**, January.

European Central Bank (2012). Corporate Indebteness in the Euro area, Monthly Bullettin, February.

Laganá, M., Peřina, M., von Köppen-Mertes, I., Persaud, A. (2006). Implications for liquidity from innovation and transparency in the European corporate bond market, *European Central Bank*, Occasional Paper, **50**, August.

Mehra, R. (ed.) (2008). *The equity risk premium* (North-Holland, Elsevier B.V.).

Moody's Investors Service (2011). European corporate default and recovery rates, *Moody's Investor service*, Special Comment, *1985-1H*, November.

Taboga, M. (2009). The riskiness of corporate bonds, *Bank of Italy*, Temi di Discussione/Working papers, **730**, October.

Chapter 5

Credit Rating Agencies

(*Rita L. D'Ecclesia, Vittorio Moriggia*)

5.1 Introduction

Credit Rating Agencies (CRAs) assess the risk of most issuers and issues, they evaluate the ability of a borrower, such as corporation, state or city government to repay its debt in full and on time. This is estimated to be a \$16 billion financial information, data and analytics market and there is also \$1.25 trillion of directly indexed to Standard & Poor's. Their risk assessments have an enormous influence on countries' and companies' borrowing costs, so it is important to understand their role and how they may influence the markets.

CRAs publish in-depth overviews of many sectors, e.g., industrial enterprises, structured financing, sovereign nations, sub-national governments, public utilities, banks, insurance companies, mutual funds, and project financings, along with general obligation bonds and revenue bonds issued by institutions such as U.S. municipalities. On their websites they offer public ratings on issuers free of charge, operating under the *issuer-pays* model. This may be an enormous conflict. They release, under subscription, additional ratings to only those parties who have subscribed to the rating service, distinguishing *Investor-pays* model, also known as "subscriber-pays", and the *public-utility* model, also known as "government" model.

CRAs stress that their ratings constitute opinions, their rating are not a recommendation to buy, sell or hold a security and do not address the suitability of an investment for an investor. Ratings have an impact on issuers via various regulatory schemes by influencing the conditions and the costs under which they access debt markets. Regulators have given to CRAs much of the responsibility for assessing debt risk. For investors, ratings are a screening tool that influences the composition of their portfolios as well as their investment decisions, [Elkhoury (2008)].

After 1997 Asian crisis the CRAs have played a critical role in the financial markets, where a financial discipline of credit risk management had been introduced. The default of Asian Blue Chip companies defaulted on major financial obligations in 1997 and of the implosion of the US two major companies, Enron and Worldcom in 2001, followed by other defaults in Europe, Cirio in 2002 and Parmalat in 2003, caused a major change in the role played by CRAs.

The Financial Crisis Inquiry Commission (FCIC, nicknamed the Angelides, the ten-member commission appointed by the United States government with the goal of investigating the causes of recent financial crises, in 2011) stated: "CRAs were key enablers of the financial meltdown. The mortgage-related securities at the heart of the crisis could not have been marketed and sold without their seal of approval. Investors relied on them, often blindly. In some cases, they were obliged to use them, or regulatory capital standards were hinged on them. This crisis could not have happened without the Rating Agencies. Their ratings helped the market soar and their downgrades through 2007 and 2008 wreaked havoc across markets and firms", [US Government Printing Office (2011)].

5.2   The CRAs

The main business of Credit Rating Agencies during the 20th century was to perform analyses and issue opinions regarding the creditworthiness of companies (*corporate* rating) and governments (*sovereign*). Over the last few decades these companies have provided ratings for a wide range of increasingly complex financial debt instruments, so-called structured finance products including Commercial Mortgage Backed Securities (CMBS), Asset Backed Securities, (ABS) and so forth. The ratings only give an indication of the soundness of the company at a given point in time and must therefore be periodically reviewed and updated to take account of recent developments.

The three biggest CRAs are Standard & Poor's (S&P), Moody's Investor Service and Fitch. S&P and Moody's are US-based, while Fitch is dual-headquartered in New York and London, and is 50% controlled by the France-based FIMALAC (Financière Marc de Lacharrière, a French holding company) and by Hearst Corporation. S&P was founded by Henty Varnum Poor in 1860 and, nowadays, is owned by McGraw-Hill. It has offices in 23 countries, 10,000 employees and carries out assessments in 128 countries. Moody's was founded by John Moody in 1909 starting to analyze the railroad stocks and bonds, it has offices in 28 countries and accounts for 6,700 employees providing ratings in 110 countries. Fitch was founded by John Knowles Fitch in 1913, has 50 offices worldwide and 2,000 employees assessing in 100 countries. In 1924 Fitch introduced the now familiar AAA to D ratings scale.

In 2001, Moody's and S&P market share was around 40% each, and Fitch's market share was around 15%; the Big Three held 95% of the market. In 2012, S&P's market share rose to 45%, Moody's to 38% and Fitch to 13%, still covering 95% of the entire market. The dominance of Moody's and S&P, is often underestimated, debt issuers aim is to obtain ratings from Moody's and S&P, and only occasionally turn to Fitch, in the event Moody's and S&P disagree.

From the mid 1990s until early 2003, the Big Three were the only "Nationally Recognized Statistical Rating Organizations (NRSROs)" in the United States (four other NRSROs merged with Fitch during the 1990s). A new CRA emerged on the international finance scene, Dagon Global Credit Rating Co. Ltd. founded in 1994 upon the joint approval of the People's Bank of China and the former State Economic & Trade Commission of the People's Republic of China. It has given the US debt a credit rating of A+ since 2010, roughly equivalent to Spain and is not recognized by the Securities and Exchange Commission (SEC) that cannot regulate it. Dagong in Mandarin means impartial and without prejudice.

In 2009 the first independent NSNRO Rating Agency was founded by Julius Kroll, the Kroll Bond Rating Agency. It aimed to establish new standards for assessing risk and offers accurate, clear and transparent ratings. The Kroll Bond Ratings is 40%-owned by pension funds and foundations, providing a built-in safeguard against conflicts of interest. It has provided accurate rating criteria for Commercial Mortgage Backed Securities becoming the third ranked agency in this sector after Moody's and Fitch.

CRAs thus contribute to solving principal agent problems by helping lenders "pierce the fog of asymmetric information that surrounds lending relationships and help borrowers emerge from that same fog."[1] In the US the SEC acts as a real supervisor of CRAs' activities promoting competi-

---

[1]Cf. [Elkhoury (2008)], p. 2, and references in it.

tion and monitoring conflicts of interest. Using credit ratings to regulate financial service entities is common in the US, where was introduced in the 1930s. These regulations not only affect banks but also insurers, pension funds, mutual funds and brokers by restricting or prohibiting their purchase of bonds with "low" ratings, [Elkhoury (2008)]. However, the SEC's authority does not extend to regulating the substance of the credit ratings or the procedures and methodologies that CRAs use to determine those ratings.

In EU regulation for CRAs' conduct was introduced on December 7, 2010 to replace previous European Directive operated by the Committee of European Securities Regulators (CESR).

5.2.1   *The role of CRAs*

Credit Rating Agencies play a vital role in global securities and banking markets: they issue creditworthiness opinions, called *ratings*, that help to overcome the information asymmetry that exists between those issuing debt instruments and those investing in them. They have to provide ratings which are independent, objective and of the highest possible quality, [COM (2011)].

The role of CRAs, according to the Communication [COM (2006)] of the EU Commission on Credit Rating Agencies, is important for two reasons: "First, although credit ratings are based on complex assessments they can be easily and instantly assimilated by investors regardless of their expertise and profile. Second, CRAs enjoy a good reputation and are seen by market participants to be providing unbiased data analysis." When a CRA downgrades a country's credit rating, it becomes more expensive for it to borrow money and more difficult to reduce its debts. The higher borrowing costs will also affect the services offered to ordinary citizens.

In Autumn 2008 the European Commission presented its first policy response in relation to the role that CRAs had played in the emerging financial crisis, [COM (2008)]. During the 2010's sovereign debt crisis again CRAs had playing a major role and, as the FCIC indicated, they were often seen as the ones who had fostered the crisis. In January 2012 nine Euro area countries were downgraded by S&P causing large speculative activity and huge increase of bond yields differentials among countries. On January 16, 2013 a new law was approved by the European Parliament to attempt to reduce investors' over-reliance on external credit ratings of sovereign debt, address conflicts of interest in agency activities and increase transparency and competition in the sector. The law set new rules on when and how CRAs may rate state debts and private firms' financial health. Agencies are allowed to issue unsolicited sovereign debt ratings only on set dates and now private investors may sue them for negligence. Sovereign debt rating can be published at least two but no more than three times a year, on dates published by the rating agency at the end of the previous year. Furthermore, these ratings can be published only after markets in the EU have closed and at least one hour before they reopen.

The European law aims to make ratings more clear by requiring Agencies to explain the key factors underlying them. Ratings must not seek to influence state policies and the Agencies themselves must not advocate any policy changes. To reduce over-reliance on ratings, credit institutions and investment firms must develop their own risk assessments. The European Commission is also considering the development of a European creditworthiness assessment scheme.

The new rules apply to all CRAs conducting business in the EU, reduce the conflicts of interest introducing a limit on CRA's shareholders in order to make them accountable for the ratings they provide. Agencies' shareholders with 10% or more of the capital or voting rights will not be allowed to hold 10% or more of a rated entity. They will also be prevented from owning 5% or more of the capital or voting rights in more than one Agency unless the Agencies involved belong to the same group. Investors or share issuers will be able to claim damages for ratings that prove to be ill-founded and harm their interests.

5.2.2 *Credit ratings*

A credit rating consolidates a large variety of information that needs to be known about the creditworthiness of the security's issuer. It takes into account the history of borrowing and repayment, as well as the availability of assets and the extent of liabilities. The credit rating is obtained using qualitative, quantitative and non public information for a company or government.

Credit ratings are not based on mathematical formulas, but on the analyst's judgment and experience to assess the creditworthiness of a particular company or government. The credit rating is crucial when buying bonds issued by companies and governments to determine the likelihood that the borrower (government or company) will pay its obligations. A poor credit rating indicates that the company or government has a high risk of default.

Credit ratings are provided for Corporations, Sovereigns and Short-Term maturity debt. The Sovereign credit rating refers to a sovereign entity, i.e., a national government and indicates the risk level of the investing environment of a country. It accounts for political risk and economic risk.

Euromoney's bi-annual country risk index monitors the political and economic stability of 185 sovereign countries. They focus foremost on economics, specifically sovereign default risk and/or payment default risk for exporters ("trade credit" risk). The ten least-risky countries for investment, out of the 185 assessed, as of June 2012, are reported in Table 5.1.

Table 5.1   Ten least-risky countries.

Country	Rank	Previous	Overall Score
Norway	1	1	90.37
Switzerland	2	2	88.83
Singapore	3	3	88.03
Luxembourg	4	5	87.90
Sweden	5	4	86.79
Finland1	6	5	84.30
Canada A2	7	7	84.26
Denmark	8	8	83.52
the Netherlands	9	9	83.07
Germany	10	7	82.24

Short-Term rating refers to the probability of an individual going into default within a year. Short-Term ratings are commonly used: the Basel II agreement, for instance, requires banks to report their 1-year default probability if they applied an internal-ratings-based approach for capital requirements. Many institutional investors can easily manage their credit/bond portfolios with derivatives on monthly or quarterly basis. Therefore, some CRAs simply report Short-Term ratings.

Corporate ratings mainly refer to a financial instrument such as a bond, rather than the whole corporation and incorporates the risk that the company will not be able to repay that rated obligations.

Ratings are used to evaluate or estimate the risk exposure of a single position or a whole portfolio both for investment and regulatory purposes. The ratings issued by the CRAs play an important role in the regulatory framework as well as in the investment selection process, [BIS (2006)].

Under Basel II, the new Regulatory Capital Requirements for banks provided additional importance to Credit Ratings. Ratings can be used to assign the risk weights determining minimum capital charges for different categories of borrower. Under the Standardized Approach to Credit Risk, Basel II establishes credit risk weights for each supervisory category which relies on "external credit assessments". Credit Ratings are also used for assessing risks for some of the other rules of Basel II, [Elkhoury (2008)].

In addition to credit ratings, CRAs also publish "rating outlooks", a relatively new concept providing an opinion on the likely future direction of a credit rating.

S&P rates each of the 17 sovereign Governments that belong to the Euro area and has transfer and convertibility (T&C) assessments for each country. The rating and assessment histories are reported yearly on Rating Agency websites. In the case of S&P, the rating histories start on January 1, 1975. For most, they start on the day S&P's first assigned a rating. In Table 5.2 the credit ratings and the Outlook assigned to the major 10 European countries during the recent Sovereign Crisis according to S&P's and to Moody's are reported.

S&P uses current and historical information in their assessment of corporate credit risk. As corporate credit ratings are forward looking, the Agency may rate *through-the-cycle*, accounting for anticipated ups and downs in the business cycle that may affect the corporation's creditworthiness, thereby adopting a Longer-Term perspective in their rating methodology. Past studies, as [Blume et al. (1998)] and [Gray et al. (2006)] use historic averages of financial information in credit rating models to reflect the use of this Longer-Term perspective. While the CRAs claim that ratings measure default risk over long investment horizons, the sudden downgrade of AAA-rated structured finance securities to junk status, in the wake of the financial crisis, suggests that rating *through-the-cycle* is selectively applied. Historical financial information that corresponds to periods of economic stability can only be used to forecast a firm's future prospects, on the assumption that the underlying economic environment of the forecast period is as stable as in the past. As the US Sub-prime Mortgage Crisis unraveled in 2006 there was great uncertainty in the business environment, reflected by the volatility in the financial markets during the crisis period. Historical information was of limited use in assessing the future of a firm during the crisis period. Rating Agencies may rely on the most relevant and recent financial information in their rating methodologies, as current information should be a better forward looking estimator of the firm's prospects than using historical information.

Table 5.2   Credit ratings and outlooks for 10 European countries.

Standard & Poor's

Country	2013		2012		2011		2010	
	Rating	Outlook	Rating	Outlook	Rating	Outlook	Rating	Outlook
Austria	AA+	Negative	AA+	Negative	AAA	Stable	AAA	Stable
Belgium	AA	Negative	AA	Negative	AA+	Negative	AA+	Negative
France	AA+	Negative	AA+	Negative	AAA	Stable	AAA	Stable
Germany	AAA	Stable	AAA	Watch Negative	AAA	Stable	AAA	Stable
Greece	B-	Stable	CC	Negative	CC	Negative	BB+	Negative
Ireland	BBB+	Negative	BBB+	Negative	BBB+	Stable	BBB+	Stable
Italy	BBB+	Negative	BBB+	Negative	A	Negative	A+	Stable
the Netherlands	AAA	Negative	AAA	Watch Negative	AAA	Stable	AAA	Stable
Portugal	BB	Negative	BB	Negative	BBB-	Negative	A-	Negative
Spain	BBB-	Negative	A	Negative	AA	Negative	AA	Negative

Moody's

Country	2013		2012		2011		2010	
	Rating	Outlook	Rating	Outlook	Rating	Outlook	Rating	Outlook
Austria	Aaa	Negative	Aaa	Stable	Aaa	Stable	Aaa	Stable
Belgium	Aa3	Negative	Aa1	Rur-	Aa1	Stable	Aa1	Stable
France	Aa1	Negative	Aaa	Stable	Aaa	Stable	Aaa	Stable
Germany	Aaa	Negative	Aaa	Stable	Aaa	Stable	Aaa	Stable
Greece	C	Negative	Ca	Developing	Ca	Developing	B1	Negative
Ireland	Ba1	Negative	Ba1	Negative	Ba1	Negative	Baa3	Negative
Italy	Baa2	Negative	A2	Negative	Aa2	Under Review	Aa2	Stable
the Netherlands	Aaa	Negative	Aaa	Stable	Aaa	Stable	Aaa	Stable
Portugal	Ba3	Negative	Ba2	Negative	Ba2	Negative	A1	Under Review
Spain	Baa3	Negative	A1	Negative	Aa2	Under Review	Aa1	Under Review

5.2.3 *Taxonomy of rating*

Ratings are first assigned by Rating Agencies at the time of issuance and are periodically reviewed by these companies. A rating change reflects an estimate that the credit quality of the issuer has improved or worsened.

Rating criteria are adopted in the market to discretize the probability of default in a finite number of scores, [De Laurentis (1998)]. Rating gradations are broken down into a small number of distinct symbols, each symbol representing a group of ratings in which the quality characteristics are broadly the same. These symbols, which comprise two distinct rating groups of *strong* and *weak* companies or of *investment* and *speculative* securities, range from those used to designate the greatest financial strength or the highest investment quality to those denoting the least financial strength or the lowest investment quality. Table 5.3 is an example of credit scores adopted on bond assessments. Note that Moody's adopts numeric modifiers to refer to the ranking within each class – with 1 being the highest and 3 being the lowest, even if the financial strength of companies within a generic rating symbol (Aa, for example) is broadly the same, [Moody's (2000)]. The meaning of the various rating systems can be summarized as follows.

AAA/Aaa Credits rated AAA are judged to be of the best quality. They carry the smallest degree of credit risk. Issuers with this rating offer exceptional financial security. While the creditworthiness of these entities is likely to change, such changes as can be imagined are most unlikely to impair their fundamentally strong position.

AA/Aa Credits rated AA are judged to be of high quality by all standards. Issuers rated AA offer excellent financial security. Together with the AAA class, they constitute what are generally known as high-grade names. They are rated lower than AAA-rated entities because margins of protection may not be as large as in AAA securities or because fluctuation of protective elements may be of greater amplitude or there may be other elements present which make the long-term risk appear somewhat larger than the AAA credits.

A As issuers rated A offer good financial security, credits in this class possess many favorable investment attributes and are to be considered as upper-medium-grade obligations. Factors giving security to principal and interest are considered adequate, but elements may be present which suggest a susceptibility to impairment some time in the future.

Table 5.3   Ratings scales.

	Standard &Poor	Moody's	Fitch
Investment-grade Rating			
Highest credit quality	AAA	Aaa	AAA
High credit quality	AA+	Aa1	AA+
	AA	Aa2	AA
	AA-	Aa3	AA-
Strong payment capacity	A+	A1	A+
	A	A2	A
	A-	A3	A-
Adequate payment capacity	BBB+	Baa1	BBB+
	BBB	Baa2	BBB
Last rating in investment grade	BBB-	Baa3	BBB-
Speculative-grade ratings			
Speculative	BB+	Ba1	BB+
Credit risk developing	BB	Ba2	BB
due to economic changes	BB-	Ba3	BB-
High Speculative	B+	B1	B+
Credit risk presents	B	B2	B
limited margin safety	B-	B3	B-
High default risk	CCC+	Caa1	CC+
	CCC	Caa2	CCC
	CCC-	Caa3	CCC-
	CC		CC
Default	C	Ca	C
	D	C	D

BBB/Baa   Securities rated BBB are considered neither highly protected nor poorly secured. Issuers rated BBB offer adequate financial security. However, certain protective elements may be lacking or may be unreliable over any great period of time.

BB/Ba   Issuers rated BB offer questionable financial security. Often the ability of these issuers to meet obligations may be moderate and not well safeguarded in the future. Issues in this class are judged to have speculative investments; their future cannot be considered as well-assured.

B Issues which are rated B generally lack characteristics of a desirable investment. Issuers in this class offer poor financial security. Assurance of interest and principal payments or of maintenance of other terms of the contract over any long period of time may be small.

CCC+/Caa Issuers and issues rated CCC+ offer very poor financial security. They may already be in default on their obligations or there may be present danger with respect to punctual payment of obligations. The issues are likely to be in arrears on dividend payments.

CCC/Ca Issuers rated CCC offer extremely poor financial security. Such entities are often in default on their obligations or have other marked shortcomings. CCC issues represent obligations which are highly speculative.

CCC–/C Issuers rated CCC– are the lowest-rated class of entity, are usually in default on their obligations, and potential recovery values are low. This class rates the lowest issues, and can be regarded as having extremely poor prospects of ever attaining any real investment standing.

Two different rating gradations used by Moody's to classify issuers according to both financial strength, see Table 5.4, [Moody's (2000)], or management quality, see Table 5.5, are shown.

Table 5.4   Moody's financial strength rating.

	Rating	Description
Secure Companies	Aaa	Exceptional
	Aa	Excellent
	A	Good
	Baa	Adequate
Vulnerable Companies	Ba	Questionable
	B	Poor
	Caa	Very Poor
	Ca	Extremely Poor
	C	Lowest

5.3   Regulation of CRAs

CRAs' activity has been put under scrutiny by policymakers and Regulators given that they have been unable to predict events such as the 1997

Table 5.5   Moody's management quality ratings.

Rating	Description
MQ1	Excellent and strong management and control environment.
MQ2	Very good and above-average management and control environment.
MQ3	Good and average management and control environment.
MQ4	Adequate, but with a certain elements of weakness in the management and control environment.
MQ5	Unsatisfactory and poor management and control environment.

Asian Crisis, and the collapse of US corporations such as Mutual Benefit, Universal Life, Enron, Worldcom and the European Parmalat and Cirio.

In April 2002 the European Economic and Financial Affairs Council (ECOFIN) started to monitor CRAs activity and in February 2004, the European Parliament passed a resolution on the basis of MEP Katiforis' report on the role and methods of CRAs. In March 2004, following the Parmalat scandal and the European Parliament resolution, the Commission presented to the European Securities Committee (ESC) the four core issues to be examined:

- potential conflicts of interests within Rating Agencies;
- transparency of Rating Agencies' methodologies;
- legal treatment of Rating Agencies' access to inside information;
- concerns about possible lack of competition in the market for provision of credit ratings.

In June 2004 the Basel Committee on Banking Supervision achieved a critical milestone named Basel II. The major objective of Basel II is to revise the rules of the 1988 Basel Capital Accord which first set banks' regulatory capital adequate to their risks. A major concern was posted on the risk measurement and management techniques and their use to set the adequate banks capital requirements. Under Pillar 1 of Basel II, banks are required to measure their risks using two alternative approaches: the Standardized Approach; and the Internal Ratings-Based Approach. So basically Financial Institutions were required to provide a local or own measure of their risk.

In July 2004 the European Parliament addressed a call to the Committee of European Securities Regulators (CESR) for technical advice on CRAs. As the role of credit ratings is being reinforced by developments in the Basel II banking legislation, the Commission recommends that CESR works in collaboration with the Committee of European Banking Supervisors (CEBS). The aim of the call was for CESR to provide the Commission with technical analysis and advice relating to the introduction of European legislation or other solutions in this field.

In March 2005, the Commission decided not to present new legislative proposals in the area of CRAs deciding that the existing financial services directives applicable to CRAs were sufficient for all the major issues of concern raised by the European Parliament.

In 2006, the Commission on Credit Rating Agencies adopted various financial services directives, combined with self regulation by the CRAs themselves on the basis of the Code of Conduct Fundamentals for CRAs of the International Organization of Securities Commissions (IOSCO), that could provide a satisfactory answer to the major issues of concern in relation to CRAs, [COM (2006)].[2] Continuous monitoring of developments in this area and compliance with the IOSCO code was required by the Commission. On March 11, 2006 the EU Commission published a communication setting out its position regarding CRA.

Starting in August 2007 a major lack of confidence occurred in most financial markets. In many respects, the Global Financial Crisis started with the Lehman's default in September 2008 validated a number of long-standing concerns in the CRAs industry, prompting the need for reforms in regulation and in practice. CRA have been criticized for failing to monitor the creditworthiness of corporations over time, and failing to adjust ratings in a timely manner to reflect any changes in their findings.

At the moment the European Securities Market Authority (ESMA) carries out policy work to prepare future legislation, such as regulatory technical standards, and guidelines. This work is undertaken through the CRA Technical Committee, which has representatives from all relevant national authorities.

Within the EU at present there are three Financial Services Action Plan (FSAP) Directives that are relevant to CRAs, for more details see [CESR (2008)].

- **The Market Abuse Directive 2002 (MAD)** approved on December 2002 by the Commission Directive 2003/125/EC . It tackles the issue

---

[2]The International Organisation of Securities Commissions (IOSCO) is an international non mandatory standard setting organization composed of securities markets supervisors. Securities markets supervisors cooperate within IOSCO in order to promote high standards of regulation aiming at maintaining just, efficient and sound securities markets, [SEC (2008b)].

of insider dealing and market manipulation, and states that "Credit Rating Agencies issue opinions on the creditworthiness of the particular issuer or financial instrument as of the given date. As such these opinions do not constitute a recommendation within the meaning of the Directive. However CRA's should consider adopting internal policies and procedures designed to ensure that credit ratings published by them are fairly presented and that they appropriately disclose any significant interests or conflicts of interest concerning the financial instruments or the issuers to which their credit ratings relate." There is however no requirement imposed on CRAs or any established means of monitoring whether or how they seek to comply with this recommendation.

- **The Capital Requirements Directive 2005 (CRD)** providing for the use of external credit assessments in the determination of risk weights applied to a firm's exposures. It regulates the capital adequacy of banks and other financial institutions, based on Basel II requirements. In July 2011, a proposal for a revision of the CRD (CRD IV) based on the new Basel III standards was presented. The new rules, which have not yet been adopted, are expected to take effect in 2013. The CRD allows banks to choose among various methods of fulfilling the capital requirements. Key aspects of the directive are broader risk management, flexibility and greater sensitivity to risk. Only the use of assessments provided by recognized External Credit Assessment Institutions (ECAIs), mainly CRAs, are acceptable to the competent authorities. The CRD allows Member States to recognize an ECAI as eligible in two ways: direct recognition, in which the competent authority carries out its own assessment of the ECAI's compliance with the CRD's eligibility criteria; indirect recognition, in which the competent authority recognises the ECAI without carrying out its own evaluation, relying instead on the recognition of the ECAI by the competent authority of another Member State.

- **The Markets in Financial Instruments Directive, 2007 (MiFID)**, in force since November 2007, is a core pillar in EU financial market integration. Adopted in accordance with the "Lamfalussy" process, MiFID establishes a regulatory framework for the provision of investment services in financial instruments (such as brokerage, advice, dealing, portfolio management, underwriting etc.) by banks and investment firms and for the operation of regulated markets by market operators. It also establishes the powers and duties of national competent authorities in relation to these activities. Its aim is to foster the integration, competitiveness, and efficiency in EU financial markets. In concrete terms, it abolished the possibility for Member States to require all trading in financial instruments to take place on traditional exchanges and enabled Europe wide competition between those exchanges and alternative venues. It also granted banks and investment firms a strengthened "passport" for providing investment services across the EU subject to compliance with both organisational and reporting requirements as well as comprehensive rules designed to ensure investor protection. In Annex I to MiFID, it is mentioned that the issuing of a rating will normally not result in the CRA also providing 'investment advice', however, CRAs that also provide investment services and activities on a professional basis, may require authorization.

Regulation (EC) No 1060/2009 on CRAs (CRA Regulation, CRA I) came into on December 7, 2010 and requires CRAs to comply with rigorous rules of conduct in order to mitigate possible conflicts of interest, ensure high quality and sufficient transparency of ratings and the rating process. Several amendments to this Regulation followed in 2011 and 2012 to strengthen the rules on the disclosure of rating methodologies, with a view to promoting sound credit rating processes and, at the end, improve rating quality. Some efforts were directed specifically to improve the quality of sovereign ratings and to enhance competition in the credit rating market. The amendment to the CRAs Regulation introduced in 2011 (CRA II)[3] entrusts the ESMA with exclusive supervisory powers over CRAs registered in the EU. ESMA is also in charge of any new application for registration.

The various amendments brought the European Parliament on January 16, 2013 to approve new rules on when and how credit rating agencies may rate Sovereign debts and private firms' financial health. They allow agencies to only issue unsolicited sovereign debt ratings on set dates, and enable private investors to sue them CRAs for negligence. The new Rules for CRAs basically aim to:

- avoid relying solely or mechanistically on external credit ratings. Financial institutions are required to make their own credit risk assessment with the supervision of competent authorities. So these internal risk assessments have to be monitored in order to verify that these firms won't over-rely on credit ratings.

---

[3]Regulation (EU) No 513/2011 of the European Parliament and of the Council of 11 May 2011 amending Regulation (EC) No 1060/2009 on CRA, OJ L 145, 31.5.2011.

- increase the quality of the credit ratings given to specific structured instruments. They require issuers (or originators or sponsors) to disclose specific information on structured finance products on the main elements of underlying asset pools, necessary for investors to make their own credit assessment and thus avoid the need to rely on external ratings.
- gauge competition: issuers (or their related third parties) should solicit a rating to engage two CRAs, independent from each other, to issue two independent credit ratings in parallel on the same structured finance instruments.
- set independence rules aimed at addressing conflicts of interests with regard to the issuer-pays model and CRA shareholder structure.

The overall impact of each sovereign credit rating can only be fully perceived in a cross-border context. This is because ratings can be issued in one country for financial instruments issued in another, so that action taken on a national level might not have any effect, as ratings could continue to be issued and used if they were produced in a different EU or even third country jurisdictions. As a result, national responses to credit rating issuance risk being circumvented or ineffective without EU-level action. Therefore any further actions in the field of CRAs can best be achieved by a common effort.

The CRAs Regulation renders a CRA liable in case it infringes, intentionally or with gross negligence, the CRAs Regulation itself, thereby causing damage to an investor having relied on a credit rating of such CRA, that provided the infringement in question, affecting the credit rating.

Discussions on regulating CRAs have been very lively not only in Europe but also on the international scene.

The current US regulation of CRAs appears to be very detailed and exhaustive from regulating the recognition process of the NRSRO status, to defining the features that qualify their activity and specifying illegal behaviors and the relevant sanctions. The current regulation defines very clearly all the steps of the process and the duties concerning the rating activity. It is important to point out that such ruling has also been issued timely as a consequence of the most recent financial scandals and of the responsibility that the CRAs were claimed to have. Accurate provisions for different kind of abuses and conflicts of interest, together with the appointment of a compliance officer within each NRSRO, who is accountable for the conformity and for the continuous compliance with the regulation in force, are set. The recent financial crisis has pushed SEC to intervene again in June 2008 to reshape the regulation cocerning NRSROs, which according to Section 6 of CRA Reform Act of 2006, played a key role in rating the spread and the placement of the securities largely responsible of the market collapse as Residential Mortgage Backed Securities (RMBS) and collateralized debt obligations (CDO). In order to protect unsophisticated investors by such dangerous securities and to prevent further spread of the ongoing crisis. The SEC proposed the following amendments to its existing NRSRO rules with the goal of proving the quality of credit ratings:

- enhance the disclosure and comparability of credit ratings performance statistics;
- increase the disclosure of information about structured finance products;
- require more information about the procedures and methodologies used to determine credit ratings for structured finance products;
- strengthen internal control processes through reporting requirements;
- address conflicts of interest arising from the process of rating structured finance products;
- reduce undue reliance in the Commission's rules on NRSRO ratings, thereby promoting increased investor due diligence, [SEC (2008a)].

5.3.1 *Conflicts of interest*

In the early 1970s, the basic business model of the large CRAs changed. In place of the *investor pays* model that had been established by John Moody in 1909, the CRAs converted to an *issuer pays* model, whereby the entity issuing the bonds also pays the rating firm to rate them. Various reasons have been addressed for this change among which the following in our opinion stands as the most likely. The bond rating business, like many information industries, involves a two-sided market, where payments can come from one or both sides of the market. Information markets for the quality of bonds have a similar feature, in that the information can be paid for by issuers of debt, buyers of debt, or some mix of the two and the actual outcome may sometimes shift in idiosyncratic ways. The change to the *issuer pays* business model opened the door to potential conflicts of interest. A CRA might shade its rating upward so as to keep the issuer happy and forestall the issuer's taking its rating business to a different Rating Agency. However, the CRAs' concerns about their long-run reputations apparently kept the conflicts in check for the first three decades of experience with the new business model, [White (2010); Caouette et al. (2008); Smith and Walter (2002)]. There were two important and related characteristics of the bond issuing market that helped. First, there were thousands of corporate and government bond issuers, so that the threat by any single issuer (if it was displeased by an agency's rating) to take its business to a different Rating Agency was not important. Second, the corporations and governments whose plain vanilla debt was being rated were relatively transparent, so that an obviously incorrect rating would quickly be spotted by others and would thus potentially tarnish the rater's reputation. There is empirical evidence that large issuers of structured finance instruments received more favourable ratings than smaller issuers during the 2006- 2007 period. This could be explained by the fact that larger issuers were major contributors to a CRAs' income and basically might influence them to issue higher credit ratings, [SEC (2011b)]. Under the *issuer pays* model, CRAs have a financial incentive to generate business from rated issuers, risking the issuance of overinflated ratings in order to increase or keep business.

In 2002, Fitch and the Egan-Jones Rating Companies accused the big two CRAs, Moody's and S&P of *notching*. Notching refers to the general practice of making rating distinctions among the different liabilities of a single entity or of closely related entities. Notching occurs when CRAs reduce their ratings on structured financial collateral based on ratings provided by another Agency without rating the collateral themselves. Notching arises when collateral, such as Mortgage Backed Securities (MBS), and other Asset Backed Securities (ABS) are included within investment vehicles that are rated, such as Collateralized Debt Obligations (CDO). According to Moody's, notching is intended to ensure that two securities with the same rating have the same expected loss rate. An obligation's Expected Loss Rate (ELR) is defined as the product of the Probability of Default (PD) and the expected severity of Loss Given Default (LGD). According to a study by Greenberg Quinlan Rosner Research company, [GQRR (2002)], it emerged that the two largest CRAs employing notching were maximizing their market share and undermining competition. Fitch accused Moody's and S&P of initiating an automatic downgrading of structured securities, if the two agencies were not hired to rate them. Moody's response to Fitch's accusations was to say that unsolicited ratings usually result in a lower rating for debt securities because of either lack of information or the use of different methodologies to determine the PD.

Unsolicited ratings raise potential conflict of interests. Both Moody's and S&P state that they reserve the right to rate and make public ratings for SEC-registered corporate bonds, whether or not requested by an issuer. If the issuer does not request the rating, the rating will simply be based on publicly available information. If the issuer requests the rating, then it may provide information to the CRAs and pay the fees. Many new entrants in the Credit Rating industry issue unsolicited ratings to gain credibility in the market. Some issuers have accused CRAs of using unsolicited ratings and the threat of lower ratings to induce issuers to cooperate in the rating process and pay the fees of solicited ratings, [Elkhoury (2008)].

Since 2001, Moody's and S&P claim that no unsolicited rating was issued in Europe. As unsolicited ratings are based on public information and thus lack issuer input, the issue of unsolicited ratings could be addressed by requiring CRAs to disclose whether it has been solicited or not. Moody's and S&P regularly specify whether the ratings have been solicited and give issuers the opportunity to participate at any stage of the process, if they wish.

Conflicts of interest arise due to

(1) *issuer-pays* model. For instance, an important issuer may decide to be rated on a continuous basis by his "preferred CRA", creating an incentive for this CRA to positively rating this issuer contributing to increase his income. Increased transparency does not help as long as the issuer-pays model applies on such a broad basis, so that it is difficult for investors to find a CRA whose remuneration model is less conflicted.
(2) *the investor-pays and public utility* models. The reputation in rating business has a "lock-in effect" so issuers tend to remain with the same CRA for long periods. In the occurrence of a change of the existing Rating Agency would cause a lack of investor's confidence toward the issuer. The lock-in effect is even stronger when issuers consider moving to new approved CRA.
(3) the shareholder structure. A CRAs' independence may be compromised if an issuer they are rating is also one of their shareholders.
(4) sovereign ratings. In Europe, which European CRA should issue the sovereign credit ratings to be considered reliable? [SEC (2011a)].

CRA Regulation introduced some provisions to mitigate conflicts of interests related to the *issuer-pays* model:

- *transparency*;

- *disconnecting the interest* of the staff involved in the rating activity from the remuneration paid by the rated entity;
- *regular rotation* of the staff within the CRA so that analysts only deal with a specific entity for a limited time.

5.4   The Importance of Competition

The analysis of the structure of the market for rating services unveils a level of concentration which is significantly high. The credit rating market is oligopolistic and is dominated by the three major CRAs: S&P, Moody's and Fitch. In the United States, the SEC reported that in 2011 the three CRAs issued 97% of the outstanding ratings and earned over 98% of ratings revenues.

Medium and smaller CRAs often cater to very specific market needs, with ambitions to develop their international market presence. There are also a number of local Rating Agencies active in different countries and regularly approved by the local Regulators. They issue rating opinions both for general and specialized purposes; their impact on the global financial markets is nonetheless marginal. For instance, in December 2012 the ESMA which is exclusively responsible for the registration and supervision of CRAs in the European Union, had approved new CRAs in addition to the local subsidiaries of the major three CRAs, as reported in Table 5.6

The market is characterized by relevant "reputational" barriers which can prevent new potential competitors to enter the market. High profit margins and limited pricing transparency my cause very high prices for the rating services.

The limited availability of service providers reduces the elasticity of the demand, i.e. issuers cannot easily change their CRA if they are not satisfied with its performance. Furthermore, some segments of issuers, particularly the Small-Medium Enterprises (SMEs) or small sovereigns, might experience difficulty to obtain a rating as not all market segments are adequately covered by the existing CRAs or ratings might be too expensive for these issuers. This can substantially limit the SME access to the capital markets.

Strong economies of scale in the sector as well as reputation of CRAs, which is a crucial asset, limit the market entry. New entrants to the credit rating business face a particular challenge to develop and demonstrate a track record to acquire credibility with investors which is necessary to persuade issuers to buy their rating service. Additionally, the oligopolistic

Table 5.6 List of registered and certified CRAs in Europe in 2012.

Name of CRA	Headquarter	Registering competent authority of Member State	Status	Effective Date
Euler Hermes Rating GmbH	Germany	Bundesanstalt für Finanzdienstleistungsaufsicht (BaFin)	Reg.	16 Nov 2010
Japan CRA Ltd	Japan	Autorité des Marchés Financiers (AMF)	Cert.	6 Jan 2011
Feri EuroRating Services AG	Germany	Bundesanstalt für Finanzdienstleistungsaufsicht (BaFin)	Reg.	14 Apr 2011
Bulgarian CRA AD	Bulgaria	Financial Supervision Commission (FSC)	Reg.	6 Apr 2011
Creditreform Rating AG	Germany	Bundesanstalt für Finanzdienstleistungsaufsicht (BaFin)	Reg.	18 May 2011
Scope Credit Rating GmbH	Germany	Bundesanstalt für Finanzdienstleistungsaufsicht (BaFin)	Reg.	24 May 2011
ICAP Group SA	Greece	Hellenic Capital Market Commission (HCMC)	Reg.	7 Jul 2011
GBB-Rating Gesellschaft für Bonitätsbeurteilung mbH	Germany	Bundesanstalt für Finanzdienstleistungsaufsicht (BaFin)	Reg.	28 Jul 2011
ASSEKURATA Assekuranz Rating-Agentur GmbH	Germany	Bundesanstalt für Finanzdienstleistungsaufsicht (BaFin)	Reg.	16 Aug 2011
Companhia Portuguesa de Rating, S.A. (CPR)	Portugal	Comissão do Mercado de Valores Mobiliários (CMVM)	Reg.	26 August 2011
AM Best Europe-Rating Services Ltd. (AMBERS)	UK	Financial Services Authority (FSA)	Reg.	8 Sep 2011
DBRS Ratings Limited	UK	Financial Services Authority (FSA)	Reg.	31 Oct 2011
Fitch France S.A.S.	France	Autorité des Marchés Financiers (AMF)	Reg.	31 Oct 2011
CRIF S.p.A.	Italy	Commissione Nazionale per le Società e la Borsa (CONSOB)	Reg.	22 Dec 2011
Capital Intelligence Ltd	Cyprus	Cyprus Securities and Exchange Commission (CySEC)	Reg.	8 May 2012
European Rating Agency, a.s.	Slovakia	National Bank of Slovakia	Reg.	30 Jul 2012
Axesor SA	Spain	ESMA	Reg.	1 Oct 2012
CERVED Group S.p.A.	Italy	Commissione Nazionale per le Società e la Borsa (CONSOB)	Reg.	20 Dec 2012

CRAs market structure, which reflects the dominant market position of the major Agencies, few of which have over one hundred years of experience, makes it more difficult for new players to enter the market. The lack of competition is also supported by the existing capital requirements rules, Credit Ratings for regulatory capital purposes have to be issued by Agencies recognized as External Credit Assessment Institution (ECAI) by banking supervisors. So it may be difficult for a newly registered and approved CRAs to become recognized as ECAI by the banking supervisory authorities.

The European Securities Markets Expert (ESME) Group believes that the oligopolistic structure could have contributed negatively to the quality/integrity of the rating process causing over-reliance on the few international CRAs.

Recent concerns and criticism on the CRAs' main activity may help new CRAs to have easier access to the market. New CRAs have to follow a long and slow process to become reliable entites.

Steps can be taken to encourage and facilitate the entry of new competitors. One option would be to encourage the development of specialist niche CRA that would focus on specific industry segments or asset classes to differentiate themselves from the existing players. Another option would be to encourage new CRAs to carry out unsolicited ratings to help build market awareness and credibility. Encouraging more CRAs to operate would also require vigilance against "ratings shopping", although issuers who engage untested CRAs with questionable standards are unlikely to be considered reliable by the market.

To improve credit rating market conditions and guarantee independence of CRAs and high quality ratings, as well as improved transparency and comparability of ratings are all considered to be cost-effective options.

Encouraging the creation of a network of small and medium-sized rating agencies is seen as a preferred option to reduce the barriers to entry into the market, [SEC (2011a)].

Some additional issues have to be considered for the rating of specific instruments. For instance, in the case of structured products or bonds it is important to have access to a large database containing all the information on corporate bonds over a long period in order to provide accurate and reliable ratings. In the case of complex structured products "Dual ratings could allow a further reduction in reliance on ratings for these complex products", [SEC (2011a)].

5.5   Rating Methodologies

The processes and methods used to establish credit ratings varies widely among CRAs. Traditionally, CRAs use quantitative and qualitative assessment approved by their rating committee.

Recently, there has been increased interest in using quantitative statistical models based on publicly available data assuming the assessment process could be more objective and not relying as much on confidential information. Quantitative models may play an important role in the assessment process but have to be combined with a set of qualitative information which contribute to provide the final credit rating. However, it is not possible to identify the optimal assessment criteria given that the model performance depends heavily on various circumstances. The CRAs have recently publicly committed themselves to an enhanced standard of transparency. Priority focus should be on the rating methodologies, the key risk factors and the key assumptions for the different asset classes and the individually distinct sub-asset classes.

Ratings gaming occurs when an issuer uses his understanding of a CRAs' criteria to optimise the pooled portfolio while still staying officially within the criteria which reinforces the need for qualitative review (e.g. in rating committees) relative to a purely quantitative model-driven approach.

The regulatory capital requirements linked to the different company's credit risk are set using different approaches:

(1) the *Standardised Approach* (SA) the measurement of credit risk is based on external credit assessments provided by External Credit Assessment Institutions (ECAIs) or export credit agencies.
(2) The *Internal Ratings-Based Approach* (IRBA), subject to supervisory approval as to the satisfaction of certain conditions. Banks use their own rating systems to measure some or all of the determinants of credit risk.
(3) The *Foundation Version*, banks calculate the PD on the basis of their own ratings, but rely on their supervisors for measures of the other determinants of credit risk.
(4) The *Advanced Version*, banks also estimate their own measures of all the determinants of credit risk, including the LGD and the Exposure at Default (EAD).

The measurement of the PD has challenged various scholars in the Finance and Quantitative world. In the last 30 years different approaches have been used, starting from the first accounting based credit-scoring models to the relatively newer structural and market-based models. The accounting-based models use various key accounting ratios to produce either a credit risk score or a PD measure. If the credit risk score, or default probability, attains a value above a critical benchmark, the company or financial institution which is applying for a loan is considered risky and may fail in getting the loan. An accurate review of the articles on the subject can be found in the special issue of the Journal of Banking and Finance published in 1984, [Journal of Banking & Finance (1984)].

The main criticism of accounting-based models is due to the fact that book value accounting data are measured at discrete intervals and so they may fail to detect the fast-moving changes in borrower conditions. The use of market data, available at higher frequency, and recent pricing theoretical models gave birth to newer models. In particular a seminal work in the estimation of the PD for a company is based on the use of the Black and Scholes [Black and Scholes (1973)] and Merton option pricing models [Merton (1974)]. The first commercial models using the Merton's approach were developed by Kealhofer, Merton and Vasiceck (KMV)[4] in 1996 and were based on the firm's capital structure, the volatility of the assets returns and the current asset value, they applied to publicly traded companies whose equity value are market determined.

The main assumption is that a firm goes bankrupt when the market value of its assets falls below its debt obligations to outside creditors. Crucial inputs into the estimation of the probability of default are the asset values and its volatility (σ_A), both of which have to be estimated. The underlying constructs are two theoretical relationships. First, the value of equity can be viewed as a call option on the value of a firm's assets. Second, assuming a theoretical link exists between the observable volatility of a firm's equity value and its (unobservable) asset value volatility, the implied values for both asset values and its volatility can therefore be estimated for all publicly traded companies with adequate stock return data. Given any initial values of the company's asset values and its short-term debt outstanding, an Expected Default Frequency (EDF), basically a distribution of the PDs, can be calculated for each borrowing firm. Default then occurs in some future period when (or if) the value of a firm's assets falls below its outstanding (short-term) debt obligations.

The translation of the public information into probabilities is carried

---

[4]KMV Corporation that was founded in 1989.

out estimating:

(1) The asset value and the volatility of asset return: financial models usually consider market values of assets, and not book values which only represent historical costs of the physical assets, net of their depreciation. The calculation of the market value of the firm's assets and their volatility would be simple if all the liabilities of the firm were traded and marked-to-market every day. Alternatively, KMV use the option pricing model to value corporate liabilities assuming that the firm's capital structure is composed of equity, E_t, short-term debt, D_{st}, which is considered equivalent to cash, long-term debt, D_{lt}, which is assumed to be a perpetuity, and convertible preferred shares. The KMV's model estimates the market value, A_t and volatility, σ_{A_t}, of the firm using the market value of its stock, E_t, the volatility of its stock, and the book value of its liabilities, $D_t = D_{st} + D_{lt}$. The market value of the company's equity may be expressed as the value of a call option as follows:

$$E_t = f(D_t, A_t, \sigma_A). \tag{5.1}$$

(2) The Distance-to-Default (DD): the default occurs when the asset value reaches the Default Point (DP), which is a level somewhere between the value of total liabilities and the value of short-term debt. The DP in the KMV's model is estimated as the short-term debt plus half the long-term debt, $\text{DP} = D_{st} + 0.5 \cdot D_{lt}$.

Given the firm's expected value at the horizon, and its default point at the horizon, KMV determines the percentage drop in the firm value that would bring it to the default point. By dividing the percentage drop by the volatility, KMV controls for the effect of different volatilities. DD is therefore the number of standard deviations that the asset value must drop in order to reach the DP. The DD is a normalized measure and it is used to compare one company with another. DD is also an ordinal measure akin to a bond rating but it still does not provide the default probability measure. In order to have a cardinal or a probability measure, KMV uses historical default experience to determine an expected default frequency as a function of distance to default. It does this by comparing the calculated DD and the observed actual default rate for a large number of firms from their proprietary database. A smooth curve fitted to those data yields the EDF as a function of the DD.

(3) The Probabilities of Default (PD): The value of the firm, projected to a given future date, has a probability distribution characterized by its expected value and standard deviation (volatility). The EDF, or the company's PD, is the area of the part of the probability distribution which is to the left of the book liabilities of the firm. A mapping is determined between a firm's distance to default and the default rate probability based on the historical default experience of companies with similar DD values. In the case of private companies, for which stock price and default data are generally unavailable, KMV estimates the value and volatility of the private firm directly from its observed characteristics and values based on market comparables, in lieu of market values on the firm's securities. For a firm with publicly traded shares, the market value of equity may be observed. The expected asset value at the horizon and the default point are determined. An investor holding the asset would expect to get a payout plus a capital gain equal to the expected return. Using a measure of the asset's systematic risk, KMV determines an expected return based upon historic asset market returns. This is reduced by the payout rate determined from the firm's interest and dividend payments. The result is the expected appreciation rate, which when applied to the current asset value, gives the expected future value of the assets. The firm would default when its total market value falls below the book value of its liabilities. Based upon empirical analysis of defaults, KMV has found that the most frequent default point is at a firm value approximately equal to current liabilities plus 50% of long-term liabilities.

To estimate the current value of risky cash flows one needs to measure the default-free component and the component exposed to credit risk (risky component). This is done estimating:

- the present value of the cash flows;
- the future value of the cash flows;
- the Loss Given Default (LGD), which is defined, given the firm's Recovery Rate (RR), by[5]

$$LGD = 1 - RR$$

from the definition of RR:

$$RR = 1 - LGD$$

---

[5]RR is the rate of face value recovered through bankruptcy procedure in event of default.

- the 1-year risk-free rate;
- the probability that the issuer defaults in 1 year, which is derived from EDF.

Variations in the stock price, the leverage ratio, and the asset volatility can all change the firm's EDF. Higher volatility of asset return implies that the market has more uncertainty on the firm's business value. KMV's methodology relies almost exclusively on equity market information so it has been most successfully used for publicly traded companies. Major concerns arise when the volatility of a firm's stock price is not an accurate proxy of the variability of asset values and its use for non-publicly traded equity companies.

The market-based models estimate the PD using the term structure of yield spreads between default free and risky corporate securities [Jonkhart (1979)], [Iben and Litterman (1989)]. These models derive implied forward rates on risk-free and risky bonds and use these rates to extract the "markets expectation" of default at different times in the future. A market based model widely adopted by CRAs is the mortality rate model proposed by Altman [Altman (1989a,b)] and the aging approach [Asquith et al. (1989)]. These mortality-default rate models are used by CRAs in their structured financial instrument analysis. They derive actuarial-type PD using historical data on bond defaults classified by both credit grade and years to maturity. They rely on the availability of large loan default data base: to have stable estimates of PDs the data base has to include between 20,000 and 30,000 "names". Very few financial intermediaries worldwide come even remotely close to approaching this number of potential borrowers.

Recent applications of the neural network approach to the credit risk classification problem has also proven to be successful. These models aim to develop non-linear bankruptcy prediction function using as inputs the predictive variables and some potentially "hidden" correlations among them. A commercial model of rating replication using neural networks is available from Finance FX (Atlanta, GA) [Altman et al. (1994); Coats and Fant (1993)].

Further studies adopt the Logical Analysis of Data (LAD) in this kind of classification problems, cf. [Hammer (1986); Cavalli and Moriggia (2002)].

The key measure in credit risk models is the measure of the PD but exposure is also determined by the expected timing of default and by the Recovery Rate (RR) after default has occurred, [Elkhoury (2008)].

- S&P ratings seek to capture only the forward-looking probability of the occurrence of default. They provide no assessment of the expected time of default or mode of default resolution and recovery values.
- By contrast, Moody's ratings focus on the Expected Loss (EL) which is a function of both PD and the expected RR: $sEL = PD \cdot (1 - RR)$.
- Fitch's ratings also focus on both PD and RR. They have a more explicitly hybrid character, in which analysts are also reminded to be forward-looking and to be alert to possible discontinuities between past track records and future trends, [Bhatia (2002)].

The rating given to an issuer or security will affect their cost of raising capital. Very often, a deterioration in a debtor's creditworthiness, reflected in a rating change, may trigger particular contractual obligations (e.g. immediate debt repayment or increasing collateralization needs).

The rating, according to CRAs, is a relative measure of risk: a *BB*-rated company provides a better performance in terms of risk (it is less risky) than a *BBB*-rated company, and a worst performance (riskier) than a *B*-rated company.

Investors use ratings as a key piece of information to determine their investment decisions, depending on the risk they are willing to assume, so they use the historic long-term default series by rating category as an indicator or a measure of future anticipated default. However a specific rating cannot be seen as a mathematical prediction of the future PD.

Ratings are usually requested – and paid for – by the issuers themselves. In these cases, they are based on both publicly available data and information not accessible to the public, but which is voluntarily disclosed by the issuer being rated (e.g. by means of interviews with senior financial officials of the rated entity). However, CRAs sometimes issue unsolicited ratings which are usually prepared without access to non-public information of the issuer but may use other sources.

An increase in the number of rating opinions would improve the quality of the ratings, decrease the risk of conflict of interest and improve investor information, [ESME (2008)].

5.5.1 *General principles of the rating process*

S&P Ratings Services employs fundamental credit analysis, supplemented by quantitative models, as appropriate, in accordance with its methodology and criteria. The analysis follows a systematic framework, called the Rating

Methodology Profile (RAMP), tailored to the type of obligor. Business risk and financial risk are the main elements of corporate and financial institution analysis. Credit ratings are often identified with financial analysis, especially ratios. But it is critical to realize that ratings analysis starts with the assessment of the business and competitive profile of the private company or the economic and political profile of the government. The credit ratings of Moody's and S&P are assigned by its rating committees and not by individual analysts. There is a large part of judgement in the committees' final ratings. CRAs provide little guidance as to how they assign relative weights to each factor, though they do provide information on what variables they consider in determining sovereign ratings. Identifying the relationship between the CRAs' criteria and actual ratings is difficult, in part because some of the criteria used are neither quantitative nor quantifiable but qualitative. The analytical variables are interrelated and the weights are not fixed. The quantitative variables are then combined according to specific criteria adopted by the various Agencies so it is not possible to provide a final formula to assign a credit rating. In addition to traditional debt ratings, which are opinions as to the credit quality of a specific instrument, Rating Agencies produce different ratings, like Moody's Management Quality Ratings, and Moody's National Ratings. These are opinions on the overall quality of an organization, including the management characteristics and operational practices of either, for more details see [Moody's (2000)]:

- asset management companies whose principal activity involves the investment management of institutional and/or retail assets;
- custodian banks whose principal activity involves the processing and safekeeping of securities, or
- administrative service providers whose principal activity involves the pricing and accounting of securities, funds and other pooled investments.

These kind of ratings are used within that portion of a portfolio that is exposed to a given country's local market, taking into consideration the various risks implied by that country's foreign and local currency ratings.

5.5.1.1 *Private firm credit rating*

Country risk, industry characteristics, competitive position, cost efficiency, and profitability relative to peers, are the main factors to consider when assessing business risk. Industry characteristics typically encompass growth prospects, volatility, and technological change, as well as the degree and nature of competition.

Broadly speaking, the lower the industry risk, the higher the potential credit rating on companies in that sector will be.

The economic environment is especially important for bank credit quality. Regulatory structure affects utilities, insurance companies, banks, and other sectors. A company's product/service diversity, especially any risk concentration of a financial institution, is considered.

Risk management ability is an increasingly important analytical factor in the financial services sector to assess credit, market, and trading risks. S&P Ratings Services attaches great importance to management's philosophies and policies concerning financial risk: the firm's employed accounting principles are going to be considered as well as profitability, leverage, cash flow adequacy, liquidity, and financial flexibility.

For financial institutions and insurers, critical factors are asset quality, reserves for losses, asset/liability management, and capital adequacy, other ratios may include profit margins, return on investment, debt/capital, debt/cash flow, and debt service coverage. Cash flow analysis and liquidity assume heightened significance for firms with speculative-grade ratings ('$BB+$' and lower).

Off-balance sheet items, such as leases and pension liabilities, are considered. Where appropriate, S&P Ratings Services may adjust reported financial statements to arrive at a more faithful representation of credit measures and to improve comparability. S&P Ratings Services makes extensive use of risk-adjusted asset quality indicators and risk-adjusted capital analysis to compare financial institutions in different countries.

They also employ proprietary quantitative models to measure the capital and earning adequacy of insurance companies, including firms that insure US municipal bonds and other obligations.

Ratings assigned to insurance companies may be substantially determined by quantitative models that evaluate publicly available financial data. Combining business and financial risk RAMP categories may be scored, but there is no precise recipe for combining the scores to produce ratings. The analytical variables are interrelated and the weights are not fixed. A company's business-risk profile determines the level of financial risk appropriate for any rating category. A well-positioned firm can tolerate greater financial risk, for a given rating, than a poorly positioned organization. Two firms with identical financial metrics may be rated very differently to the extent their business challenges and prospects differ.

5.5.1.2 *Government credit rating*

For sovereign governments, the key determinants of credit quality are political and economic risk. Economic risk addresses a government's ability to repay obligations on time. Political risk addresses the sovereign's willingness to repay, a qualitative factor that distinguishes sovereigns from most other issuers. Political risk encompasses the stability and legitimacy of political institutions. At the regional and local government level, the analysis includes the supportiveness and predictability of the public sector system and the matching of revenue to service responsibilities. The foundation of government creditworthiness is the economic base. The economic structure, demographics, wealth, and economic growth prospects play a key role in credit analysis. Budgetary performance is a central component of financial analysis. Special attention is paid to revenue forecasting, expenditure control, long-term capital planning, debt management, and contingency plans, debt structure and funding sources. Off-balance sheet obligations are recognized. Quantitative elements are captured in a number of ratios that can be compared to those of peers. For sovereigns, financial analysis includes fiscal and monetary flexibility. The financial sector may be viewed as a significant contingent liability for a sovereign government. External liquidity is also analyzed. Similar to the rating process for the private sector, analytical judgment, rather than a formulaic approach, is employed to weigh the individual RAMP categories and reach a rating decision.

5.5.1.3 *Other organization credit rating*

The Issuer Credit Ratings (ICR), which indicates the obligor's default risk, is generally the starting point when rating individual insurance companies. The issue's credit rating may also take account of ultimate recovery in the event of default. For the same obligor, secured debt is often rated higher than unsecured debt, and subordinated debt is typically rated below senior debt. Debt of a holding company may be rated below debt of its operating subsidiary. Recovery expectations dictate whether an obligation is rated above, below, or the same as the ICR. S&P Ratings Services is in the process of expanding its recovery analysis for speculative-grade issuers, in response to the market's increased interest in post-default recovery. As a result, a growing number of issues will be rated 1-3 designations (notches) above and below the ICR. Certain obligations, including municipal revenue bonds, are serviced from a dedicated source, such as water and sewer charges and road tolls. Analysis of these instruments is generally project-specific and focuses on revenue generation relative to debt service, facility maintenance, and other requirements, often cushioned by reserve funds.

5.5.2   *Input factors for the rating process*

Ratings are based on information relating to revenue stream and balance sheet (with particular focus on the debt) of the rated entity. Past financial performance is also considered. Different factors enter into ratings of different sectors of the economy.

The credit ratings effectively classifies issuers into corresponding grades, depending on whether they are considered more or less default-prone. Even those issues theoretically considered default-free, typically the Government bonds, recently have presented different class of Ratings.

The precise factors and the weights that influence the assessment provided by a specific Rating Agency are usually unknown. It is reasonable to suppose that if a Rating Agency reveals the scoring system and the exact criteria to determine that score, its services would not be needed anymore. The rating of an issue or issuer should depend on some or all of the following factors:

- financial ratios and other economic values;
- strategic factors likely to support future cash flow and critical factors that will inhibit future cash flow;
- the issuer's capacity to respond favorably to uncertainty;
- risk elements such as: interest rate risk, prepayment and extension risk, liquidity and concentration risks, currency risk, and derivatives risk;
- prospective performance with respect to price appreciation or yield;
- the company's organizational structure and other management characteristics;
- the company's financial profile, risk management and controls, information technology, operational controls and procedures, regulatory and internal/external compliance activities and client servicing performance;
- leading of market positions under highly valuable and defensible business franchises, financial fundamentals strength, and the operating environment stability;
- a conservative capitalization structure with reliance on debt and asset protection;
- internal cash generation and margins width in earnings coverage of fixed financial charges;

- assurance of alternate liquidity and access range to financial markets;
- liquidity maintenance;
- any other issues related to the issue or issuer under review. For example, the corporation's credit quality depends also on both the bond rating assigned to its traded indebtedness and on the national rating.

Although CRAs have different concepts and measurements of the PD, various studies which have compared Moody's and S&P ratings, have found a great similarity for investment grade ratings [Cantor and Packer (1996a,b); Ammer and Clinton (2004)].

In the case of speculative-grade issues, Moody's and S&P assign divergent ratings much more frequently to sovereign bonds than to corporate bonds. The literature also finds clear evidence of differences in rating scales once we move beyond the two largest agencies. For example, ratings for the same issuer tend to be lower for the two largest agencies than for other agencies such as Fitch.

5.5.3 *Grading process for the rating agencies*

Credit rating is by nature subjective. Long-term credit judgments involve so many factors unique to particular industries, issuers, and countries, so any attempt to reduce credit rating to a formulaic methodology may lead to serious mistakes. A multidisciplinary approach to risk analysis aims to bring an understanding of all relevant risk factors and viewpoints,[De Laurentis (1998)]. A diverse group of credit risk professionals weigh those factors, considering a variety of plausible scenarios for the issuer, and thus come to a conclusion on what the rating should be. Several analytical principles guide this reasoning process.[6]

Rating is the result of a comprehensive analysis of each individual issue and issuer by experienced, well-informed and impartial credit analysts. Even if the ratings of these analysts are not based on a defined set of financial ratios or rigid computer models, quantification is essential to their

---

[6]The credit rating is an interesting argument for diverse practitioners who consider the credit quality involving the incomes and, consequently, the price of a security, as well as bond investors, mark-to-market analysts, credit derivatives traders, etc. Rating Agencies do not guarantee the accuracy of their ratings and neither do want recommend to buy or sell because they consider their ratings simply opinions that can be used solely as one factor in an investment decision. Any single investor should make his/her own study and evaluation of any issuer whose securities or debt obligations they consider buying or selling.

analysis, particularly since it provides an objective and factual starting point for each rating committee's analytical discussion.

How does rating affect the cost of borrowing? Since the high bond rating, like e.g. AAA, indicates low credit risk to the investor, borrowing will cost less for a high rated issuer. When and if the rating drops, say e.g. to A, bond issuers will have to pay higher bond yields.

For instance, let's consider a firm that issues a €10 million 30-year bond. If the bond is AAA rated the issuer can pay an interest of 2%, so the bond will pay a yearly coupon which amounts to 0.02X€10.000.000=€200.000 for the next thirty years. In addition the bond may be also sold "at premium" on the market, i.e. the investor will pay a issue price higher than the reimbursement (the face value received back on maturity). If the bond is BBB rated, the issuer will be asked to pay an higher interest rate, for instance a 7% yearly coupon of face value, and he also issues the bond "at discount", i.e. a price lower than the face value. If we compare these two bonds, the total interest paid on the AAA rated bond is €3,275,888.16,[7] while the total cost of the BBB rated bond is €38,965,608.44.[8]

5.5.4   *Rating announcement*

The main goal of credit rating is to facilitate a comparison between issuer's underlying long-term creditworthiness by means of standardized categories, so rating decisions are typically not influenced by events whose impact on credit quality is expected to be temporary [Micu et al. (2006); Weinstein (1977)]. For this reason, Rating Agencies provide various kinds of announcement:

The Outlook : reflects the likely direction of an issuer's credit quality over the medium term (usually two years). It is modified when a change in the issuer's risk profile has been observed, but it is not regarded as

---

[7]Assuming the issuer pays €200,000 per year for the next 30 years and on the market we compound these coupon payments at a constant 2% market rate (very simple and conservative hypothesis) the total amount to pay for coupons is:

$$\Sigma_{t=1}^{30} 200,000.00 \cdot (1 + 0.02)^t = 8,275,888.16 \qquad (5.2)$$

and we assume the premium he pays at the moment of issuance is €5,000,000.00.

[8]Assuming the issuer pays €700,000 per year for the next 30 years and on the market we compound these coupon payments at the same constant 2% market rate the total amount to pay for coupons is:

$$\Sigma_{t=1}^{30} 700,000.00 \cdot (1 + 0.02)^t = 28,965,608.44 \qquad (5.3)$$

and we assume the additional cost the issuer pays at the moment of issuance is €10,000,000.00.

permanent enough to review the credit rating. Rating outlooks fall into four categories: Positive (POS), Negative (NEG), Stable (STA), and Developing(DEV). Outlooks may be assigned at the issuer level or at the rating level. Where there is an outlook at the issuer level and the issuer has multiple ratings with differing outlooks, an '(m)' modifier to indicate multiple will be displayed. A designation of RUR (Rating(s) Under Review) indicates that an issuer has one or more ratings under review, which overrides the outlook designation. A designation of RWR (Rating(s) Withdrawn) indicates that an issuer has no active ratings to which an outlook is applicable. Rating outlooks are not assigned to all rated entities. In some cases, this will be indicated by the display NOO (No Outlook). A stable outlook indicates a low likelihood of a rating change over the medium term. A negative, positive or developing outlook indicates a higher likelihood of a rating change over the medium term. A rating committee that assigns an outlook of stable, negative, positive, or developing to an issuer's rating is also indicating its belief that the issuer's credit profile is consistent with the relevant rating level at that point in time. A positive or negative outlook has historically been followed by a rating change in the same direction over the next year about one third of the time;

The Review : provides stronger signals than the Outlook about future changes in rating; it highlights that there is a high probability of change (upgrading or downgrading). The review is usually concluded over 90 days, after receipt of additional information to clarify the impact of a particular event on credit quality. A rating can be placed on review for upgrade (UPG), downgrade (DNG), or more rarely with direction uncertain (UNC). A review may end with a rating being upgraded, downgraded, or confirmed without a change to the rating. Ratings are placed on review when a rating action may be warranted in the near term but further information or analysis is needed to reach a decision on the need for a rating change or the magnitude of the potential change. A review for upgrade or downgrade has historically been concluded with a rating change in the same direction about two thirds of the time.

Confirmation of a Rating : is a public statement that a previously announced review of a rating has been completed without a change to the rating.

Affirmation of a Rating : is a public statement that the current credit rating assigned to an issuer or debt obligation, which is not currently under review, continues to be appropriately positioned.

Outlooks and Reviews were introduced in the 80's to meet investor demand for more timely indicators and forewarn investors of possible changes in creditworthiness. Like the credit rating need not be on review to be changed, a review or a change in outlook does not always imply a change in rating. There are three main hypotheses that could be applied to explain the ratings announcement effects:

(1) The information asymmetry content hypothesis states [Zaima et al. (1988)] that rating agencies are supplied with considerable nonpublic information about a certain company and thus a rating reclassification may provide additional information to the market about the total firm value. According to that, rating re-classification has an impact on the market value of the firm, therefore common stock prices should also be affected by the rating re-classification. When re-classifications provide information about changes in firm value, then the securities of downgraded (upgraded) firms should decline (increase), this means that CDS spreads should increase (decrease).

(2) A credit-rating change provides signals to the market about future earnings and cash flows of the respective issuer, as well as to its competitors in the industry. In particular, a downgrade for one firm can signal good news for rival firms. For instance, if a firm is close to the default, a downgrade can signal that a competitor is in a weak business [Akhigbe et al. (1997)].

(3) The wealth redistribution hypothesis [Zaima et al. (1988)] states that there is a conflict of interest between bondholders and stockholders. Consequently, a credit rating downgrade reduces bond value, which is expropriated from bondholders to stockholders, causing the share price to increase. The hypothesis predicts that a rating downgrade (upgrade) will result in the respective issuer's share price increasing (decreasing). It also predicts that a rating downgrade (upgrade) will result in a decrease (increase) in the bond price therefore in an increase (decrease) in the CDS spread.

Many research papers have investigated the effects that ratings announcements have on financial markets and in particular on the price of stocks, bonds and derivative products, see [Hull et al. (2004)], [Norden and Weber (2004)], [Ammer and Clinton (2004)], and [Micu et al. (2006)]. However, many of the previous studies were performed only on stock, see [Best

(1997)], [Akhigbe et al. (1997)] and on bond prices [Bremer and Pettway (2002)], [Kliger and Sarig (2000)], [Gropp et al. (2001)] but still may be useful for comparison.

Generally, with a few exceptions, [Jonkhart (1979)], [Kliger and Sarig (2000)], the findings show that upgrades or reviews for upgrade do not have a significant impact on prices. In the case of downgrades or review for downgrades most studies find that they do impact on prices with most of the price adjustment taking place prior the announcement. In some cases most of the changes in bond spreads occurred six months before the rating downgrade. Most of the studies find similar results in equity and credit markets. The potential impact of rating announcements on equity prices is ambiguous and depends on the motivation of the announcement. When the rating announcement is motivated by changes in the issuer's financial perspectives, it should have the same impact on the equity and bond markets; a negative (positive) rating announcements should cause a fall (rise) in equity prices. On the contrary, rating announcements caused by changes in leverage should have opposite effects in the equity and bond markets; negative (positive) announcements motivated by an increase in leverage should result in a rise (fall) in equity prices.

All types of rating announcements, outlooks, reviews and rating changes, whether positive or negative, have a significant impact on CDS prices [Norden and Weber (2004)], [Micu et al. (2006)] [Mayordomo et al. (2010)], [Castellano and D'Ecclesia (2011)], [Castellano and D'Ecclesia (2012)]. This is particularly true given that CDS quotes are considered the market price of credit risk, so they are supposed to convey information in a more timely fashion. The CDS markets' features and development is described in Chap. 8.

Glossary

Asset-backed security Security whose value and income payments are derived from a group (pool) of small and illiquid assets that are unable to be sold individually that are collateralized (or "backed"). Pooling the assets into financial instruments allows them to be sold to general investors.

Basis point Hundreds of percentage point usually used to measure spread between interest rates.

CDO Collaterized Debt Obligations backed by bonds.

CEBS Committee of European Banking Supervisors.

CESR Committee of European Securities Regulators.

CMBS Commercial Mortgage Backed Securities are backed by mortgages on commercial rather than residential real estate.

CR Credit Rating: assessment of the creditworthiness of individuals and corporations.

CRA Credit Rating Agencies: companies that assign credit ratings for issuers of financial assets, often used to finance a type of debt.

CRD Capital Requirements Directive provides criteria for the determination of risk weights for firms exposed to credit risk.

ECAI External Credit Assessment Institution, those recognized by authorities.

ECOFIN European Economic and Financial Affairs Council, responsible for economic and financial matters.

ESC European Securities Committee.

ESMA European Securities Market Authority, in charge to policy work for future legislation on securities market.

FCIC Financial Crisis Inquiry Commission is a U.S. government commission charged to investigate the causes of the financial crisis of 2007-2010. It is also nicknamed the New Pecora Commission in comparison to the Pecora Commission charged to investigate the causes of the Great Depression in the 1930s.

Fitch Credit Rating Agency.

Investor-pays model Subscribed rating service in which the ratings are available only to whom have paid a subscription.

Issuer Legal entity that issues (sells) securities to finance its debts, investments or activities.

Issuer-pays model Typical public rating service where the ratings on issuers are distributed (consulted) free of charge.

LAD Logical Analysis of Data is a classification methodology used to classify new observations in a way consistent with past classifications.

Lamfalussy process Approach to a four-level development of financial service industry regulations, involving the European Parliament and Council of EU (first level), the committees and regulators (second level), the national regulators (third level) for the compliance and enforcement of the new rules (fourth level).

MAD Market Abuse Directive: it tackles the issue of insider dealing and market manipulation.

MiFID Markets in Financial Instruments Directive: it establishes a regulatory framework for the provision of investment services in financial instruments.

Moody's Credit Rating Agency.

Mortgage-backed security Asset-backed security that represents a claim on the cash flows from mortgage loans through a process known as securitization.

Neural networks Artificial neural networks are composed of interconnecting artificial neurons (programming constructs that mimic the properties of biological neurons).

Notching General practice of making rating distinctions among different liabilities of a single entity.

NRSRO National Recognized Statistical Rating Organization: type of recognition for the CRAs.

RAMP Rating Methodology Profile: a systematic framework for the rating process.

RMBS Residential Mortgage Backed Security: asset backed security by residential mortgage.

SEC Security and Exchange Commission: in USA it is in charge of control on market securities.

S&P Standard & Poor's Credit Rating Agency.

Securitization Financial practice of pooling various types of contractual "consolidated" debt (residential mortgages, commercial mortgages, auto loans, etc.) and selling them as bonds, or similar obligations, to investors.

Spread Distance (difference) between risk-free asset interest rate and risky asset interest rate.

References

Akhigbe, A., Madura,J., Whyte, A.M. (1997). Intra-Industry Effects of Bond Rating Adjustments, *The Journal of Financial Research*, **20**(4), pp. 545-561.

Altman, E.I. (1989). Default Risk,Mortality Rates,and the Performance of Corporate Bonds, *Research Foundation*, Institute of Chartered Financial Analysts,Charlottesville.

Altman, E.I.(1989). Measuring corporate bond mortality and performance, *Journal of Finance*, September, pp. 909–922.

Altman, E.I., Marco, G., Varetto, F. (1994). Corporate distress diagnosis: Comparisons using linear discriminant analysis and neural networks (The Italian Experience), *Journal of Banking and Finance*, pp. 505-529.

Altman, E.I. , Saunders, A. (1998). Credit risk measurement: Developments over the last 20 years, *Journal of Banking & Finance*, **21**, pp. 1721-1742.

Ammer, J. and Clinton, N. (2004). Good News is no News? the Impact of Credit Rating Changes on the Pricing of Asset-Backed Securities, *Board of Governors of the Federal Reserve System (U.S.)*, International Finance Discussion Papers, **809**.

Asquith, P. ,Mullins Jr., D.W., Wol, E.D. (1989). Original issue high yield bonds:Aging analysis of defaults, exchanges and calls, *Journal of Finance*, pp. 923-953.

Bhatia, A.V. (2002). Sovereign credit ratings methodology: an evaluation. *International Monetary Fund*, Working Paper, **02/170**.

Best, R.W. (1997) The role of default risk in determining the market reaction to debt announcements, *The Financial Review*, **32**(1), February, pp. 87–105.

BIS (2006). *International convergence of capital measurement and capital standards*, Basel Committee on Banking Supervision, June, Bank for International Settlements.

Black, F., Sholes, M. (1973). The Pricing of Options and Corporate Liabilities. *Journal of Political Economy*, **81**, 3, May-Jun, pp. 637–654.

Blume, M.E., Lim, F., MacKinlay, A.C. 1998.The declining credit quality of U:S: corporate debt: myth or reality?, *Journal of Finance* 53, 1389-1413.

Bremer, M., Pettway, R.H. (2002). Information and the market's perceptions of Japanese bank risk: Regulation, environment, and disclosure, *Pacific-Basin Finance Journal*, **10**, pp. 119–139.

Caouette, J.B., Altman, E.I., Narayanan, P., Nimmo, R. (2008). Managing Credit Risk; The Great Challenge For Global Financial Markets, Chapter 6, Wiley Finance, 2nd edition.

Cantor, R. and Packer, F. (1996). Sovereign risk assessment and agency credit ratings,*European Financial Management*, **2**(2), pp. 247–256, July.

Cantor, R. and Packer, F. (1996). Determinants and Impact of Sovereign Credit Ratings, *Economic Policy Review*, **2**(2), October.

Castellano, R., D'Ecclesia, R.L. (2011). Credit Default Swaps and Rating Announcements. *The Journal of Financial Decision Making*, **6**, pp. 234–256.

Castellano, R., D'Ecclesia, R.L. (2012). CDS Volatility: the Key Signal of Credit Quality, *Annals of Operation Research* (DOI: 10.1007/s10479-012-1244-9)

Cavalli, E., Moriggia, V. (2002). Logical data analysis vs. neural networks in the creditworthiness, *Neural Network World*, 4/02, pp. 371–392.

Coats, P. ,Fant, L. (1993). Recognizing financial distress patterns using a neural network tool, *Financial Management*, pp.142-155.

CESR (2008). The role of credit rating agencies in structured finance, consultation paper, February.

COM (2006). Communication from the commission on credit rating agencies. *Official Journal of the European Union*, March, 2006/C 59/02.

COM (2008). Regulation of the European parliament and of the council on credit rating agencies, November, 704.

COM (2011). Amending regulation (EC) no 1060/2009 on credit rating agencies, Proposal for a Regulation, November, 747.

De Laurentis, G. (1998). La misurazione e la gestione del rischio di credito, chapter I processi di rating e i modelli di scoring, Bancaria Editrice, Roma (I).

Elkhoury, M. (2008). Credit rating agencies and their potential impact on developing countries, *United Nations Conference on Trade and Development (UNCTAD)*, Discussion papers, **186**, January.

ESME (2008). Role of credit rating agencies, ESME's report to the European Commission, June.

EU (2006). Directive 2006/48/ec of the European parliament and of the council of 14 june 2006. *Official Journal of the European Union*, June.

Fitch Ratings (2012). Definitions of ratings and other forms of opinion, Fitch Ratings, August.

Gray, S., Mirkovic, A., Ragunathan, V. 2006. The determinants of credit ratings: Austrlian evidence, *Australain Journal of Management*, **31**(2), pp. 333-354.

Gropp, R., Richards, A. J. (2001). Rating Agency Actions and the Pricing of Debt and Equity of European Banks: What Can we Infer About Private Sector Monitoring of Bank Soundness?. *Economic Notes*, **30**, issue 3, pp. 373–398.

Greenberg Quinlan Rosner Research Inc. (2002). Most Structured Finance Senior Executives Oppose Notching, `http://gqrr.com/repository/documents/545.pdf`

Hammer P. L. (1986) Partially Defined Boolean Functions and Cause-Effect Relationships, *Lecture at the International Conference on Multi-Attribute Decsion Making via OR-Based Expert Systems*, University of Passau.

Hull, J.C. (2000). Options, Futures, & Other Derivatives, Prentice-Hall Inc., Upper Saddle River NJ (USA).

Hull, J., Predescu, M., White, A. (2004). The Relationship Between Credit Default Swap Spreads, Bond Yields, and Credit Rating Announcements, *Journal of Banking and Finance*, **28**, pp. 2789-2811, January.

Iben, T., Litterman, R. (1989). Corporate bond valuation and the term structure of credit spreads, *Journal of Portfolio Management*, pp. 52–64.

Katz, S. (1974). The price and adjustment process of bonds to rating reclassifications: a test of bond market efficiency, *Journal of Finance*, **29**, pp. 477–433.

Kliger, D., Sarig, O. (2000). The information value of bond rating, *Journal of Finance*, **55**, pp. 2879-902.

Jonkhart, M. (1979). On the term structure of interest rates and the risk of default, *Journal of Banking and Finance*, **3**, September, pp. 253–262.

Mayordomo S., Pena J.I., Schwartz, E.S. (2010). Are all credit default swap databases equal? *NBER Working Paper*, **16590**.

Merton, R. (1974). On the Pricing of Corporate Debt: The Risk Structure of Interst Rates. *Journal of Finance*, **29**, 2, May, pp. 449–470.

Micu, M., Remolona, E., Wooldridge, P. (2006). The price impact of rating announcements: which announcements matter?, *BIS Working Papers*, **207**.

Moody's (2000). About Moody's.

Norden, L. and Weber, M. (2004). Informational efficiency of credit default swap and stock markets: The impact of credit rating announcements, *Journal of Banking and Finance*, **28**, pp. 2813-2843.

SEC (2008). Proposed Rules for Nationally Recognized Statistical Rating Organizations, available on-line, June

SEC (2008). Proposal for a regulation of the European parliament and of the council on credit rating agencies, available on-line, November. SEC(2008) 2745.

SEC (2011). Executive summary of the impact assessment, Commission staff Working paper, 1355.

SEC (2011). Impact assessment, Commission staff Working paper, 1354.

Van Roy, P. (2005). Credit ratings and the standardise approach to credit risk in Basel II, *The European Central Bank*, Working paper series, **517**, August, http://www.ecb.int/pub/pdf/scpwps/ecbwp517.pdf.

Smith, R.C., Walter, I. (2002). Rating Agencies:Is there an Agency Issue?, in *Ratings, Rating Agencies, and the Global Financial System*, ed. R.M. Levich, C. Reinhart and G. Majnoni, 289-318, Kluwer, Boston.

US Government Printing Office (2011). The Financial Crisis Inquiry Commission, The Financial Crisis Inquiry Report 2011.

VV.AA.. (1984). *Journal of Banking & Finance*, Elsevier, **8**, 2, June.

Weinstein, M. (1977). The effect of a rating change announcement on bond price, *Journal of Financial Economics*, **5**, pp. 329–350.

White, L. J. (2010). Credit Rating Agencies, *the Journal of Economic Perspectives*, **24**(2), pp. 211–226.

Zaima, J. K. and McCarthy, J. (1988). The Impact of Bond Rating Changes on Common Stocks and Bonds: Tests of the Wealth Redistribution Hypothesis, *Financial Review*, **23**, pp. 483–498.

Chapter 6

Securitization Market

(*Rosella Giacometti*)

6.1 Introduction

Securitization — the process by which an asset is transformed into a security i.e. a capital market instrument — has been one of the most innovative developments in financial markets in the last two decades. Securitization is the financial practice of pooling various types of contractual debt such as residential mortgages, commercial mortgages, auto loans or credit card debt obligations and selling the consolidated debt to various investors.

Securities backed by mortgage receivables are called Mortgage Backed Securities (MBS), by bonds are called Collateralized Debt Obligations (CDO) while those backed by other types of receivables are broadly grouped as other Asset Backed Securities (ABS).

Securitization has evolved from the late 1970s, when 'Ginnie Mae' — a government sponsored entity — sold its first MBS, to an estimated outstanding volumes of €6,685 billion in the United States and €1,959 billion in Europe as of the 4-th quarter of 2011. In 2011, ABS issuance amounted to €1,014 billion in the US and €372 billion in Europe.

One of the principal characteristics required for assets to be securitized is that they can be decomposed into a series of cash flows or 'receivables', which can then be packaged and re-packaged with other cash flows. In other words, securitization is a process by which the Originator identifies the claims that it would like to transfer to the market. Banks and private organisations have incomes that are due to them in the future in payment for loans or services that they have offered to third parties. By making these debt instruments available to the capital markets in a format they can easily handle, the Originators transform assets into liquid tradable securities. By pooling and repackaging these illiquid assets the Originators transform them into marketable securities. The motivation is to raise funds and transfer the risk of the underlying portfolio of assets to other investors. The funds raised can then be used for some other productive purpose.

The overall securitization process is a bit more complicated than a simple transformation from assets to securities.

The Originator transfers the assets to a separate entity, typically a SPV, Special Purpose Vehicle, which transforms the assets into new securities, generally with different risk profiles. The typical structure is comprised of multiple tranches of different credit quality. This transformation process is critical since by the principle of 'credit enhancement' the credit quality of the combined products is increased above that of the original underlying assets' pool. One of the key features of 'credit enhancement' is the repackaging of the asset portfolio into a set of securities, tranched into different classes according to their risk profile or credit quality: senior, mezzanine and junior or equity tranches. It is important to stress that through the securitization process we must relieve any claim against the Originator: all the claims are against the SPV. This feature is a critical difference when compared a traditional funding instrument of corporate finance. Securitization is an example of structured finance where, by term of structured product, we mean a financial instrument designed to offer different choices to investors with different risk appetites. If the securitizing transaction is properly structured and the pool performs as expected, the credit risk of all tranches of structured debt improves; if improperly structured, the affected tranches may experience dramatic credit deterioration and losses.

6.2 Asset Classes

The final product of the securitization process sold to the capital market are generically called 'Asset Backed Securities' (ABS) since they are backed by the pool of assets also called collateral or reference assets. The different nature of the assets in the pool of collateral gives rise to the different categories of securities. We adopt the following classification:

- MBS, Mortgage Backed Securities; further subdivided into RMBS and CMBS, backed by residential mortgages and commercial mortgages respectively;

- CDO, Collateralized Debt Obligations backed by bonds; a further subdivision is CLO, collateralized loan obligations;
- Other ABS, backed by other receivables not included above.

In 1968, Ginnie Mae issued the first RMBSs. They were the first application of securitization and nowadays their volume exceeds that of any other securitization application. Since that time RMBSs have been issued by a variety of Government Sponsored Agencies (GSAs) and by private issuers. Three major US government sponsored agencies, Ginnie Mae, Fannie Mae and Freddie Mac, are the leaders in the huge secondary market. Fannie Mae and Freddie Mac were initially created by the U.S. Congress with the goal of expanding the residential mortgage market. For this reason, they are also referred to as GSAs, even though both eventually were converted into private companies.

Government National Mortgage Association (GNMA), also known as Ginnie Mae, is a government-owned corporation within the Department of Housing and Urban Development (HUD). It performs a similar function to Fannie and Freddie. But, it has the explicit backing of the full faith and credit of the United States government.

Private Issuances are commonly referred to as 'non-agency'. An agency buys residential mortgages that conform to their conditions in term of size and underwriting standards. A non-agency collects non conforming mortgages either in terms of size (called Jumbo loans) or in terms of underwriting standards such as debt-to-income ratio, borrower history or loan-to-value ratio (commonly referred to as sub-prime). An important milestone in securitization was the first US public Securitization of Community Reinvestment Act (CRA) loans which started in 1997. CRA loans were those targeted to low and moderate income borrowers and neighborhoods.

RMBSs are designed to provide liquidity in the mortgage market which is vital for the social economy. Through RMBSs the mortgager is able to refinance its positions since securitization provides a secondary mortgage market where the pooled mortgages can be transferred to other investors.

CMBSs are Mortgage-Backed Securities collateralized by Commercial real estate i.e. non residential properties. In contrast to Residential properties, Commercial properties are managed for economic benefits and include, for example, retail centers, hotels, restaurants, hospitals, etc. The distinction between RMBS and CMBS is made because of the significant difference between the two in term of risks, structural features, and type of obligors. In particular a CMBS is different from any other type of securitization since it is a business loan, while the RMBS, CDO and ABS markets are driven largely by consumer behavior.

A final distinction is made by looking at the nature of the reference portfolio since it can be made up of physical debts, of which we could find examples in CLOs (Collateralized Loan Obligations) and CBO (Collateralized Bond Obligations), or on the other hand it could be made up of structured debts, as in the case of CDO of ABS, CDO of CDS and squared CDO.

Finally with Other ABS we refer to all those securities backed by all other types of receivables. Auto loans, credit card debt and leases are the mainstays of the Other ABS market. Auto loans are the products of the auto finance world, the most common way to finance a car purchase. In most markets a large part of the sales of vehicles are funded by a financial organisation which collaborates with the vehicle sellers. In the US market, and increasingly in the EU, car sales are financed. The securitization of auto loans provides a way to give liquidity and refinance the market. Credit card transactions are also interesting receivables. They are short term loans and fairly constant in volume over time. Consequently they represent a steady stream of predictable cash flows that can be securitized.

Securitization is also a significant way of funding leasing companies. The leases backing the securities have been written for various types of equipment, such as furniture, personal computers, telecommunications equipment, medical machines, and aircrafts. The relatively high and increasing use of securitization by leasing companies is explained by the benefits they receive from securitization - most important of which is an alternative source of funding. The cost of a lessor's funding directly affects its competitive position in the leasing market.

Although a majority of securitizations are related to consumer debt, in principle any cash flow receivable can potentially be securitized. Two interesting examples are revenues from movies and music royalties. In 1998 receivables form David Bowie's music albums were securitized and sold with the name of 'Bowie Bond'. The securitization of the collections of other artists, such as James Brown and the Isley Brothers, later followed. The revenues from James Bond's films were also securitized in 2000.

Finally we mention SME (Small-Medium Enterprise) and WBS (Whole Business Securitization) which are securitizations for companies. SME Loan Securitization is an important tool to support SMEs where the loans of different SMEs can be pooled and refinanced. They are generally supported with public guarantees, which foster issuance. For example,

"District Bonds" are CDO whose underlying portfolio comprises loans to SME's within a well defined geographical area. In a WBS the whole business of an operating company is securitized. The receivable is the future cash-flows of the company business. It has been common to finance businesses trying to emerge from actual or near bankruptcy. It is similar to other traditional asset securitizations in the sense that an Originator attempts to get funding at a lower cost than its creditworthiness allows. By isolating certain assets from the Originator's own credit risk it is possible to achieve a higher credit rating through credit enhancement. The main difference is that in a WBS the company securitizes its entire business for funding purposes and not just a residual part.

In Fig. 6.1 we present the outstanding amount of the securitization products in Europe in the first quarter of 2012. We observe that 60% of the amount is concentrated in RMBS compared with 6% in CMBS. CDOs and SMEs account for 10% whilst overall ABSs account for 14%.

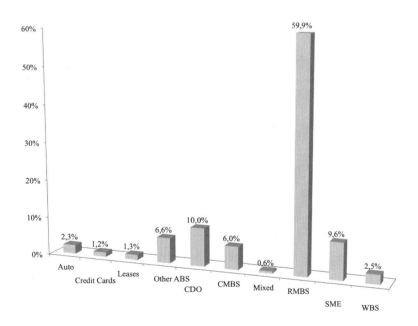

Fig. 6.1   European Securitization in the first quarter of 2012, outstanding volume.

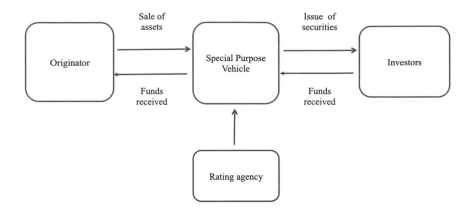

Fig. 6.2   Parties in a securitization.

6.3   The Securitization Process

In order to understand securitization we introduce the four principal parties involved in these contracts and their functions. In Fig. 6.2 we present a map of the involved parties.

- The Originator who selects a portfolio of receivable and sells or transfers it to a Special Purpose Vehicle.
- The Special-Purpose Vehicle (SPV) which buys and restructures the pool of assets into new securities.
- The Rating Agency which gives a rating to the issued financial instrument.
- The Investors of the Capital Market who buy the new securities.

The entity which decides to securitize its assets is called the Originator. It could be a bank or a company. Typical Originators are real estate finance companies, automobile financing companies, car rental companies, credit card companies, hoteliers and real estate rentiers, electricity and telephone companies and banks.

For example, a bank or an automobile financing company identifies which loans will form a particular pool for a securitization, a real estate finance company identifies a set of homogeneous mortgages, and so on.

The Originator sells the assets and receives the funds generated from the sale which are transferred to the SPV.

The Special-Purpose Vehicle (SPV) or Special-Purpose Entity (SPE), is typically a Trust created solely for the purpose of the transaction. It may be a company that offers SPV services. The SPV acts as an intermediary between the Originator and the Investors: it is a legal entity created with the sole purpose of holding the assets and nothing else. It cannot engage in any other business activity and it cannot have any employees. This protect the SPV from conflicts of interest. It must subcontract all activities such as designing the enhancement procedures, managing the portfolio of collateral and secretarial work. These are performed with the help of ancillary service providers. It is usual for both an investment bank and a servicer to be involved.

The investment bank assists the SPV with structuring the transaction, providing the appropriate procedure to improve the credit quality of the new securities and placing them in the capital market for a fee. The servicer collects payments and monitors the collaterals. This service is often provided by the Originator itself, since the servicer needs very similar expertise to the Originator and wants to ensure that loan repayments are paid directly to the Special-Purpose Vehicle. The underlying portfolio may be dynamically or statically managed during the life of the securitization. In a managed securitization the assets in the portfolio may be changed to improve the yield of the portfolio and maintain a fixed risk profile. This is generally referred to as a CDO in which the collateral are tradable assets. With static management the collateral remains unchanged.

In the most common securitization structure the asset movement from the Originator to the SPV is a true sale. With a true sale, the Originator is allowed to remove the transferred assets from his balance sheet. In the case of a subsequent bankruptcy of the Originators the rights of investors in assets held by the SPV is not affected and assets cannot be distributed to the creditors of the Originator i.e. the SPV is bankruptcy-remote. There are other examples where such a transfer is not a true sale but a synthetic transaction, in which the underlying assets remain on the balance sheet of the Originator, this is then referred to as securitized funding. In this case protection against the credit risk of the Originator would normally be achieved by using credit derivatives. A typical example of funding in a WBS is one in which the Originator transfers almost the entire business (substantially all the assets) into a SPV but it does not actually sell it. The property of the business is retained by the company. In both cases, the Originators receive an amount of cash equal to the value of the collateral portfolio and it is isolated from the inherent credit risk.

The SPV holds the assets and repackages them into tranches creating new securities backed by the collateral of receivables in the pool. The tranches are created in such a way that the lowest risk tranche receives a AAA rating from the Rating Agency. The nature of rating is described as ex-ante, meaning the structure and the required enhancement level in order to reach the desired rating class is indicated by the Rating Agency. The Rating Agency analyses the asset pool, the enhancement procedures undertaken and a review of the historical performance of the Originators assets. Using this information it makes an estimate of the worst case scenarios for the performance of the collateral portfolio. The level of credit enhancement and the capital structure may need to be modified based on the results of the stress test in order to get the desired rating class for the different tranches.

Credit enhancement is used to describe the various means designed to protect investors against losses in the assets collateralising the investment. These losses may vary in severity and timing and depend on the asset characteristics, as well as how they are originated and administered. Credit enhancements are essential to secure a high credit rating and a low cost of funds. The enhancements may require either external or internal procedures. External Credit Enhancements include insurance and third party guarantees which involves a limited/full guarantee by a third party to cover losses that may arise on non-performing collateral. Internal Credit Enhancements are based on credit tranching and over-collateralisation, where the Originator provides assets in excess of the collateral required to be assigned to the SPV.

Finally the tranches are issued and sold to Investors: for this reason the SPV may also be called the Issuer. The securities enter into the Capital Market as tradable securities: certificates, bonds or notes are issued and they can be referred to as Asset-Backed Bonds, Obligations or Notes.

Each tranche is represented by its own Bond or Note and is characterized by a specific risk-return profile determined by both the performance of the underlying portfolio and the tranche's seniority in the capital structure. At the top of the capital structure are low-risk AAA rated tranches, also called Senior. They commonly include 70 to 90% of the total nominal value of the portfolio, depending on the quality of the collateral loan pool. The middle tranche of the capital structure is referred to as Mezzanine the highest risk — lowest quality tranche — is at the bottom. Generally the high risk —

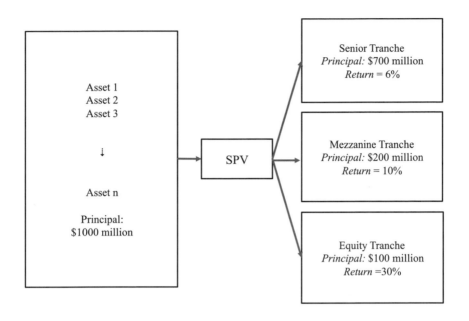

Fig. 6.3   An example of tranches in the securitization.

low quality tranche — is retained by the Originator and it is referred Equity tranche, further improving the credit quality of the remaining tranches sold to the Capital Market. The typical structure is presented in Fig. 6.3.

The incoming cash flows generated by the portfolio of collateral are allocated to the Asset Backed Bonds according to a precisely defined priority: this priority of payments is called the Waterfall Principle and creates the different risk levels of the various tranches.

In Fig. 6.4 we can have a graphic example of the Waterfall Principle.

Incoming cash flows are paid to the most senior tranche (AAA) first and then top-down. Let us consider the example in Fig. 6.3. If no defaults have occurred, the holders of the Senior Tranche receive overall an interest of 6% on the nominal value of the tranche. The interest received is equal to $42 million ($700 million × 6%=$42 million). If the cash flows generated by the collateral portfolio are sufficient, in cascade, the holders of the Mezzanine receive $20 million ($200 million × 10%=$20 million) and Equity Tranche holders $30 million of interest.

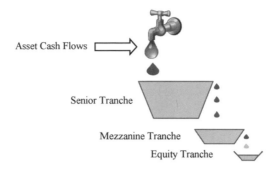

Fig. 6.4   Waterfall Principle.

There are two different structures to manage the interest payment for different structures: Pass-Through and Pay-Through. In a Pass-Through structure the interest earned on the receivables is directly passed to the Investors. In this case the SPV is only a distribution device for the interest generated by the pool. The opposite holds for a Pay-Through structure: the interest received from the receivables is not passed immediately to the holder of the tranche: the SPV issues new securities to them and pays the interest only at fixed and pre-determined points in time.

When it comes to losses the Waterfall Principle is reversed and losses are allocated "bottom up". Any shortfall in incoming cash flows, mainly due to default of loans contained in the securitized portfolio, first hit the Equity Tranche. Accordingly, the lower-rated Equity tranches form a protection for the more senior tranches, as investors in higher-rated tranches are protected from losses by more junior tranches which have to absorb the first losses.

If we look at the example in Fig. 6.3, the Equity Tranche accounts for 10% of the nominal value of the pool, the Mezzanine Tranche accounts for 20% and the Senior Tranche for 70%. The Equity Tranche will bear all losses stemming from defaults on the securitized loans up to 10% of the notional value. Only if losses exceed this threshold (in our example: 10%), will investors in the Mezzanine Tranche have to bear losses. Therefore, Mezzanine investors are protected by the Junior Bond (corresponding to the Equity Tranche) and only run the risk that losses exceed that threshold. The protection by the subordinated Junior Bond is reflected in a better rating of the Mezzanine Tranche. The Mezzanine tranche will bear the losses occuring between 10% and 30%. Only if losses exceed this threshold (in our example: 30%) will investors in the Senior Tranche be affected.

By using a tranching technique, it is possible to create very highly AAA-rated bonds in the portfolio. A rating of 'AAA' implies that the bond is a very secure investment with a very low probability of default. This tranche is theoretically almost as secure as an investment in most government bonds, and it is highly improbable that those investors will miss any of the contractual payments on their bonds.

6.4 Rationale for Securitization

The success of securitization can be explained by the benefits they offer to Originators and Investors. There are three major reasons for Originators to securitize their assets:

(1) Raise funds at reduced funding costs. Through securitization, a company rated less than AAA but with AAA ratable cash flow could be able to borrow at AAA rates. This is the principal reason to securitize a cash flow and can have tremendous impact on borrowing costs. The Originator receives an amount of cash approximately equal to the securitized portfolio, incurring into only the cost of transferring to the SPV all the cash flows of the receivables.

(2) Risk transfer. Securitization represents a sort of insurance for the underlying portfolio. The credit exposure attached to the loans of an Originator is transferred from the Originator to the Investors. The Originator pays the Investors a periodic fee (the cash flows of the receivables) for protection against credit risk. In case of default of the underlying loans, the Investors suffer the losses.

(3) Off balance-sheet debt financing. By securitizing some of its assets in a true sale to the SPV, the Originator is able to remove them from his balance sheet and lower his capital requirements. This is particularly attractive for Banks that have to satisfy some capital requirements under Basel II and III. Securitization of the loans does not have any impact on the relationship with the clients since the Originator does not have to notify third parties when their loans have been transferred to an SPV.

Securitization has also important advantages for the Investors:

(1) Investors have access to a wider range of investment types and can increase their portfolio diversification. Given the wide range of assets

that can be securitized it is possible to invest in securities that show a lower correlation with other traditional asset classes.

(2) The ability to satisfy different risk appetites of Investors. Asset Backed Bonds and Notes are available in all kind of risk and credit categories, ranging from AAA to the very risky equity first-loss pieces.

(3) Possible higher returns: in the past, ABS's offered higher yields than many other assets with the same rating class e.g. AAA rated government debt.

Asset Backed Securities are structured products which contain the same risk as that of the collateral portfolio. However the risk is not allocated uniformly to different classes of Investors. In the evaluation of the risk of an investment in a securitization product, it is critical to consider both the risk of the Originator and the risk of the selected collateral portfolio.

The risk of the Originator's bankruptcy is directly related to its business and financial risk. By business risk and financial risk we mean the possibility that a company will have lower than anticipated profits due to negative market conditions as well as those tied to the financial structure and management of the Originating company. These are the factors which affect the creditworthiness of every corporation. Consequently we need to readdress the issue of true and synthetic sale. In the case of true sale the Originator becomes 'bankruptcy remote'. In a true sale the rating of the tranches in an ABS are enhanced at most by one notch above the current rating of the Originator. Should the Originator become insolvent, other creditors of the Originator cannot make a claim against the receivables sold to Investors. As long as the Originator continues to operate, even in bankruptcy, Investors will receive payments on the receivables. However in a synthetic sale the credit enhancement needs to include credit derivatives which protect Investors against Originator's default.

There are additional risks related to the ongoing generation of the receivables which may be not directly controlled by the Originator. These risks include, but are not limited to:

(1) Poor performance of the underlying portfolio of collateral. This risk may be mitigated through over-collateralisation.

(2) Prepayment. Unlike corporate bonds, most securitizations are amortized, meaning that the principal amount is paid back gradually over the specified term of the loan, rather than in one lump sum at the maturity of the loan. ABS's are derived from a pool of loans so if the

loans prepays, the ABS prepay's as well. Prepayment uncertainty is an important concern with amortizing an ABS. Prepayment implies only some obligors are exiting the pool. Generally the prepayment is done by good quality obligors, so the concentration of bad quality increases and therefore so does the probability of default among those remaining in the pool.

(3) Multiple obligor default. The risk of a reduction in the nominal value invested in a tranche is a function of the default correlation. The default correlation represents the possibility of the joint default of multiple obligors. When the correlation is low, the junior or equity tranche is almost certain to sustain all the realized losses and the senior tranche is relatively safe. However, in periods of crisis, the default correlation increases and multiple losses become more probable. An appropriate estimate of the default correlation is not easy to obtain. In the past the evaluation was done using the Gaussian copula model(see [Li (2000)] and [Schonbucher (2003)]). Copulas functions are used to describe the dependence among random variables. Given the marginal distributions of each component of a random vector, the copula describes the dependence structure among the components. In a Gaussian copula the marginals are univariate Gaussian distributions and the dependence structure follow a multivariate Guassian distribution. During the recent and still ongoing financial crisis, this model has shown its weakness and its inability to appropriately capture tail dependence.

To quantify the risk of an ABS tranche is not an easy task as we need to evaluate the joint default probability in the collateral pool. Since, in principle, any receivable can be securitized, a security created as a result of securitization can be included in a new collateral pool to issue new securities. If the initial security was hard to analyze, when multiple securities are pooled together and re-packaged, the final security may be almost inscrutable.

6.5 The Market Evolution

The technique of securitization was first introduced in the US in the 1970s. The market first developed in response to a need in the US housing market. Before the 1990s, subprime borrowers typically found it hard to qualify for bank loans. The desire to own houses was growing rapidly, interest rates were low and securitization provided an easy way to refinance the mortgage market. After a mortgage had been sold, it was usually packaged with other home loans into a Residential Mortgage-Backed Security (RMBS). CDOs helped drive the U.S. mortgage boom by purchasing some of the riskier parts of MBS's that other investors did not want. Low quality tranches were packaged in financial products and sold to investors transferring all the risk to the capital market. This is an example of re-securitization.

By the second half of the 1990s, with relatively low interest rates, investors were seeking opportunities with higher yields. The securitization market became very attractive to these investors since the risk was considered manageable. There was an overall optimistic feeling in the marketplace and the first public issuance under the Community Reinvestment Act (CRA) of 1997 led to further growth. Banks found it profitable to invest in the AAA rated tranches because the promised return was significantly higher than the cost of funds and capital requirements were low. Refinancing home loans became an additional large source of revenue for the Banks. Re-securitization again boomed.

Starting in 2000, mortgage Originators in the US relaxed their lending standards and created large numbers of subprime first mortgages. Securitization increased the affordability of loans even to those with low income or bad credit history. In this context with very low interest rates, the demand for real estate increased and prices rose. Lending standards were relaxed even further, to continue to attract first time buyers and keep prices increasing.

By 2007 the real estate bubble burst and U.S. real estate prices fell. Products created from mortgage collateralisation, previously thought to be safe became much riskier. RMBSs and CDOs were sadly and deeply implicated in the 'Credit Crunch of 2007': even though initially the dramatic increase in subprime mortgages in the United States was seen as a good thing, allowing more people to buy their own houses, it subsequently exploded into a crisis as more and more highly leveraged borrowers defaulted.

The current financial crisis has revealed several shortcomings in the securitization process, which include:

(1) conflicts of interest for participants along the securitization chain,
(2) over-reliance on Rating Agency risk models,
(3) a lack of transparency with respect to collateral and the deal structure.

These shortcomings contributed to freezing the market demand for securitized products.

The European market evolved in a different manner. The European market started later than the US market and until 2008 was constantly increasing. The decline would start a year later than the US in 2009. In contrast, although volume in the US securitization markets fell sharply in 2007 and 2008, they slowly increased in 2009 and 2010. This increase is attributable in particular to support for the RMBS market from the US government sponsored agencies (GSAs) Freddie Mac, Fannie Mae and Ginnie Mae.

We can see the evolution of the US and the European markets in Fig. 6.5.

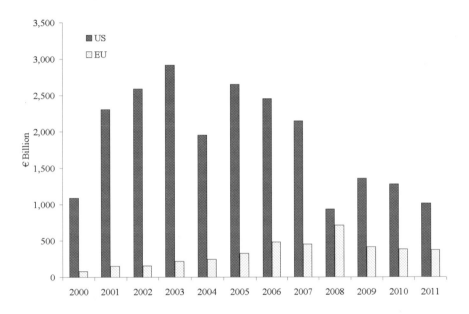

Fig. 6.5 European and US securitization issuances.

The outstanding volumes by collateral type in the EU and the US are given in Fig. 6.6 and Fig. 6.7. In both markets the RMBSs are the most important securitization instrument. In Europe, RMBSs represent by far the most prominent asset class, with the greater issuance volume in the period 2008-2010. The issuances of RMBSs was around 60% of the total in 2012. In the last 3 years there was a slight decrease in the outstanding volumes of all the types of collateral (excluding RMBS in US) confirming that currently, securitization is still very weak and the market has not yet found a stable path and investors remain sidelined.

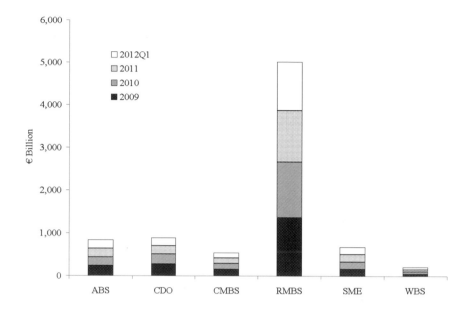

Fig. 6.6   European outstanding volumes by collateral from 2009 to 2012 Q1.

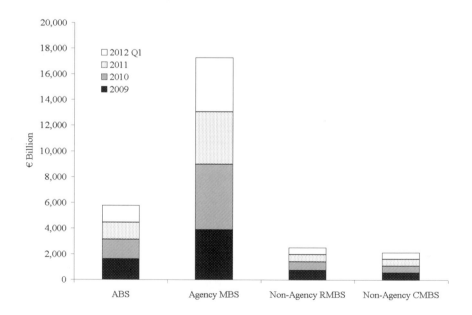

Fig. 6.7   US outstanding volumes by collateral from 2009 to 2012 Q1.

Table 6.1   Issuance by Collateral and Country in €billion.

Country	ABS	CDO	CMBS	RMBD	SME	WBS	Total
Belgium	-	-	-	1.0	-	-	1.0
Denmark	-	-	-	-	-	-	-
France	0.5	-	-	1.4	1.4	-	3.3
Germany	3.7	0.2	-	-	-	-	3.9
Greece	-	-	-	-	-	-	-
Ireland	-	-	-	-	-	-	-
Italy	-	-		20.9	-	-	20.9
the Netherlands	-	-	-	5.2	-	-	5.2
Portugal	-	-		1.1	-	-	1.1
Spain	0.4	-	-	0.5	4.5	-	5.4
UK	2.5	-	2.0	10.4	1.8	1.1	17.9
Other	0.3	-	-	-	-	-	0.3
Pan Europe	0.0		0.2	2.0			2.3
Multinational	-	-	-	-	-	-	-
European total	7.4	0.2	2.0	40.5	7.7	1.1	58.9

In Table 6.1 we can see that the securitization activity in Europe varies considerably by country. Issuance is mainly concentrated in a few markets (the United Kingdom, Spain, the Netherlands and Italy). In the first quarter of 2012 Italy showed the highest volume issuance (35% in RMBS), followed by the UK (30%). Spain and the Netherlands, had an issuance share of 9%. RMBS's are the dominant asset class in all countries except Germany, where auto loan securitization represents the biggest market.

In Fig. 6.8 we see the evolution of outstanding volumes by country. In 2012 UK outstanding volumes represented almost 40% of the market. Among the remainder only the Netherlands (16%), Spain(14%) and Italy(11%) held a share larger that 10%. While in the UK and Spain the volumes are decreasing, in Italy and the Netherlands the volumes are stagnant.

In Table 6.2 we report the outstanding country volumes by collateral amount. It is interesting to observe that, when we compare this table with the previous one, the issuance in most countries is quite limited. Mortgages are always the main collateral for which there is an issuance in most countries. Some common factors show that investors have learned from the crisis and that they are avoiding excessively complex or risky products. Specifically, there have been successful publicly placed issuances in Germany, the Netherlands, the United Kingdom and, very recently, in Italy with the securitization of collateral with a low risk profile. Only the best quality auto

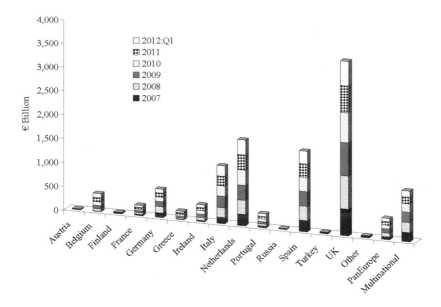

Fig. 6.8　European outstanding volumes by country and collateral from 2009 to 2012 Q1.

Table 6.2　Outstanding volumes by Collateral and Country in €billion.

Country	ABS	CDO	CMBS	RMBD	SME	WBS	Total
Austria	0.0	-	0.2	2.0	-	-	2.2
Belgium	0.1	-	0.1	71.1	14.5	-	85.9
Finland	-		-	-	3.7	0.0	3.7
France	18.1	0.2	3.8	18.3	3.8	-	44.2
Germany	35.3	2.5	16.2	19.0	8.5	0.1	81.6
Greece	15.2	3.0	-	6.0	9.4	-	33.6
Ireland	-	0.3	0.4	57.4	2.5	-	60.5
Italy	47.8	4.8	10.2	131.0	17.1	1.4	212.3
the Netherlands	5.7	1.3	6.3	281.6	12.2	-	307.2
Portugal	6.5	-	-	38.2	9.6	-	54.3
Russia	0.9	-	-	2.7	-	-	3.5
Spain	21.7	1.2	0.3	163.0	80.4	-	266.5
Turkey	3.2	-	-	-	-	-	3.2
UK	38.0	7.8	61.9	354.6	7.2	53.8	523.2
Other	2.2	1.8	-	0.3	0.4	-	4.6
Pan Europe	2.8	40.2	20.9	0.2	5.8	0.1	70.1
Multinational	1.9	123.7	2.7	0.2	0.8	0.6	130.0
European total	199.5	186.8	123.1	1149.1	172.2	55.9	1,886.7

ABSs (Germany) and prime RMBSs (UK and the Netherlands) have been able to access the public market.

In light of the recent financial crises, Basel III has given precise rules for securitization with respect to capital charges applied to securitized products on a bank's trading book. Re-securitization exposures (CDO's of ABS and CDO's of RMBs) will be treated differently from first securitization exposures to reflect that they are more complex and riskier. Capital requirements for re-securitization positions will be approximately double the requirements of a first issuance for securitized products.

Glossary

Trust A Trust is basically a private agreement between parties. Trust structures are created and used to place assets under the ownership of a separate legal entity.

GSA Government Sponsored Agencies or Entities. Three GSAs dominate the market for mortgages in the United States: The Government National Mortgage Association (GNMA) (or Ginnie Mae), The Federal National Mortgage Association, better known as Fannie Mae (or just Fannie), and the Federal Home Loan Mortgage Corporation, or Freddie Mac (Freddie).

Securitization It is the process of pooling and repackaging relatively homogeneous illiquid assets into marketable securities that can be sold to investors.

ABS The final products of the securitization process which are sold to the capital market are called 'asset backed securities'

MBS MBSs are mortageges backed securities i.e. asset securities backed by mortgages;

CDO CDOs are collateralized debt obligations i.e. asset securities backed by bonds;

CLO CLOs are collateralized loan obligations i.e. asset securities backed by loans;

SPV Special Purpose Vehicle is a Trust created for the purpose of the secutitization transaction or a company that offers SPV services

Credit enhancement It is the term used to describe the various means to protect investors against losses in the assets collateralising their investment.

CRA Community Reinvestment Act 1977 is a United States federal law designed to encourage commercial banks and savings associations to help meet the needs of borrowers in all segments of their communities, including low- and moderate-income neighborhoods. The Community Reinvestment Act was passed so that banks would have an incentive to do more business in previously ignored areas.

Waterfall Principle The waterfall principle is characteristic of securitisation transactions. The payments received are distributed to the investors in a established sequence. The investors in the highest ranking tranche are the first to have their claims for payment of capital and interest satisfied. The payment flow resembles a waterfall in the sense that the incoming payments are distributed to the investors in descending order.

Pass-Through In a Pass-Through structure the interest earned on the receivables is directly passed to the Investors. The SPV is only a distribution device for the interest generated by the pool.

Pay-Through In a Pay-Through structure the interest received from the receivables is not passed immediately to the holder of the tranche. The SPV issues new securities to them and pays the interest only at fixed and pre-determined points in time.

References

Donnelly, C., Embrechts, P. (2010). The devil is in the tails: actuarial mathematics and the subprime mortgage crisis, *ASTIN*, Bulletin, **40**(1), pp. 1–33.

Fabozzi, F. J., Kothari, V. (2008). *Introduction to securitization* (Wiley Finance).

Gorton, G. (2008). The Panic of 2007, *Yale School of Management*, Working Paper.

Hull, J. C. (2008). The Financial Crisis of 2007: Another Case of Irrational Exuberance, in *The Finance Crisis and Rescue: What Went Wrong? Why? What Lessons Can be Learned*, (University of Toronto Press).

Hull, J. C. (2009). *Risk Management and Financial Institutions*, 2nd Edition (Upper Saddle River, Pearson).

Hull, J. C., White, A. (2009). The Risk of Tranches Created from Subprime Mortgages, *University of Toronto*, Working paper.

Keys, B. J., Mukherjee, T., Seru, A., Vig, V. (2008). Did securitization Lead to Lax Screening? Evidence from Subprime Loans, *University of Michigan*, Working paper.

Kothari, V. (2006). *Securitization: The Financial Instrument of the Future*, 3rd edition (Wiley Finance).

Krinsman, A. N. (2007). Subprime Mortgage Meltdown: How Did it Happen and How Will It End, *The Journal of Structured Finance*, Summer, pp. 13–19.

Mian, A., Sufi, A. (2008). The Consequences of Mortgage Credit Expansion: Evidence from the 2007 Mortgage Default Crisis, *Graduate School of Business*, Working Paper, University of Chicago.

X. Li, D. (2000), On Default Correlation: A Copula Function Approach *The RiskMetrics Group*, Working Paper, **99-07**.

Schönbucher, P. J. (2003). *Credit Derivatives Pricing Models: Model, Pricing and Implementation.*, 2nd edition (John Wesley & Sons Ltd: Chichester, West Sussex England), January.

Zimmerman, T. (2007). The Great Subprime Meltdown, *The Journal of Structured Finance*, **13**(3), Fall, pp. 7–20.

Chapter 7

Market Bond Products

7.1 The Covered Bond Market

(*Giorgio Consigli*)

7.1.1 *Introduction*

Covered Bonds are bonds issued by (or offering recourse to) a credit institution (the *Coverer*) and with priority recourse to a pool of collateral. Investors have a claim against the issuing institution in the first instance, and, in the event of default of the issuer, a priority claim on the cover pool. *Covered Bonds* (CB) are dual-recourse bonds issued mainly to fund long term investments under specific legislation.

The recourse to the issuer and consequent inherent credit risk distinguishes CB from Asset-Backed Securities.

In most European countries, the issuance of CB is regulated by specific rules concerning eligible assets, assessment criteria, asset-liability management guidelines and so forth. The eligible cover assets range from public sector entities, mortgage and housing loans, credit institutions, to senior *Mortgage-Backed Securities* (MBS) issued by securitization entities.

The CB market in 2011 represented the most important European fixed-income market after the sovereign bond market with €2.67 trillion of outstanding notional, of which Germany, Spain and France made up more than 50%. Germany is still the largest CB market (€590 billion), then Spain (€401 billion), France (€365 billion) and Denmark (€350 billion). Also the Swedish CB market gained importance in the last 3 years. The growth of this market segment can be attributed to its solid underlying legal and regulatory framework and consequent increasing liquidity. Looking at the past competition between CB and securitisation products the on-balance treatment of CB seems to have the edge. The *European Central Bank* (ECB) clearly states that CB are a valuable alternative to the US Mortgage Backed Security model, [ECBC (2010)].

The essential features of CB as agreed by the the *European Covered Bond Council* (ECBC), [ECBC (2011)], are:

(1) The bond is issued by a credit institution which is subject to public supervision and regulation, to which bondholders otherwise have full recourse.
(2) Bondholders have a claim against a pool of financial assets or loans in priority over unsecured creditors of the credit institution.
(3) The credit institution has ongoing obligations to maintain sufficient assets in the cover pool to satisfy the claims of CB holders at all times.
(4) The obligations of the credit institution with respect to the cover pool are supervised by public or other independent bodies.

7.1.2 *Basic features*

Compared to other debt securities issued by financial institutions, such as senior unsecured debt or Asset-Backed Securities, CB can be viewed as *senior secured debt*. During the summer of 2012 the issuance of international debt securities resumed its overall growth as a result of the unprecedented effort by the ECB through it's three-year collateralised *Longer-Term Refinancing Operations* (LTROs). By improving market confidence, the ECB's policy action was influential in reopening the debt securities' primary markets for Euro zone financial institutions.

Global issuance of financial international debt securities during the first quarter of 2012 increased by roughly 40% respect to the last quarter of 2011 showing the largest increase since 2008. For long periods in the second half of 2011, much of the debt issuance by European banks had been confined to CB, as unsecured bond funding was available only for top-rated banks and banks headquartered in jurisdictions with a AAA sovereign rated debt. It was primarily high-rated European banks that reopened the market for senior unsecured bonds at the beginning of 2012. The senior secured debt segment represents still the largest share of banking sector liabilities and it is used, being the most liquid segment of market as the *benchmark*. A benchmark CB is a Euro-denominated, bullet maturity, fixed annual coupon bond with a defined minimum outstanding volume (nowadays min

Table 7.1   Main features of CB and Asset-Backed Securities.

Motivation of issuer	Covered bonds refinancing	Asset-Backed Securities risk reduction, regulatory arbitrage, refinancing
Issuer	loan originator	special entity
Recourse option	yes	generally no
Structure	assets generally remain on balance sheet	assets transferred to special entity
Impact on issuer's capital Requirements	none	reduction
Legal restrictions on issuer's eligible collateral	yes	generally none
Management of asset pool	dynamic	static
Asset pool transparency	limited (but regularly controlled)	limited
Prepayment of assets	no pass-through as assets are replaced	generally full pass-through
Coupon	predominantly fixed	predominantly floating

€500 million). The current total outstanding volume of the Euro area benchmark CB market is approximately €1 trillion (approx. 12% of liquid Euro-denominated bonds).

Covered bonds are distinct from *Asset-Backed Securities* (ABS) as well as *Mortgage-Backed Securities* (MBS). Their difference is at the origin of the different performance occured in this market over the 2008-2012 period. Under certain conditions, credit institutions might have incentives to issue ABSs, as happened in Spain during the last few yearswhere a particular regulatory framework combined with the low cost of securitisation made Spanish banks to become a major issuer of ABSs in Europe (second only to the United Kingdom). In this case, the differences between ABSs and CB tend to disappear.

From the issuer's perspective the purpose of CB is basically to use a pool of high quality assets to not only reduce the cost of funding and increase its duration, but to also extend and stabilize the investment base. Compliance with Article 52(4) of the UCITS Directive has already led to some standardisation in cover pool monitoring and banking supervision. Most CB systems have established an external, independent cover pool monitor who must have appropriate qualifications. In most countries national banking supervisors (and in some cases, financial market regulators) exercise special supervision of CB in order to fulfil Article 52(4) UCITS. Investors are attracted to CB because of their legal status, higher recovery rates and better transparency than a senior unsecured bank bond. The asset pool of a CB may legally or generally include:

- Exposures to (or guaranteed by) central governments, central banks, public sector entities, regional governments and local authorities in the EU.
- Exposures to third country central Governments, non-EU central banks, multilateral development banks, international organisations with a minimum rating of 'AA-', non-EU public sector entities, non-EU regional governments and non-EU local authorities with a minimum rating of 'AA-' and up to 20% of the nominal amount of outstanding CB with a minimum rating of 'A-'.
- Substitute assets from institutions with a minimum rating of AA- for no more than 15% of the nominal outstanding amount.
- Loans secured by residential property.
- Loans secured by commercial immovable property.
- Ship mortgage loans with Loan-to-Value (LTV) of up to 60%.

Asset-liability guidelines exist in most of the CB systems, but large differences in technical details and regulatory frameworks make a comparison difficult. The strong relationship between CB liabilities and cover pool on the banks' asset portfolio leads to a classical ALM problem in banks balance sheets with liabilities valued according to the assets included in the cover pool. To cover heterogeneous CB systems few tools can be used:

- the *cover principle*
- some CB net-present value asset-liability matching rules: in specific CB markets *Mandatory over-collateralisation* (on a nominal or net-present value basis) plays an important role in mitigating the risk of a negative difference between cover pool and CB nominal value. Derivatives have

also been considered as market-based intruments to mitigate the risk in CB asset-liability management recently.

7.1.3   *Market evolution*

The modern age of the CB market started in 1995 when the first German Pfandbrief in benchmark format (Jumbo) was issued. The bond was issued to meet liquidity needs of investors and to provide additional funding for public sector loans. Since then, the Jumbo market has expanded dramatically. The introduction of the Euro currency caused investors to intensify their demand for liquid products. Banks needed to look for new funding sources (i.e. high credit-quality liquid bonds) to attract international capital investors. Therefore, banks in Western countries revitalised their CB systems to create a competitive capital market instrument. Figure 7.1 illustrates the growth of the CB market since 2003.

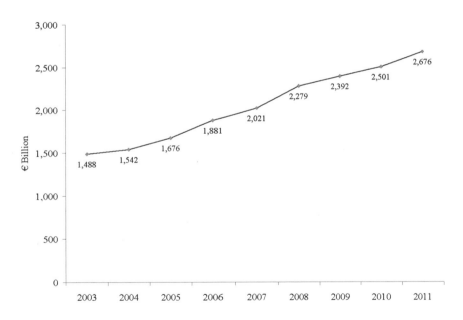

Fig. 7.1   Total outstanding volume of CB market.

European banks are the primary players in the market, with just two Countries dominating half of the market at the end of 2011, although the market context is evolving. Over the last two years Swedish and Norwegian

banks have become relevant market players on the supply side. Germany
has the largest market share for CB liabilities in 2011, but new issuances
keep declining while banks headquartered in France, Spain, Denmark and
Sweden show an increasing market share year after year, with the Danish
banks to report the largest new issuance amount.

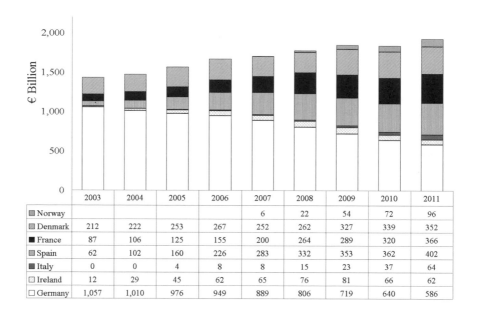

	2003	2004	2005	2006	2007	2008	2009	2010	2011
Norway					6	22	54	72	96
Denmark	212	222	253	267	252	262	327	339	352
France	87	106	125	155	200	264	289	320	366
Spain	62	102	160	226	283	332	353	362	402
Italy	0	0	4	8	8	15	23	37	64
Ireland	12	29	45	62	65	76	81	66	62
Germany	1,057	1,010	976	949	889	806	719	640	586

Fig. 7.2   CB outstanding volumes by country.

Besides the clear and effective legal framework which in many countries
has facilitated the success of the CB market, several reasons explain the
success of CB as banks' liabilities in Germany, Denmark and Spain.

In *Germany*, cover assets are registered and identified. The register
records the cover assets being used to cover the Pfandbriefe as well as any
associated derivative claims. The legal effect of registration is that in the
case of insolvency of the issuer, the assets which form part of the cover pool
are clearly known and therefore not part of the insolvency estate. While
the bank carries out the daily administration of the cover register, it is
the cover pool monitor who supervises the required cover and registration.
Covered Bond holders enjoy preferential treatment as the law stipulates the
separation of the cover assets on the one hand and the insolvency estate

on the other. The satisfaction of the Pfandbrief creditors is not limited to the cover assets and these creditors also participate to the insolvency proceedings with respect to the Pfandbrief bank's other assets.

In *Denmark* the Act on CB (SDOs) came into force on July, 1 2007. It was passed to implement the new set of rules on CB from the EU (capital requirements directive- CRD 1) and gave both, mortgage banks and commercial banks, the opportunity to issue SDOs. The CB legislation in Denmark allows for joint funding, i.e. two or more institutions joining forces to issue CB in order to achieve larger issues. Danish mortgage banks operate according to Danish law, which confines the activities of issuers to the granting of mortgage loans funded by the issuance of mortgage bonds. The cover pool may include unsecured loans to public authorities and guarantees issued by public authorities. Cover assets, mortgages and eligible securities are assigned to specific capital centres which constitute the cover pools of the bonds issued in accordance with Danish legislation.

The *Spanish* CB system was recently reformed helping the CB market to grow significantly over the last two years. The institution issuing CB keeps a special accounting register. The legislation does not require a special pool monitor other than the Bank of Spain prudential supervision, on a continuous basis, which includes the periodic disclosure of information regarding cover assets by credit institutions. The issuer is also responsible and liable for cover and eligible assets pool monitoring. The quantitative mandatory limits have to be maintained at all times, thus the monitoring is carried out continuously by the issuer as a part of the risk management and auditing of its activity. The *special* supervision is carried out by the *Comisión Nacional del Mercado de Valores* (CNMV) which may also monitor and supervise compliance with statutory requirements and limits upon approval of the issuance and of the placing process. In case of insolvency of the Spanish issuer CB holders have to be treated as privileged claims against the insolvency estate.

7.1.4 *Primary market*

The CB market is one of the key components of European capital markets. The amount of outstanding mortgage CB represents around 20% of outstanding residential mortgage loans in the EU.

The major categories of cover assets are mortgage loans, public sector loans and ship loans. Covered bonds backed by mortgage loans exist in all countries with CB systems. Covered bonds to fund public sector lending

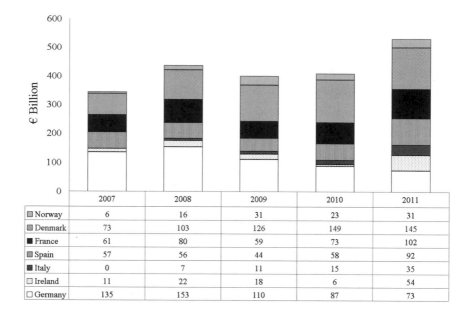

	2007	2008	2009	2010	2011
▨ Norway	6	16	31	23	31
▨ Denmark	73	103	126	149	145
■ France	61	80	59	73	102
▨ Spain	57	56	44	58	92
■ Italy	0	7	11	15	35
▨ Ireland	11	22	18	6	54
□ Germany	135	153	110	87	73

Fig. 7.3   New Issues of CB in selected EU countries.

(national, regional and local authorities) are relevant in most European countries (Austria, France, Germany, Ireland, Italy, Luxembourg, Poland, Portugal, Spain and UK). Covered bonds backed by ship loans transact mainy in Denmark and Germany.

Being secured by the underlying assets, CB spreads and market dynamics depend on the evolution of these markets.

A robust legal framework and investor protection schemes in the case of issuer's insolvency have fostered market expansion, see Figure 7.4. The various European CB systems use different techniques to protect CB holders against claims from other creditors in case of insolvency of the issuer. Most systems establish, by law or by contract, the segregation of CB and cover pools from the general insolvency estate.

One important and widespread unifying characteristic is that CB in Europe do not automatically become part of bailout schemes if the issuer becomes insolvent. Numerous CB systems have provisions that allow derivatives to become part of the cover pool with the sole purpose to hedge interest rate or currency mismatches.

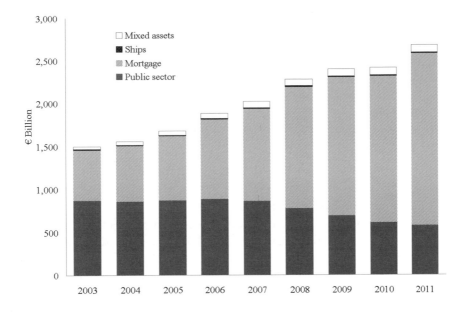

Fig. 7.4   CB market outstanding by cover pool.

7.1.5   *Secondary market*

During the last two years CB prices have been driven by the sovereign crisis in combination with central bank activity such as the ECB *long-term-refinancing operation* (LTRO) and the second 2011 *Covered Bond Purchase Program* (CBPP2). The LTRO reduced the spreads in all sectors. In that context, CB have outperformed sovereign bonds with the exception of Spain and Italy where CB represent the most attractive products when compared to sovereign or senior unsecured bank debt. The CB has been affected by the debt crisis and higher volatility can be expected for the next future. The main determinants of CB prices dynamics in secondary markets are:

- correlation with cover asset market dynamics and increased overcollateralisation requirements;
- sovereign and senior unsecured bond spreads;
- banking sector systemic fragility (concentration, risk exposure, asset-liability mismatching and so forth);
- primary market volumes.

Figure 7.5 shows the evolution of the EMTX Euro area Government Bond Indices (quoted on the EuroMTS market) in a limited number of relevant markets. The performance over the 2009-2011 period reflects the high volatility of sovereign spreads and the widening of the spread with respect to senior unsecure banking debt. Over 2011 and 2012 Rating Agencies have tightened the standards for credit rating of issuing banks and increased the required over-collateralisation, CB ratings have followed the downgrades of the sovereign ratings in many cases. As of November 2012, CB downgrades have been significant over the last 18 months: in Italy 40 negative rating revisions were recorded, 54 in Portugal and 51 in Spain, numeorus downgrades occurred also in Germany, France, Greece, Ireland, etc., most of which from October 2011-February 2012.

On average CB spreads have evolved preserving a positive differential with respect to senior unsecured debt and MBS and a negative differential compared to government bonds. Such stylised evidence has some exceptions: in 2012 CB spreads were actually tighter than those of sovereign bonds for Spain and Italy, whose sovereign rating went through a series of negative shocks. The difference between senior debt and CB spreads has been decreasing in general, still remaining positive in all countries. At the beginning of May 2012, the difference was on average 133 bps for Italy, 131 bps for Portugal, 102 bps for Germany, 91 bps for Danish banks, 62 bps for Spain and 61 bps for France. Except for Spain and Italy, the difference has been decreasing over the years.

The correlation between secured (CB, RMBS) and unsecured liabilities is generally driven by the issuer credit risk and its rating assessment. A negative premium may be induced on CB by their collateralisation, higher liquidity and lower risk weights, according to the Basel III framework.

Diverging dynamics between sovereign and CB spreads can be explained by several factors:

- collaterals: high quality collaterals within the same market provides a favourable influence on CB spreads relative to sovereign;
- rating: in general a downgrade of sovereign debt will typically drive down CB ratings also, the opposite effect doesn't hold;
- liquidity: sovereign bond markets exhibit historically a much higher liquidity leading to lower liquidity premiums relative to CB;
- ECB cuts: interest rate cuts by the ECB have an immediate impact on the sovereign yield curve not the same on banking sector liabilities. In

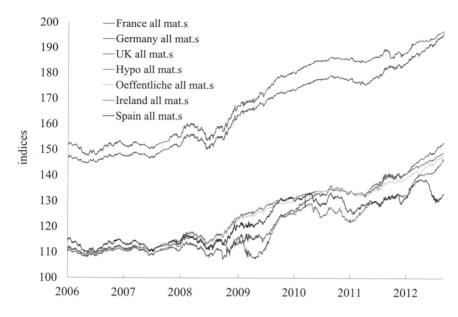

Fig. 7.5   EMTX total return indices by country.

general banking liabilities cost of funding also depends on other factors related to the credit cycle;

- Risk weights and capital charges: have a positive impact on sovereign spreads relative to CB.

All these factors will drive the sovereign-CB spreads dynamics over time. In principle, reflecting the different cost of funding of local Governements relative to the banking sector and in consideration of the relevant share of public debt in bank portfolios, the two spreads tend to be correlated. Furthermore, as for any fixed income security, CB prices will be determined by the fluctuations of the term structure of interest rates, thus by the monetary policy.

The dynamics of CB by maturity analyzed using the EMTX CB indices, show an increasing market volatility and contracting investment horizons in tha last years as reported in Figure 7.6. The main changes occurred for longer maturiities CBs.

Since 2010 the indices on the different maturity buckets have converged and have been affected by increasing volatility and, in the first half of 2012 by a sequence of severe market shocks. At European level, banks are

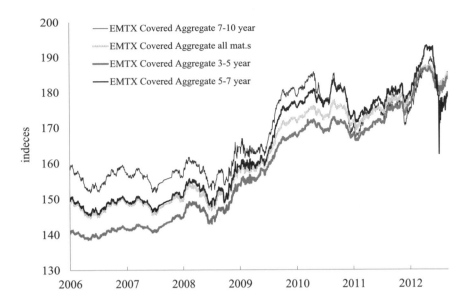

Fig. 7.6   EMTX total return indices, global and by maturity buckets.

finding difficult to raise long-tergm capital and CB yields are suffering from historically high volatility and depend increasingly on short-term interest rate movements.

7.1.6   *Covered bonds in the sovereign debt crisis*

Covered bonds traditionally trade at a discount to sovereign bonds in a well-behaved market. This spread may widen significantly during a financial crisis. Even German Pfandbriefe, often perceived as one of the most secure forms of collateralised debt, traded at a discount up to 100 bps to the Bunds during the 2008 crisis. This occures during financial crises originated by the banks and not by the sovereign. In contrast, during a sovereign debt crisis, the bank debt, in particular that backed by a strong pool of assets, can trade below that of the sovereign, as is currently the case for primary European banks. Banking and sovereign debt crises are generally linked together and, as in the case of Ireland, and more recently Spain, bank assets often end up on the sovereigns' balance sheet and vice versa. Now, as part of the Basel III proposals, banks will be required to hold a greater amount of sovereign debt in order to maintain liquid asset buffers.

The link between the credit spread of a CB and sovereign debt is evident in the case of public CB. Such instruments are backed by loans granted to central, regional and municipal governments. In the event of default by sovereign or sub-sovereign entities, the value of the collateral pool decreases, thereby lowering the expected recovery value. The link between sovereign debt and mortgage-backed CB is less direct: CB are correlated with the senior unsecured claims of other investors, which in turn are correlated with sovereign debt. In the event of insufficient value of mortgages in the collateral pool is insufficient to cover full redemption, investors' remaining claims will follow those of senior unsecured debt.

Rating Agencies activity directly affects CB price dynamics. For example, a Moody's downgrade of an issuer, will result in a one-for-one downgrade of its CB programs. In addition, banks' are typically not rated above that of the sovereign. This link is most severe when a housing bubble bursts. The economy and therefore the sovereigns' finances decline. The value of assets underlying the collateral pools, typically mortgages, declines. In Ireland and Spain, during a period of prolonged house price declines, issuers often struggled to 'top-up' these pools. Therefore overall quality of the collateral pool can come under threat. Given these dynamics, sovereign and CB debt share a mutual macroeconomic risk factor, which cannot be mitigated. The correlation between CB and sovereign debt can often be tenuous and can increase in period of crises, when systemic macroeconomic risk affect both instruments.

There have been two distinct trends in the performance of CB relative to their sovereign over the course of the debt crisis, depending whether we look at the EU core or periphery. The European peripheral PIIGS economies have all seen 10-year sovereign borrowing costs temporarily exceed 7.00% over the 2011-2012 period. These high rates brought the spreads with respect to the German borrowing costs over 500 bps, an unsustainable level especially in a monetary union. In these markets, Covered Bonds have outperformed sovereign debt in times of stress and underperformed during periods of relief. For example, between October and November 2011, when the sovereign debt crisis was arguably at its peak, investing in Spanish government debt would have returned a negative 7.6% over the period. Both single and pooled CB were considerably less vulnerable to this price decline, with a loss of 2.00% and 3.40% respectively. Similarly an investment in Spanish sovereign debt starting on January 2012 to present would have yielded a negative return of 7.20%, while single and pooled CB gained 0.52% and 4.10%, respectively.

The outperformance of CB during the last three years is due to their significantly lower volatility relative to that of the sovereign. While prices follow the same trend, the magnitude of this move is less for Covered Bonds given the dual nature of the claim afforded to investors. Moreover, in response to the bank funding stress, the European Central Bank (ECB) has initiated two Covered Bond Purchase Programmes - CBPP1 and CBPP2. Under CBPP1, the ECB purchased €60 billion of Euro-denominated CB issued by Euro area banks and, under CBPP2, on October 31 2012, €16.42 billion. This has contributed to the lower volatility observed in the CB market over the past 3 years.

Idiosyncratic factors can create persistent deviations in the regional performance of CB versus sovereign debt. CB and sovereign debt are highly correlated in times of crisis, when sovereign debt sells off, CB will outperform and conversely, when sovereign debt rallies, CB will underperform. In other words, the spread between CB and sovereign debt is highly dependent on the level of domestic sovereign rates. This relationship holds for all major European markets.

Take for example the diverging performance of Portuguese and Irish CB relative to their respective sovereigns. Irish CB have traded at heavy discount to sovereign debt for over 18 months, while the opposite is true for Portuguese CB. This can be attributed to fundamental differences in the housing markets of these countries. Irish house prices grew at a fast pace for almost 15 years. This fuelled a housing bubble, which upon bursting, forced the government to nationalise 5 out of the 6 Irish banks (and take a significant stake in the sixth). In contrast, the Portuguese market experienced only modest growth in the two decades leading up to the financial and sovereign debt crises.

The risk-adjusted return from owning Spanish CB was significantly higher than for sovereign debt. It is the lower volatility of CB in times of crisis that provides the greatest benefit to investors. This trend has been more strongly reflected in the Italian market, where in presence of a more resilient banking sector and stable property market, Italian CB have traded up to 100 bps over the sovereign.

The dynamics of the CB-sovereign relationship is of interest also in core markets such as UK and Sweden. These markets have indeed received considerable inflows to sovereign debt from investors looking for security in volatile and uncertain market conditions. Covered bonds, with a less liquid nature of the asset class, received far less 'safe-haven' buying during these periods. As a result, CB tend to underperform sovereign debt in core markets that receive such flows.

As of today the perspective of the CB market is strictly related to the end of the sovereign debt crisis, the continuation of the regulatory and legal harmonization (see ECBC [ECBC (2012)]) and, thanks to a positive economic cycle the recovery of the housing market. All these can be considered exogenous to the banking sector, but more importantly the achievement in the second half of 2012 of sufficient capitalization ratios in most large commercial banks in Europe, calls for a recovery of the credit activity funded not only through the interbank market but increasingly through CB. The endogenous nature of the asset-liability strategies pursued by the banking sector and its positive and multiplicative impact on banks' profit generation has put several European banking sectors at the centre of the economic and financial debate.

7.2   Inflation-Linked Bonds

(Sergio Ortobelli Lozza)

7.2.1   *Introduction*

Inflation-Linked Bonds (also known as linkers) are bonds that provide protection against inflation, their principals are linked to inflation, which serve to minimize inflation risk.

The principal amount of the bond increases with inflation, thus the interest rate is applied to the increased amount. This causes the increase in interest payment over time. At maturity, the principal is repaid at the inflated amount. This ensures that an investor has complete inflation protection. In most countries, the Consumer Price Index (CPI) or its equivalent is used as an inflation proxy. Inflation-linked bonds can be properly understood by comparing them to vanilla bonds.

An inflation-linked bond protects the investor from unexpected changes in the consumer price index. Investors do not necessarily expect inflation to be high, since they do not know what the future will bring they are willing to sacrifice some current yield for inflation protection on the principal. During the recent sovereign risk crisis the role of these instruments has shown a slower pace compared to the previous evolution.

Inflation risk hedging has always been of critical importance in portfolio management and in particular for pension funds which have liabilities directly tied to an inflation index. An Inflation-Linked Bond (ILB) is a bond whose coupons are linked to a consumer price index. For ILBs issued within the Euro area this is the "Harmonized Index of Consumer Prices, excluding tobacco" (ex-HICP), an index monthly published by Eurostat. For few ILBs, the national Consumer Price Index (CPI) excluding tobacco is used.

An Inflation Swap is a contract between an inflation "receiver" who pays a fixed rate versus an inflation-indexed rate (floating or fixed). It defines the dates when the cash flows are to be paid and the way in which they are calculated. Usually at the time when the contract is initiated at least one of these series of cash flows is determined by an unknown random variable that for most of the inflation swaps in the Euro area is the Euro ex-HICP. The inflation "payer" pays the indexed rate. Specifically, the two counterparties agree to exchange one stream of cash flows against another stream, also called the "legs" of the swap. Inflation derivatives markets are still in their infancy and their development could complete the set of instruments available for efficient hedging against inflation risk together with specific equities and commodities, see, among others, [Amenc (2009); Ang et al. (2011)].

7.2.2 The development

First known ILB was issued by th Massachuttes Bay Company in 1780. The British Government began issuing Inflation-Linked Guilts (ILG) in 1981. Most common ILBs are:

- the Canadian Real Return Bond (RRB);
- the British ILG;
- the new US Treasury Inflation-Protected Securities (TIPS).

The first sovereign bond linked to Euro area inflation was issued by the French Treasury in 1998 and was indexed to the French CPI excluding tobacco. On October 2001 the French Treasury decided to issue a new 10-year bond indexed to ex-HICP with maturity July 2012. From this slow start the market for ILBs in the Euro area grew significantly until 2007. Greek, Italian and German bonds have similar characteristics to French ILBs: they offer guaranteed redemption at par and they are linked to the Euro area ex-HICP which became the benchmark index methodology. In July 2004, the electronic trading platform EuroMTS launched a market for trading inflation-linked securities. An index of ILBs composed of nine

Table 7.2   ILBs issued in the last decade.

	Issued 1999-2003	Issued 2004-07	Issued 2008-11
France	27	37	8
Germany	0	2	2
Greece	0	0	3
Italy	2	51	18
Global	29	90	31

bonds of different European countries was also created to provide a reliable benchmark and to contribute promoting the liquidity of the bonds included in the index.

Recent studies have proposed corporate inflation-linked bonds, as an appropriate substitute for sovereign inflation-linked bonds. Martellini and Milhau [Martellini and Mihau (2011)] have shown that the optimal capital structure of a firm depends on the chosen debt structure. In particular, higher levels of correlation of asset value with inflation should encourage the issuer to offer less fixed-rate debt and more inflation-linked debt.

The main investors in continental Europe of ILBs have been insurers, banks, mutual funds and French institutional investors. Life insurers need to hedge long term inflation indexed liabilities and several pension reforms are ongoing in the major European countries and an increasing demand for ILBs should be expected in the future. ILBs represent an appropriate instrument for pension liability matching especially in those countries where an increase in life expectancy is occurring.

Since the recent sovereign risk crisis the Euro area ILB markets has changed drammatically with a large reduction of its liquidity, due to lower rate of return provided by these bonds and to increased sovereign issuers' credit-worthiness. For instance Greek and Italian ILBs bear a much higher credit risk than German or French ones. The issued sovereign ILB by maturity and country is reported in Table 7.2 which shows the large reduction occurred in the period 2008-2011.

7.2.3   *The role of ILBs*

A Government should issue an ILB for theee reasons: the first is provided by Milton Friedman (see [Farcia and Rixtel (2007)] and the reference therein) according to whom the government (monetary authority) is responsible for creating inflation and should allow others to manage it; a mean to hedge it. The second, suggested by [Campbell and Shiller (1996)], says that the proper role of the government is to provide public goods such as new financial markets and instruments. The third, supported by [Campbell and Viceira (2002)], suggests that, from the point of view of long term investors, sovereign ILBs are unique risk free assets, since they provide protection against both inflation and credit risk. The recent crisis suggests ttaht the concept of risk free asset is being seriously challenged, see [NGE (2011)].

There are two main drivers for issuance of inflation-linked bonds by a government:

- its costs of financing can be reduced;
- it allows a more precise matching of the government's assets and liabilities.

The first idea suggests that the government should pay a lower yield since it provides a protection from inflation. Several empirical studies (see, among others, [Reschreiter (2004)]) have shown that the issuance of ILBs have generated ex-post savings in the governments financing cost. We should also note that (as shown by [Towned (1997)]) ILBs are less liquid than nominal bonds since the issuer pays a liquidity premium. This lower liquidity does not affect much the financing cost given that ILBs are generally purchased by "buy and hold" investors.

[Barro (1997)] suggests that an optimal fiscal policy should favour the issuance of long term ILBs. The same kind of arguments have been made by Martellini and Milhau [Martellini and Mihau (2011)] in favour of corporate ILBs.

There are two reasons why private investors should benefit from the availability of ILBs:

- ILBs may provide the most natural hedge against inflation risk;
- portfolio diversification benefits since inflation is uncertain. The diversification benefit (see [Fischer (1975)]) for holders of ILBs allows a positive inflation risk premium, as shown, among others, by [Kothari and Shanken (2004); Hunter and Simon (2005); Roll (2004)] for US market and by [Bardong and Lehnert (2004)] for the Euro market.

The ILB could also represent a fundamental component of any pension fund portfolio. The existence of ILBs in such a portfolio means that pension holdings, and social security pensions, have inflation indexed annuities (and government guarantees). The idea that the existence of ILBs generates social welfare gains is summarized in three points:

(1) distributional arguments (see [Drudi and Giordano (2000); Issing (1973)])
(2) portfolio diversification and market completeness (see [Farcia and Rixtel (2007)])
(3) incentives to savings (see [Bach and Musgrave (1941); Sarnat (1973)]).

7.2.4 *ILBs and monetary policy*

According to the Fisher theory (see [Fischer (1975)]), the nominal interest rate is the sum of three components: the real interest rate, the inflation expected by the market, and an inflation risk premium. Therefore using the sovereign nominal bond and ILB with the same maturity we are able to derive a market measure of real interest rates and inflation expectations. This is one of the main arguments in favour of ILBs issuance and provides the central bank with useful information for the monetary policy chosen.

Denote $n_{t,M}$ the nominal bond yield and $il_{t,M}$ the ILB's yield at time t with maturity M. The spread between the yields of a conventional nominal bond and an ILB of the same maturity is called "Break-Even Inflation Rate" (BEIR), i.e.:

$$BEIR_{t,M} = n_{t,M} - il_{t,M} \tag{7.1}$$

BEIR is the theoretical rate of inflation which makes the expected rate of return of the two bonds equal (i.e. break-even). BEIR is a linear approximation of the market participants' average inflation expectation (denoted by π) over the residual bonds maturity. This linear approximation holds a compound bias and does not take into account the inflation risk premia (denoted by ρ) as suggested by the Fisher relationship:

$$(1+n)^M = (1+il)^M \left[(1+\rho)(1+\pi)\right]^M \tag{7.2}$$

If investors are risk neutral and demand the same expected return from the nominal and the ILB, the inflation compensation would approximate the expected average rate of inflation for the maturity of the bond. Investors are generally risk averse and require an higher expected return on nominal securities requiring a premium for bearing that inflation risk. Even when the inflation risk premium is zero, i.e. $\rho = 0$, from (7.2) we can deduce that

$$(1+n)^M = E_t \left(\frac{(1+il)^M}{(1+\pi)^M} \right) \tag{7.3}$$

which implies:

$$n_{t,M} - il_{t,M} \approx \frac{1}{E_t \left(\frac{1}{(1+\pi)^M}\right)^{1/M}} - 1 < E_t\left(\pi\right) \qquad (7.4)$$

where the last inequality follows from Jensen's inequality (see [Jensen (1906)]). The BEIR therefore underestimates the expected inflation when we have no inflation risk premium and provides an indicator of expected inflation and an important tool for the central bank's monetary policy.

According to formulas 7.3 and 7.4, it is possible to estimate a term structure of expected inflation given the term structures of real and nominal interest rates. The estimation of the real interst rates term structure and the inflation risk premium require specific assumptions and procedures. Some examples are provided in the next Sections.

7.2.4.1   *Real term structure and inflation risk premia*

Generally, central banks use the Nelson Siegel parametric method or its extensions (see [Nelson and Siegel (1987); Gurkaynak (2007, 2010)]) to approximate the nominal and the real yield curves. According to [Nelson and Siegel (1987)] assumes that the zero coupon yield y_m for maturity m is described by:

$$y_m = \beta_1 + (\beta_2 + \beta_3)\frac{\tau}{m}\left(1 - \exp(-\tfrac{m}{\tau})\right) - \beta_3 \exp(-\tfrac{m}{\tau})$$

The parameters $\beta_1, \beta_2, \beta_3$ and τ are estimated by minimizing the distance between the bond prices implied by the theoretical formula and the observed bond prices. The same methodology is applied to estimate the real yield curve (with ILBs) and the nominal yield curve (with nominal bonds). The BEIRs are computed as the difference between the two curves. These estimates allow us to compute implied forward BEIR for longer periods providing information about the credibility of the central bank's commitment to keep consumer price stability. BEIRs also include risk premia to compensate investors for inflation risk, and for differential liquidity risk between the nominal and ILB markets. The inflation risk premia complicate the interpretation of BEIRs as measures of inflation expectations, so different models for its valuation have been proposed. Deacon and Derry [Deacon and Derry (1994)] were among the first to determine the inflation term structure assuming a zero inflation risk premium. Evans, Anderson and Sleath [Evans (1998); Anderson and Sleath (2001)] extend their analysis to find a significant time-varying inflation risk premium in the UK term structure. The inflation term structure of the Euro area is discussed and analyzed in [Cappiello and Guene (2005); Farcia and Rixtel (2007); Hordahl and Tristani (2010)]. In particular, Hordahl and Tristani [Hordahl and Tristani (2010)] have applied a joint model of macroeconomic and term structure dynamics, proposed by [Hordahl et al. (2006)] to estimate inflation risk premia in the United States and the Euro area. They show that inflation risk premia are relatively small, positive, and with increasing maturity in both currency areas. They also prove that long term inflation premia are countercyclical in the Euro area, while they are procyclical in the US.

7.2.5 *Portfolio selection with ILBs*

In order to examine the benefits of ILBs for investors in the Euro area, we evaluate and compare the impact of the investors's choices on the ex-post final wealth for investments in ILBs or in sovereign nominal bonds.

The portfolio selection problem is traditionally studied in terms of risk and reward of the underlying portfolio, see Appendix 7.A to this Chapter. When we deal with portfolio selection for Corporate or Government bonds the most logical measure of reward is represented by the yield to maturity and/or the portfolio future wealth estimate and the risk is represented by portfolio modified duration (MD). Investors maximize their portfolio future wealth for a specific MD. In the case of ILB the concept of risk-reward is different, given that for ILB we are not always able to determine the yield to maturity and the MD. In this case we use a risk-reward approach where the risk and reward using historical data for ILB returns and applying the standard mean-variance approach for portfolio selection [Markowitz (1959)]. A description of the two approaches is given in Appendix 7.B.

7.2.5.1 *Portfolio selection with sovereign ILBs*

To build a portfolio with Euro area's ILBs, we collected all the sovereign ILBs obtained from Thomson Reuters DataStream for the period February 13,2004 through May 18, 2012 comprising 2156 trading days. 147 sovereign ILBs across Italy, Germany, France and Greece were collected. all the assets were not necessarily present for the entire period either because they had maturity before May 18, 2012 or because they were issued after February 13, 2004. The proposed portfolio selection is based on a dynamic dataset and the optimized portfolio is obtained by considering only the assets which were tradable at the date of optimization. A preliminary liquidity filter was introduced to use only highly liquid assets.

The size of the portfolio can be reduced making a selection of the admissible securities (ILBs) to include. For instance a selection criteria could be based on the existing correlations of the various ILBs. In this case, PCA on the correlations matrix of ILBs rates of return is estimated and the principal components are used to estimated the approximated rates of return. A detailed description is provided in Appendix 7.C.

Once the portfolio is built, the ex-post wealth obtained of ILBs is analyzed, see Appendix 7.B on the portfolio.

Being $x = [x_1, ..., x_n]'$ the portfolio composition, we assume that no short sales are allowed ($x_i \geq 0$) and that it is not possible to invest more than 5% in any unique asset ($x_i \leq 0.05$). We also consider proportional transaction costs of 5 basis points. We solve the portfolio optimization problem weekly over a window of 6 months of daily trading observations to compute the mean and the variance of portfolios. We derive the sample path of the final wealth which maximizes the Sharpe ratio.

We assume that the investor has an initial wealth W_0 equal to 1 (at the start date, 8/05/2004) and use as a benchmark the return of the uniform portfolio (which invests the same proportion in each asset) since we want to outperform the strategy based on a uniform portfolio. The output of this analysis is given in Figure 7.7, which shows the final wealth during the ex-post period.

There is high variability in the ex post wealth that is essentially due to the three crises (sub prime crisis, credit risk crisis and the country credit risk crisis), as well as the lower liquidity of ILBs compared to nominal bonds. The portfolio composition of the optimal choices was well diversified with a portfolio turnover, even if the trading volumes were not very high. The sovereign ILBs portfolio shows 13.44% rate of return over the selcted period.

7.2.5.2 *Portfolio selection with sovereign nominal bonds*

To build a portfolio with Euro area sovereign nominal bond we collect them from Thomson Reuters DataStream for the period May 5, 2004 through May 18, 2012. 1,173 sovereign nominal bonds across Austria, Belgium, France, Germany, Finland, Ireland, Italy and Nederlands and, as in the ILB case, assets were not present for all the period either because they had maturity before May 18, 2012 or because they were issued after May 8, 2004. A liquidity filter is also applied. The detailed procedure used to build this portfolio is described in Appendix 7.B.

We assume that no short sales are allowed ($v_i \geq 0$) and that it is not possible to invest more than 20% in any unique asset ($\frac{v_i}{W} \leq 0.2$). We solve

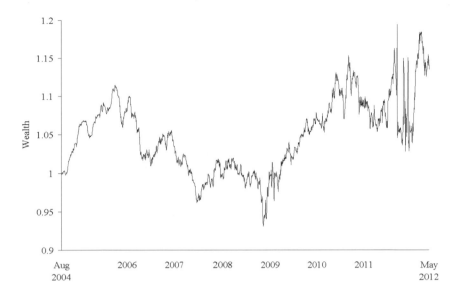

Fig. 7.7   Ex-post final wealth of 147 index linked portfolio.

the portfolio optimization problem weekly and then we consider the sample path of the final wealth obtained by solving (7.C.9). Again we assume proportional transaction costs of 5 basis points.

We summarize the ex-post empirical comparison for 20 possible modified durations in the interval between the minimum MD of 10 and the maximum MD of 19.5, in order to obtain results comparable to the ILB markets that have long maturities. Most of the ILBs used in the previous analysis have similar maturities. We consider the long term investor with at a time horizon of more than 10 years. We assume that the investor has an initial wealth W_0 equal to €100,000 (at the date 8/05/2004) and that the benchmark return is given by the return of the uniform portfolio (that invests the same proportion in each asset). As for the ILBs market we perform three main steps to compute the ex-post final wealth. First, for a fixed portfolio Modified Duration we determine the solution of optimization problem (7.C.9). Second, we compute the ex-post final wealth and we use the optimal solution starting point for the subsequent optimization problem. Third, we repeat these steps for all MDs as long as observations are available.

Figure 7.8 reports the ex-post final wealth during the ex-post period for all the modified durations. As we expect, we observe a growing

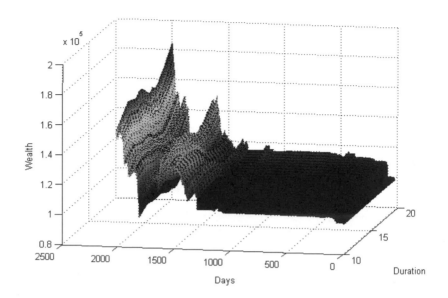

Fig. 7.8 Ex-post final wealth for different fixed modified durations sovereign bonds.

Table 7.3 Statistics for the ex post returns.

	ILBs	Sovereign Bonds 10 Years Mod. Duration	Sovereign Bonds 19.5 Years Mod. Duration
Mean	7.94E-05	0.000235	0.000307
St.Dev.	0.00581	0.005245	0.007048
$VaR_{5\%}$	0.00604	0.006637	0.010137
$CVaR_{5\%}$	0.01075	0.012178	0.015653
Final Wealth	113,439	156,461	177,033

ex-post wealth and risk when the Modified Duration of the portfolio strategy increases.

In order to compare the results obtained from investing either in sovereign ILBs or in sovereign nominal bonds, we estimate the mean, standard deviation, Value at Risk 5% ($VaR_{5\%}$), Conditional Value at Risk 5% ($CVaR_{5\%}$) of each portfolio expected wealth , see Table 7.3. In particular, for sovereign bonds Table 7.3 reports the statistics of optimal portfolios for two possible fixed Modified Durations: 10 years (minimum) and 19.5 years (maximum).

The final wealth increases of the 13.44%, 56.46% and 77.03%, when we invest respectively in ILBs, in sovereign bonds with the shortest MD (10 years) and in sovereign bonds with the longest MD (19.5 years). Even for sovereign bonds we observe very big losses during the subprime crisis, but surprisingly we did not observe big losses during the most recent country credit risk crisis. From a theoretical point of view the observed differences among the optimal choices in the two markets can be justified by three distinct effects: different liquidity in the two markets, different inflation and different inflation risk premia present across the Euro area. From a practical point of view, we observe that all the strategies on the nominal bonds generate higher return mean, $\text{VaR}_{5\%}$ and $\text{CVaR}_{5\%}$ compared to the portfolio strategy based solely on ILBs. However, the strategy valued for the minimum Modified Duration gave a lower standard deviation than the one for Inflation-Linked Bonds. We deduce that the portfolio selection based on ILBs generally may provide lower losses respect to the use of nominal bonds. This observation is consistent with the scarce liquidity of the ILBs market.

The comparison between the two portfolio selections has shown:

- ILBs market does not have a comparable number of overall choices for portfolio selection over Euro area nominal bonds;
- we cannot easily apply the classic optimization models for the fixed income market since we need the forecasted real yield to maturity and (modified) duration of each asset, when faced with a large number of maturities;
- we generally obtain lower ex post wealth and financial risk investing in Euro area ILBs compared to nominal bonds. On the other hand, portfolio selection with ILBs appears less risky than the portfolio selection for nominal bonds (and obviously for equity market).

7.3 Bond Exchange Traded Funds

(Sergio Ortobelli Lozza)

7.3.1 *Introduction*

Bond Exchange Traded Funds have shown dramatic growth over the past ten years. They provide a very liquid tool in the bond market segment. Most of the bond market remains an over-the-counter market and therefore the bond market lacks liquidity and price transparency except for the most liquid of bonds. Bond Exchange-Traded Funds (BETFs) which track bond indices offer a good attractive tool for bond investors [Longstaff (2004)]. Their versatility in terms of choice of reference index has added to their appeal [Amenc et al. (2004)]. While similar to other ETFs, BETFs are unique in the world of fixed income because, as they are traded on stock exchanges, provide the historical prices of BETF for all investors. Historically, this kind of price transparency for bonds has been available only to institutional investors.

The BETF has to closely track its respective index in a cost-effective manner, despite the lack of liquidity in the bond market given the lack of a liquid secondary market. Most bonds are held until maturity and this makes it difficult to ensure a BETF encompasses enough liquid bonds to track an index. This is more evident for corporate bonds than for government bonds. The suppliers of BETFs face the liquidity problem by using representative sampling, which simply means tracking only a sufficient number of bonds to represent an index. The bonds used in the representative sample tend to be the largest and most liquid in the index. For example, the Lehman Aggregate Bond Index contains more than 6,000 bonds, but the Barclays iShare Lehman Aggregate Bond Fund (AGG) contains only a little over 100 of those bonds. One key feature of BETFs is that they are available on a global basis. Barclays Global Investors, for example, has created BETFs that are available in the U.S., Europe and Canada.

7.3.2   The development

ETFs were first launched as proxy of equity indices in North America in the late 1980s since then they have become very popular. Bond ETFs are a relatively recent product. The first bond ETF was launched in the US in July 2002.

The ETF market in Europe kept growing in the last decade. Currently, there are several different types of Exchange Traded Product (ETP). More than 200 new ETPs have been launched each year since 2007. This analysis is shown in Table 7.4 which reports the number of ETP issued during recent years and the growing value in USD billion of the bond ETFs launched in the Euro area, [BlackRock (2012); Garcia-Zarate (2012)].

A BETF is generally used to track the performance of a specified fixed income market index.

Table 7.4   Exchange Traded Products (ETP) in Europe in USD billion.

	Issued 2003-06	Issued 2007-09	Issued 2010-12
Bond ETF	21.2	113.7	172.4
Number of Launched ETP	194	873	921

BETFs are designed using a physical replication method (where the underlying assets are used to track the benchmark) or a synthetically (swap-based) structured method. Physically-based BETFs replicate their respective indices through acquisitions of the underlying assets. Swap-based BETF indices lend its holding to a counterparty (usually an investment bank) via a collateralised repurchase agreement (REPO) and then swap the yield on that loan for the total return of the underlying index. BETF built on a swap-based method combine the value of the collateral and the marked-to-market with the swap counterparty. A two step mechanism, [Pallaris (2011)], describes how swap-based BETF works:

(1) the BETF provider raises cash by selling BETF units. The cash is placed into a collateral account held in trust with a custodian.
(2) the BETF issuer enters into an index swap with a counterparty. On a daily basis it is marked to market and the swap counterparty pays the index total return to the BETF provider in exchange for the funding rate. The funding rate is offset by the returns on the deposited collateral held in trust with the BETF issuers' custodian.

In the case of BETF built using synthetically structured funds there exists a counterparty risk which is balanced by low tracking error.

The main providers of BETFs in Europe (up to the end of 2011) were iShares, DB X-Trackers, Lyxor, ETFS, Credit Suisse, ZKB, UBS, Amundi, Comstage, Source Markets which cover more than 90% of the European BETFs market. iShares, DB X-Trackers and Lyxor have the largest share representing the 62% of the market. German DBX-Trackers and French Lyxor providers issue swap-based BETF while the UK provider iShares issue physically based BETF.

7.3.3 Basic features

BETFs provide private investors with several benefits, some particularly important for the corporate bond market. Several factors have hindered the development of corporate fixed income market:

- the higher transaction costs incurred by investors;
- the lower level of liquidity provided by these instruments;
- the difficulty of hedging easily and efficiently positions held in these markets.

BETFs have the following advantages: benefits that help to improve and overcome market limitations. The classical advantages of bond ETFs are listed in the following five points.

(1) The stock-like features offered. Investors can buy and sell them on an exchange and their prices fluctuate throughout the trading day. Consequently, prices are available for Bond ETFs at any time during trading hours and, according to supply and demand, they are updated on a real time basis. Moreover, investors can sell short, use a limit order, buy on margin, use a stop-loss order and invest as much or as little money as they wish (since there is no minimum investment requirement). Anything that is possible with a stock, can be done with an ETF. As with stocks, investors should also pay commissions to buy and sell ETFs.

(2) BETFs offer investors the ultimate diversification tool. Investors can invest directly in the overall market instead of picking individual bonds. Diversification is a major concern for any investor seeking exposure to corporate bonds.

(3) In most cases, ETFs are more tax-efficient than conventional mutual funds in the same asset classes or categories.

(4) They provide different hedging tools: inflation hedging, revenue stream creation, foreign region investing, sector hedging (sovereign, corporate, municipal), durations (short, intermediate, long). We can identify 14 types of BETF are reported in [Kennedy (2012)]:

    (a) Corporate BETF (tracking corporate bond indices);
    (b) Sovereign BETF (tracking sovereign bond indices);
    (c) Municipal BETF (tracking indices that consist of local government bond products);
    (d) International BETF(that track international bond indices);
    (e) Inflation Linked BETF (tracking Inflation Linked Bond Indices);

(f) Convertible BETF (consisting of a corporate bond that can be redeemed for common shares of stock of the debt issuer);

(g) Mortgage-Backed BETF (giving a portfolio exposure to Mortgage-Backed Securities);

(h) Junk BETF (including bonds with low credit ratings, high yields, and therefore high risk);

(i) Leveraged BETF (designed to emulate a multiple return on an underlying bond index);

(j) Inverse BETF (constructed to emulate the inverse performance of an underlying index, thus enter inverse bond ETFs represents a way to get short without selling);

(k) Short-Term BETF (tracking an index consisting in bonds with short term durations (0-3 years));

(l) Intermediate-Term Bond ETFs (tracking an index consisting in bonds with longer durations (3-10 years));

(m) Long-Term Bond ETFs (tracking an index consisting in bonds with long durations (greater than 10 years));

(n) Broad Bond ETFs (tracking an index consisting in bonds without a prefixed range of duration).

The dominant providers of Euro area sovereign debt indices are: Deutsche Bourse, Barclays Capital, the International Index Company (IIC), EuroMTS (see, among others, [Drenovak et al. (2012)]). The indices differ in terms of the geographic diversification, size thresholds, frequency of rebalancing and reinvestments and maturity spectrum. The Deutsche Bourse provides the "eb.rexx index", family that includes only the most liquid standard sovereign coupon bonds issued by the Germany Treasury,with the whole maturity spectrum requiring as minimum thresholds a size of €2 billion, with a monthly rebalancing and coupon reinvesting . Barclays Capital provides the Barclays Term indices which predominantly focus on Germany, Italy and France (about 75%), the remainder being allocated to the Netherlands and Spain; it includes bonds with a maturity near to their original maturity, a minimum threshold size €2 billion, with a monthly rebalancing and coupon reinvesting. The International Index Company develops the Market Bond Indices, Markit iBoxx, across the whole maturity spectrum which take into account prices from multiple trading platforms and track the overall exposure to the Euro area sovereign fixed income market. They provide data for fixed income research, asset allocation and performance evaluation in USD, EUR, GBP, EURHY, global inflation linked and emerging markets. They have a minimum requirement size of €4 billion, quarterly rebalancing with coupon income monthly reinvested. EuroMTS provides EuroMTS indices, as Markit iBoxx, including in similar proportion riskier countries as Belgium, Ireland, Portugal and Greece. They are real time indices on a whole maturity spectrum that represent different minimum size requirement of €2 billion and monthly rebalancing with coupon income reinvested overnight.

The classical criticisms of for BETFs follow.

a) In general, BETF do not give investors the opportunity to outperform the fixed income market.

b) BETF based on a synthetic replication method may create additional risk for investors (see [Ramaswamy (2011)]).

c) Investors can rack up significant costs by frequently buying and selling BETF during periods of high volatility. These costs will drew any potential investment gains. BETF are dependent on the market efficiency to track the net asset value (NAV). NAV could be more or less significant for BETFs that track domestic (generally less than 2%) or foreign indices.

d) They may have been used to manipulate the market in 2008 contributing to the financial crisis.

7.3.4   *Tracking errors and performance*

BETFs usually have different performance of the underlying indices. These differences are generated by market friction and imperfect replication that reduce returns on BETFs. Many studies have been performed on the ETF market to identify the adequate tool to measure the different performance, generating a set of tracking error measures which are also applied to the BETFs market. Tracking error (Te1) common measure (see [Amenc et al. (2009); Goltz and Tang (2012)]), also called "active returns" is given by:

$$Te1 = r_{BETF} - r_{ind} \qquad (7.5)$$

where r_{BETF}, r_{ind} are the returns respectively of the ETF and of the underlying index.

Another measure is the standard deviation of Te1, i.e. σ_{Te1}:

$$\sigma_{Te1} = \sqrt{\sigma_{BETF}^2 + \sigma_{ind}^2 - 2\sigma_{BETF}\sigma_{ind}\rho_{BETF,ind}} \qquad (7.6)$$

where $\sigma_{BETF}, \sigma_{ind}$ measure the standard deviations respectively of the BETF return and of the underlying index return, while $\rho_{BETF,ind}$ is the Pearson correlation between the ETF and the underlying index returns. This measure gives an idea of the variability of the active returns, but it does not provide any information about overperformance or underperformance. As suggested by [Bacon (2008)], this measure is more appropriate for passive than for active funds management. See also [Stoyanov et al. (2008); Rachev et al. (2008)] for discussion of other metrics to be used in this context.

Other approaches have been recently used to measure the tracking error. The first, estimates the relationship between the BETF returns, r_{BETF} and the index returns, r_{ind}, using a regression model [Cresson et al. (2002); Pope and Yadav (1994); Rompotis (2008)]:

$$r_{BETF} = \alpha + \beta r_{ind} + \varepsilon_{ETF} \tag{7.7}$$

where ε_{BETF} is the error term of the regression. The regression standard error can be used as a measure of tracking performance. In general, given the aim of the BETF (i.e. full replicating the index) the estimation of 7.7 should provide good fitting, tehrefore low standard error of the regression, with β not statistically different from one, and α not statistically different from zero. When BETFs do not fully replicate the index the regression shows a large standard error, with β and α far from the theoretical expected values. The second, assumes a long run equilibrium relationship between BETFs prices and indices and using a cointegration approach estimates the relationship [Alexander (1999); Alexander and Dimitriu (2004)].

The analysis of the traking error perfomance initially for the the ETF market and recently for the BETF markets has been tackled by many scholars and practitioners. In particular [Drenovak and Urošević (2011); Drenovak et al. (2012)] apply the various different tracking error models (Te1, Te2, standard error of 7.7, and cointegration approach) to estimate the Euro zone sovereign debt ETF. The results show how statistically significant higher tracking errors are found for the European market compared to the US sovereign BETFs ([Houweling (2011)]). In the case of passive management Drenovak [Drenovak et al. (2012)] have shown much larger errors in the case of European sovereign BETF. The level of underperformance of some funds was more akin to the level associated with the underperformance of corporate BETFs in line with other results that indicate that credit risk has become an important determinant of BETF's performance during the recent country sovereign crisis.

7.3.5   *Portfolio selection with BETFs*

BETFs provide an efficient diversification tool and have lower liquidity risk and transaction costs, however their performance has to be regularly compared to that of other fixed income instruments. Investor's choice will be mainly affected by the market conditions, in particular in periods of high volatility as it occurred during the recent financial crisis, BETFs may not provide the desired performance and in some cases they generate returns lower then other fixed income instruments. An ad hoc analysis has been performed to this extent and a comparison between the performance of a portfolio holding only BETFs traded in the Euro area and a portfolio comprised of corporate and sovereign bonds traded in one Member country is presented. The analysis tries to answer to the following issues:

(1) Investing in BETFs may be less risky than investing in corporate and sovereign bonds? Can BETF markets be an alternative to the corporate and sovereign bond markets?
(2) Can a high portfolio performance be obtained using weekly rebalancing portfolio strategies or the only benefits BETF portfolios generate rely on their flexibility and different uses?

The comparison is held on two different European fixed income markets, the Italian and the German one. These two markets represent the largest European fixed income markets in the Euro area, they deeply differ for their credit risk so they can provide two extreme examples of investor's behaviours in financial distress periods. In addition the German sovereign bonds still represent the "risk free asset" while the Italian sovereign bonds in the last three years have been conisdered more as corporate bonds, see [NGE (2011)], with the Italian debt being downgraded several times by the main Rating Agencies.

When building BETF portolios the standard risk and return measures used for equity portfolios cannot be used and specific measures based on the historical observations of BETF returns are estimated.

The portfolios are built using a two steps procedure. First, portfolios that maximize the future wealth for some fixed modified durations in the German and Italian fixed income markets are identified. Second, using the historical observations of these optimal porfolios we analyze their risk and returns to determine a BETF portfolio which has a similar performance. It is so possible to build optimal portfolios for the German and the Italian bond markets with no fixed duration. Precisely varying the portfolio duration it is possible to reduce other sources of the market risk. The technical details of the models are described in Appendix 7.C of this Chapter.

7.3.5.1 *BETF portfolio selection in the Euro area*

A portfolio selection using BETFs traded in the Euro area using a dynamic dataset can be developed. We propose a simple procedure using 219 BETFs traded in Belgium, France, Germany, Greece, Ireland, Italy, the Netherland, Portugal, Spain, and UK available in Thomson Reuters DataStream for the period 12/31/2005 - 05/21/2012 (1,667 trading days). The currency used is the Euro, 47 of these BETFs are related to indices of non European countries providing us with better diversification choices. The optimized portfolio is obtained considering only the assets which were active during the period of six months (125 trading days) before the date of the optimization. Only those assets whose historical observations have not been constant for more than 80% of their historical observations were considered to guarantee liquidity of the used securities.

To reduce the dimensionality of the portfolio problem we use a Principal Components Analysis (PCA) on the correlation matrix of returns.

The portfolio selection is obtained maximazing the (7.C.6) the Sharpe ratio or the Rachev ratio. No short sales are allowed and an upper bound $(x_i \geq 0)$ of 20% in an unique asset $(x_i \leq 0.2)$ is introduced. Transaction costs are assumed to be equal to 5 basis points. The portfolio optimization problem is solved on a weekly basis over a window of 6 months. The sample path of the final wealth obtained by maximizing the performance ratio is analyzed assuming the investor has an initial wealth W_0 equal to 1 (at the date 6/23/2006).

A fixed value for the Rachev Ratio is chosen equal to 3: $\alpha = \beta = 3\%$ and no benchmark return is required (i.e. $r_b = 0$). The market portfolio $x_M^{(k+1)}$ can be determined maximizing the performance ratio of the rate of returns, i.e. the solution of optimization problem (7.C.6). The ex-post final wealth, based on the optimal portfolio is given by:

$$W_{k+1} = W_k \left(\left(x_M^{(k+1)} \right)' (1 + r_{k+1}) \right), \tag{7.8}$$

where r_{k+1} is the ex-post vector of rate of returns occurred during the k-th and $(k+1)$-th period.

The estimation of the ex-post vector of returns can be determined for each of the chosen performance measures, the Rachev and Sharpe ratios, as shown in Figure 7.9 for the period June 2006- May 2012.

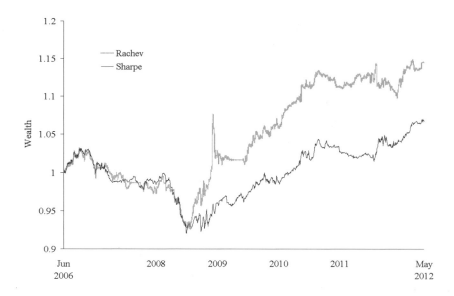

Fig. 7.9   Ex-post final wealth for BETF portfolio.

Using as performance measure the Rachev Ratio ($r_b = 1.45$)) provides a portfolio whose rate of return results higher than those of the portfolio obtained using the Sharpe Ratio ($r_b = 1.067$)). For both portfolio strategies largest losses were experienced during the sub prime crisis. The optimal portfolio composition result in both cases well diversified with a sufficient portfolio turnover.

To understand the benefits deriving from the bond ETF portfolio selection a comparison can be performed building fixed income bond portfolios in two countries of the Euro area which present different risk features: Germany and Italy. Data were provided by Thomson Reuters DataStream over the decade January 2002 May 2012 and referred to

a) 7,007 Italian fixed income sovereign and corporate bonds
b) 5,909 Deutsch fixed income sovereign and corporate bonds

AT each point in time only the actively traded securities were used for the portfolio selection. Using the same procedure used to select the ETF bond portfolio for the entire Euro area it is possible to estimate the ex post wealth for 60 portfolios which present a fixed modified duration in the interval [0.25-18] years. A specific analysis can be performed on portfolios

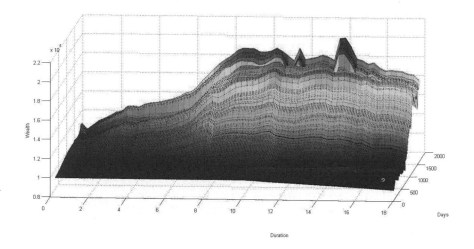

Fig. 7.10 Ex-post final wealth for fixed income and different fixed modified durations portfolio, Italy.

which present a precise modified durations (short-medium range duration (0-9 years) vs long range duration (9-18 years).

Phase 1: Portfolio selection for fixed Modified Durations. The expected future wealth is maximized choosing 60 different fixed modified durations d belonging to the interval [0.25 year, 17.95 year]for each of the two countries. No short sales are allowed ($v_i \geq 0$), it is not possible to invest more than 20% in a unique asset ($\frac{v_i}{W} \leq 0.2$), proportional transaction costs are equal to 10 basis points (twice those required for bond ETFs) and only highly liquid assets are considered. The portfolio optimization problem is solved weekly and the sample path of the final wealth is analyzed. Highly liquid assets are those assets which in the six previous months (125 trading days) present lest than 80% of constant data. If more than 100 of 125 historical returns of a given asset are null, the asset is excluded from the optimization. Given an investor's initial wealth $W_0 = e100,000$ at the date 06/23/2006 the exp-post final wealth is computed for any fixed Modified Duration portfolioobtained solving the optimization problem (7.C.9) as reported in Fig. 7.10 for the Italian market and in 7.11 for the Deutsch market.

In both markets high Modifies Duration portfolios show higher risk linked to larger ex-post wealth. However the German market present a higher volatility in particular during the sub prime crisis 2007-2009.

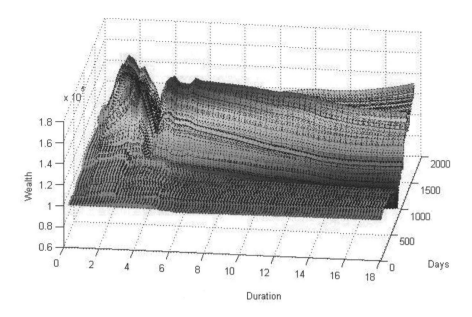

Fig. 7.11   Ex-post final wealth for fixed income and different fixed modified durations portfolio, Germany.

Phase 2: Portfolio optimization for medium and long term maturity   The 60 portfolios built in the Phase 1(7.C.9) are then selected according to specific values of the Modified Duration. Precisely, the Modified Duration ranges between 0-9 years and 9-18 years. Assuming an investor's initial wealth $W_0 = e1.0$ at the date 6/23/2006, the portfolio selection occurs using as performance measures the Sharpe Ratio or the Rachev Ratio, the results are reported in Fig. 7.12 and Fig. 7.13 for the Italian and German markets. The results show the performance of the various portfolios-for Modified Durations within (0-9) years(Sharpe 0-9, Rachev 0-9) or for the MD within (9-18) years (Sharpe 9-18, Rachev 9-18).

The optimal strategies show how in both markets most of the losses occurred during the recent period of sovereign crises, confirming how this period was dominated by high volatility. Lower losses were observed after the default of Lehman or the sub-prime crisis.

In Table 7.5 a comparison between the performance of ETF bonds in the Euro area and the Italian and German corporate and sovereign bonds. The ex-post wealth generated by the two portfolios strategies (based on the

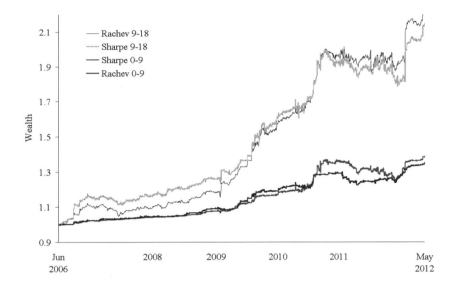

Fig. 7.12 Ex-post final wealth for Italian bonds portfolio with different modified durations.

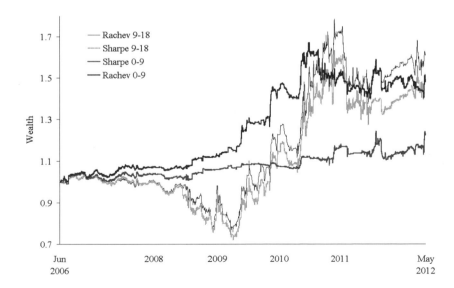

Fig. 7.13 Ex-post final wealth for German bonds portfolio with different modified durations.

Table 7.5   Statistics for the ex-post returns.

	Mean	St.dev.	VaR$_{5\%}$	CVaR$_{5\%}$	Fin. Wealth
ETF Sharpe	0.00004	0.00181	0.00283	0.00473	1.06723
ETF Rachev	0.00009	0.00252	0.00329	0.00555	1.14515
Sharpe 0-9 (Italy)	0.00022	0.00318	0.00275	0.0063	1.3859
Rachev 0-9 (Italy)	0.0002	0.00204	0.00174	0.00458	1.34864
Sharpe 9-18 (Italy)	0.00051	0.00582	0.00566	0.0108	2.14463
Rachev 9-18 (Italy)	0.00053	0.00564	0.00614	0.01025	2.22052
Sharpe 0-9 (Germany)	0.00015	0.00489	0.00454	0.01068	1.22871
Rachev 0-9 (Germany)	0.00028	0.00668	0.00743	0.01645	1.48981
Sharpe 9-18 (Germany)	0.00033	0.01156	0.01775	0.02903	1.50138
Rachev 9-18 (Germany)	0.00038	0.01183	0.01838	0.02964	1.61404

Sharpe ratio or on the Rachev ratio) result higher (in terms of risk-return measures) for portfolios selected using the Rachev Ratio.

The best performance is shown by portfolios with a Modified Duration in the interval (9-18): for the Italian market an increase of 122.05% is reported while for the German market only a a 61.4%. The yield pick up provided by Italian bonds should have encouraged investors' appetite and thus bolstered demand for these bonds. Generally, the strategies with larger Modified Duration offer higher ex-post returns (final wealth and mean) and ex-post risk (VaR, CVaR and standard deviation) than those with smaller Modified Duration. All the ex-post return/risk ratios for the Italian market result much higher than the corresponding ratios estimated for the bond ETF market and for the German market. The ex-post VaR and CVaR risk measures estimated for the the Rachev 0-9 strategy result lower for the Italian market than those estimated on the bond ETFs. It appears that bond ETFs portfolios are not less risky than Italian fixed income bond portfolios, so in general it is possible to outperform the bond ETFs market by investing in a large fixed income market.

On the one hand the observed differences among the optimal choices in the different markets can be partially explained by the role of the sovereign crisis in the European fixed income market, the difference in liquidity and costs, and the general different use as benchmark and hedge of the ETFs in strategic portfolio management (see [Amenc et al. (2004)]). Several elements that have hindered the development of the corporate bond market (a lower level of liquidity provided by these instruments, higher transaction costs incurred by investors and the difficulty of hedging easily and cheaply positions held in this market) have been the principal reasons for development of bond ETF markets.

On the other hand, the price paid for investing in a fund of funds results too high in terms of performance especially in the case used in this analysis where very basics primordial liquidity constraints and transaction costs (higher for the Italian fixed income market) were considered. The difference in the ex-post wealth presented in this example is due only to the trading activity not to the high yields provided by the Italian bond market (due to the decreasing credit risk rating). Considering that the credit risk crisis has had a stronger impact on the Italian fixed income market than other European markets (such as Germany and France) higher returns from operating in alternative countries should be expected. Bond ETFs portfolios still result less risky than equity portfolios but not than sovereign and corporate bond portfolios. During the last six years were different crisis followed the best strategy still results to invest in a sovereign bond portfolio and not in a bond ETF portfolio. In particular, the proposed analysis suggests that the advantages of investing on ETFs during the crisis are more concentrated in their flexibility (possibility of short sales; high frequency transactions; different use as benchmarks of some given sectors/markets) than in real opportunities of gains. For this reason European bond ETFs should be used together and not alternatively to the classical corporate and sovereign bonds of a given market.

Appendix 7.A. Risk and Reward of Bond Portfolios

Typically, the price of a bond is a function of the promised payments and the market required rate of return. Thus considering a fixed rate of return r, the price today of a bond P that will imply n future payments c_k at time t_k, $k=1,...,n$, is simply given by the formula:

$$P = \sum_{k=1}^{n} \frac{c_k}{(1+r)^{t_k}}. \qquad (7.A.1)$$

Generally the market required rate of return is not fixed over time and the rate r for which equality (7.A.1) holds is called *yield to maturity of the bond P*. The yield-price relationship is inverse, and we can easily measure the sensitivity of the bond price to yield changes. A classical approximation for bond price changes due to yield changes is the Modified Duration (MD)

$$D = -\frac{1}{P}\frac{\partial P}{\partial r} = \frac{1}{P(1+r)} \sum_{k=1}^{n} \frac{t_k c_k}{(1+r)^{t_k}}$$

that is obtained from the equation (7.A.1). Modified Duration is the name given to the price sensitivity and is the percentage change in price for a unit change in yield, i.e.

$$\frac{\Delta P}{P} \approx -D\Delta r. \qquad (7.A.2)$$

The promised payments c_k in equation (7.A.1) for nominal and corporate bonds are fixed while for inflation-linked bonds the values c_k are not known because they depend on the inflation rate. This fundamental difference between ILBs and sovereign bonds implies that the portfolio problem has to be dealt with using different risk and reward measures.

Appendix 7.B. Two Approaches for ILBs Portfolio Selection

Let us suppose we have a frictionless market in which no short selling is allowed and all investors act as price takers. Under these assumptions we can distinguish the two following risk and reward approaches:

1) 1st Approach.

Given a benchmark with return r_b and n bonds with a vector of returns $r = [r_1, ..., r_n]'$, the classical portfolio selection problem in the risk and reward framework consists of minimizing a given risk measure ρ provided that the expected reward v is constrained by some minimal value m. Along the efficient choices obtained by varying the value of the constraint m, there is a portfolio (commonly referred to as the market portfolio) that provides the maximum expected reward v per unit of risk ρ. So, assuming that the risk and reward are both positive, the market portfolio is obtained as the solution to the following optimization problem:

$$\max_x \frac{v\left(x'r - r_b\right)}{\rho\left(x'r - r_b\right)} \quad s.t. \quad x_i \geq 0, \forall i; \sum_{i=1}^{n} x_i = 1 \qquad (7.B.1)$$

where the vector notation $x'r = \sum_{i=1}^{n} x_i r_i$ stands for the returns of a portfolio with composition $x = [x_1, ..., x_n]'$, and the no short selling assumption is represented by $x_i \geq 0; \forall i$. Starting from the original Markowitz' analysis, Sharpe suggested that investors should maximize the so-called Sharpe ratio (see [Sharpe (1994)]) given by:

$$SR(x'r) = \frac{E(x'r - r_b)}{STD(x'r - r_b)}. \qquad (7.B.2)$$

In the Sharpe ratio, risk is approximated by the standard deviation $STD(x'r - r_b)$ of excess returns. Therefore we use historical observations of returns to estimate a reward and a risk measure of the portfolio return.

2) 2nd approach.

Consider $r = [r_1, ..., r_n]'$ the vector of the yields to maturity of the assets, $D = [D_1, ..., D_n]'$ the vector of the modified durations of each bond, and $v = [v_1, ..., v_n]'$ the vector of the wealth invested in the bonds i.e. $v_i = y_i P_i$ where y_i is the number of assets invested in the i-th bond and P_i is the price of the i-th bond. Then we can assume that the portfolio Modified Duration is approximated by the formula:

$$D_{(p)} = \frac{v'D}{\sum_{i=1}^{n} v_i} \tag{7.B.3}$$

which is true when we have a flat term structure. Thus investors in a risk and reward framework should maximize the expected future wealth approximated by $v'(1 + r)$ for some fixed risk represented by the Modified Duration of the portfolio $D_{(p)}$ and investors will choose a solution to the following optimization problem:

$$\max_{y} v'(1 + r)$$

$$\text{s.t. } \sum_{i=1}^{n} y_i P_i = W; \frac{v'D}{W} = d; \tag{7.B.4}$$

$$y_i P_i = v_i; y_i \geq 0; i = 1, ..., n$$

for some fixed Modified Duration d and an initial wealth W. Note that in this optimization problem we do not need historical observations of bond returns to estimate the reward and risk measure.

For both approaches the horizon (usually months) is divided in subperiods (usually weeks) where the optimization is performed. Each weekly optimization starts with an initial portfolio obtained by the previous optimizacion step. At the k_{th} recalibration ($k = 0, 1, 2, ...$), three main steps are performed to compute the ex-post final wealth:

Step 1: Filter the data selecting only those assets with acceptable liquidity. Approximate the returns with the PCA when we deal with the large scale portfolio problem. Determine the market portfolio $x_M^{(k+1)}$ that maximizes the Sharpe ratio, i.e. the solution of the optimization problem (7.C.6).

Step 2: The ex-post final wealth is given by:

$$W_{k+1} = W_k \left(\left(x_M^{(k+1)} \right)' (1 + r_{k+1}) \right), \qquad (7.B.5)$$

where r_{k+1} is the ex-post vector of the returns between k and $k+1$.

Step 3: The optimal portfolio $x_M^{(k+1)}$ is the new starting point for the $(k+1)_{th}$ optimization problem (7.C.6).

These steps are repeated as long as there are available observations.

Appendix 7.C. Two Approaches for BETFs Portfolio Selection

We consider n assets with returns $r = [r_1, \ldots, r_n]'$ and a benchmark with return r_b. We denote by $x = [x_1, \ldots, x_n]'$ the vector of the positions taken in the n assets. The portfolio's return is given by $x'r = \sum_{i=1}^{n} x_i r_i$. Under these assumptions we can distinguish the two following portfolio selection approaches:

1) Portfolio problem with ETFs

In order to maximize the performance of a portfolio in the risk and return framework we use the maximum expected return v per unit of risk ρ. This optimal portfolio is commonly referred to as the market portfolio and is obtained by maximizing the ratio between the return and the risk when both are positive measures. There are several possible performance ratios $G(X) = \dfrac{v(X)}{\rho(X)}$ which can be used in portfolio choices. The most important characteristic of performance ratio is "isotony" with an order of preference: that is, if X is preferable to Y then $G(X) \geq G(Y)$. Although the financial literature on investor behavior agrees that investors are non-satiable, there is not a common vision about the investors' aversion to risk. Thus investors' choices should be isotonic with non-satiable investors' preferences (i.e., if $X \geq Y$, then $G(X) \geq G(Y)$). Several behavioral finance studies suggest that most investors are neither risk averse nor risk loving.[1] A first classification with respect to the different characteristics of risk and return measures is given in [Rachev et al. (2008)]. We review two performance measures we will use in the next portfolio analysis: the Sharpe ratio and the Rachev ratio. According to Markowitz' mean-variance analysis, Sharpe [Sharpe (1994)] suggested that investors should maximize the

---

[1]See [Friedman and Savage (1948); Markowitz (1952); Levy and Levy (2002); Ortobelli (2009)].

so-called Sharpe Ratio (SR) given by

$$SR(x'r) = \frac{E(x'r - r_b)}{STD(x'r - r_b)}, \tag{7.C.1}$$

where r_b is a benchmark return and $STD(x'r - r_b)$ is the standard deviation of excess returns. Maximizing the Sharpe ratio, we get a market portfolio that should be optimal for non-satiable risk-averse investors, and that is not dominated in the sense of second-order stochastic dominance. This performance measure is fully compatible with elliptically distributed returns, but it will lead to incorrect investment decisions when returns present heavy tails or skewness. In order to account of heavy tails and skewness several other performance ratios based on tail measures have been proposed. In contrast to the Sharpe ratio, the Rachev ratio is based on tail measures and it is isotonic with the preferences of non-satiable investors that are neither risk averse nor risk lovers.

The Rachev Ratio (RR)[2] is the ratio between the average of earnings and the mean of losses; that is,

$$RR(x'r, \alpha, \beta) = \frac{CVaR_\beta(r_b - x'r)}{CVaR_\alpha(x'r - r_b)}, \tag{7.C.2}$$

where the Conditional Value-at-Risk (CVaR), is defined as

$$CVaR_\alpha(X) = \frac{1}{\alpha} \int_0^\alpha VaR_q(X)dq, \tag{7.C.3}$$

and

$$VaR_q(X) = -F_X^{-1}(q) = -\inf\{x \,|P\,(X \leq x) > q\} \tag{7.C.4}$$

is the Value-at-Risk (VaR) of the random return X. If we assume a continuous distribution for the probability law of X, then $CVaR_\alpha(X) = -E\,(X\,|X \leq -VaR_\alpha(X))$ and, therefore CVaR, can be interpreted as the average loss beyond VaR. Tipically, we use historical observations of returns to estimate a return and a risk measure of the portfolio's return . A consistent estimator of $CVaR_\alpha(X)$ is given by:

$$CVaR_\alpha(X) = \frac{-1}{[\alpha M]} \sum_{i=1}^{[\alpha M]} X_{i:M} \tag{7.C.5}$$

where M is the number of historical observations of X, $[\alpha M]$ is the integer part of αM and $X_{i:M}$ is the i-th observation of X ordered in increasing values. Similarly, an approximation of $VaR_q(X)$ is simply given by $-X_{[qM]:M}$.

---

[2]See [Biglova et al. (2004)].

Once we are able to approximate the portfolio risk and return measures, we can apply portfolio selection optimization problems to the approximated portfolio's return. When no short sales are allowed ($x_i \geq 0$) and we cannot invest more that 20% in a unique asset ($x_i \leq 0.2$), we assume that the investors will choose the market portfolio solution of the following optimization problem

$$\max_{x} G(x'r)$$

subject   to   (7.C.6)

$$\sum_{i=1}^{n} x_i = 1, \quad x_i \geq 0, \quad x_i \leq 0.2, \quad i = 1, ..., n$$

where $G(x'r)$ is either the Sharpe ratio or the Rachev ratio. To face the portfolio problem (7.C.6) we should account of other two problems: the computationally complexity and the portfolio dimensionality. Concerning the computationally complexity we observe that:

a) the maximization of the Sharpe ratio can be solved as a quadratic-type problem and thus it admits a unique solution;
b) the optimization of Rachev Ratio does not give a unique global optimum, so to overcome the computational complexity problem for global maximum, we use the heuristic proposed by [Angelelli and Ortobelli (2009)] that presents significant improvements in terms of objective function and portfolio weights with respect to the function "fmincon " provided with the optimization toolbox of MATLAB.

Concerning the portfolio dimensionality we recall that the number of observations should increase proportionally with the number of assets, see [Papp (2005); Kondor et al. (2007)]. In the portfolio problem with ETFs we deal with a large number of ETFs. It is necessary to find the right trade-off between a statistical approximation of the historical series depending only on few parameters and the number of historical observations. The most used methodology to reduce the dimensionality of the large scale portfolio problems consists of approximating the return series with a k-fund separation model (or other regression-type models) that depends on an adequate number of factors. With this methodology we identify some "good" factors and we reduce the randomness of the portfolio problem approximating the return series with a linear model that depends on the chosen factors. We use principal component analysis (PCA) and we approximate the returns by regressing on the first few components obtained with PCA. In the following empirical analysis we adopt this methodology when the number of admissible bond ETFs is bigger than 50. Thus we reduce the dimensionality of the problem by considering a number of factors which is never bigger than the 10% of the total number of assets.

In order to identify the few factors (portfolios) with the highest return variability we perform PCA on the ETFs returns. Therefore, we replace the original n correlated time series $\{r_i\}_{i=1,...,n}$ with n uncorrelated time series $\{R_j\}_{j=1,...,n}$ assuming that each r_i is a linear combination of the series $\{R_j\}_{j=1,...,n}$. We implement a dimensionality reduction by choosing only those factors whose variability is significantly different from zero. We call portfolio factors f_j $(j = 1, ..., s)$ the s time series in $\{R_j\}_{j=1,...,n}$ with a significant dispersion measure, while the remaining $n - s$ series with very small dispersion measure are summarized by an error. Thus, each series r_i is a linear combination of the factors plus a small uncorrelated noise:

$$r_i = \sum_{j=1}^{s} a_j f_j + \sum_{j=s+1}^{n} a_j R_j = \sum_{j=1}^{s} a_j f_j + \varepsilon_i \ i = 1, ldots, n \qquad (7.C.7)$$

We apply PCA to the Pearson correlation matrix obtained by the individual returns. Once we have identified the s factors f_j $(j = 1, ..., s)$ accounting for most of the historical returns variability, we further reduce the variability of the error by regressing the series on the factors f_j so that we get the approximated returns:

$$r_i = b_{i,0} + \sum_{j=1}^{s} b_{i,j} f_{j,t} + \varepsilon_{i,t+1}, \qquad (7.C.8)$$

where the regression error $\varepsilon_{i,t+1}$ is not considered in the approximation. Once we have approximated the returns we can compute the performance measure $G(x'r)$ using the approximated returns (7.C.8) and then solve the optimization problem (7.C.6).

2) Portfolio problem with sovereign bonds and corporate bonds.

In the portfolio problem with sovereign and corporate bonds we can distinguish two phases for the portfolio decisional process where we cope with two different sources of risk: the risk of variation of prices and the market risk.

(1) First phase: we compute the ex post wealth we obtain and optimize the expected future wealth of the portfolio of bonds taking into account the risk of variation of the prices by fixing the portfolio Modified Durations. We create a fund of bonds for any fixed Modified Duration. In particular, we consider 60 values of the fixed Modified Duration in the interval

[0.25-18] years. The funds change in their composition periodically to maintain the constraint of the fixed Modified Duration.

(2) Second phase: we use the historical series of ex-post wealth obtained in the first phase for different Modified Duration. Then we optimize the Sharpe and Rachev ratios on these series distinguishing short and medium range duration period (0-9 years) and long range duration period (9-18 years). With this second phase we practically reduce the market risk by obtaining optimal portfolios that are funds of other funds (the ones obtained with the phase 1) and they should have characteristics similar to those of the optimal portfolio obtained in the bond ETF market.

As in Chapter 7.2, in phase 1 we consider $r = [r_1, ..., r_n]'$ the vector of the yields to maturity of the assets, $D = [D_1, ..., D_n]'$ the vector of the modified durations of each nominal bond, and $v = [v_1, ..., v_n]'$ the vector of the wealth invested in the bonds i.e. $v_i = y_i P_i$ where y_i is the number of assets invested in the i-th bond and P_i is the price of the i-th bond. Then in a risk and return framework we consider, as return measure, the expected future wealth approximated by $v'(1+r)$ and, as risk measure, the modified duration of the portfolio approximated by the formula $D_{(p)} = \frac{v'D}{W}$ where $W = \sum_{i=1}^{n} v_i$ is the initial wealth. Thus, when no short sales are allowed ($y_i \geq 0$) and supposing that cannot be invested more that 20% in a unique asset ($\frac{y_i P_i}{W} \leq 0.2$), the investor that wants to minimize the risk of variation of the prices, will choose a solution of the following optimization problem:

$$\max_{y} v'(1+r)$$

$$\text{subject to}$$

$$\sum_{i=1}^{n} y_i P_i = W, \quad \frac{v'D}{W} = d, \quad y_i P_i = v_i$$

$$y_i \geq 0, \quad \frac{y_i P_i}{W} \leq 0.2, \quad i = 1, ..., n$$

(7.C.9)

for some fixed Modified Duration d and an intial wealth W. Observe that in this first phase we do not need historical observations of bond returns to estimate the risk and return measure.

In Phase 2 of the portfolio decisional process we consider the observations of the ex-post wealth obtained with each fixed Modified Duration as the prices of a fund buildt in Phase 1. Then we perform a risk and return portfolio optimization for different modified duration ranges. We distinguish two different Modified Duration ranges: 0-9 years and 9-18 years and as done in the first phase we optimize the portfolio problem (7.C.6) for each Modified Duration period (0-9 years and 9-18 years) and for each performance measure $G(x'r)$ (Sharpe ratio and Rachev ratio) using the historical observations of the 30 return funds corresponding with the associated Modified Duration period.

Glossary

Asset-backed security A financial security backed by a loan, lease or receivables against assets other than real estate and mortgage-backed securities. Asset-backed securities (ABS) differ from mortgage-backed security (MBS) because the securities backing it are assets such as loans, leases, credit card debt, a company's receivables, royalties and so on, and not mortgage-based securities.

Asset pool This is the asset portfolio explicitly defining the backing of covered bonds, or ABS or MBS. In the case of assets backing covered bonds, this is also referred to as cover pool

CNMV Comision Nacional del Mercado de Valores: Spanish organism in charge to supervise the issuance and placing activity in the financial market.

Covered bond purchase program following-up on its decision of 7 May 2009 to purchase Euro-denominated covered bonds issued in the Euro area, the Governing Council of the European Central Bank (ECB) decided upon the technical modalities today. These can be found at `http://www.ecb.int/press/pr/date/2009/html/pr090604\_1.en.htmlforthefirstCBPP`.

Dual-recourse covered bonds offer dual recourse for payment. Bondholders can rely on recourse to the assets in the cover pool as well as to the issuer.

EMTX EuroMTS indeces: they are a Euro-denominated total return indices designed to measure the performance of Euro area Government bond market.

Jumbo covered bond In the past, covered bonds, known in German as Pfandbriefe, were typically bought by investors and held until they matured. There was no active trading of these absolutely safe investments. In order to promote the trading of covered bonds and to make these investment vehicles attractive for foreign investors, jumbo covered bonds, or jumbos, were introduced in 1997. Several smaller issues were combined to form one large bond called a jumbo. Jumbo covered bonds must fulfill the following criteria: - the issue volume has to be at least €1 billion - it can only be divided into tranches of at least €125 million - at least five market makers set bid and ask prices simultaneously during normal trading hours of 9am to 5pm with order volumes of up to €15 million.

LTV Loan-to-Value: ratio of a loan underwritten of a value of an asset purchase.

LTRO Longer Term Refinancing Operation: it is a process by which the ECB provides financing the Euro area banks.

Over collateralisation Cover pools are called dynamic (rather than static) because their contents can be enhanced over time by adding more or different assets. If some assets in the pool deteriorate, they can be replaced. Unlike with mortgage-backed securities (MBS) or collateralized debt obligations (CDOs), if the overall value of the assets declines, the drop can be mitigated by increasing the amount of over-collateralization.

SDO Saerligt Daekkede Obligationer: Denmark covered bond

BEIR Break-Even Interest Rate: theoretical rate of inflation that makes the expected rate of return nominal bond and inflation-linked bond equal..

CPI Consumer Price Index.

CVaR Conditional Value at Risk, the expected value of profits than one would expect lower than VaR.

ETF Exchange Traded Fund, a particular collection of investment that is traded on an exchange.

ETP Exchange Traded Product.

ex-HICP Harmonized Index of Consumer Prices excluding tobacco.

IIC International Index Company.

ILB Inflation-Linked Bond: a bond whose coupn are linked to a consumer price index.

MD Modified Duration: risk measure for bond, defined as a linear combination of coupon maturities.

NAV Net Asset Value.

OLS Ordinary Least Square, statistical technique for finding coefficients in a regression.

PCA Principal Component Analysis, statistical technique to find the main drivers of an historical time series.

RR Rachev Ratio, measure representing the average of earnings versus the average of losses

SR Sharpe Ratio, measure of return for unit of risk.

TER Total Expence Ratio.

TE Tracking Error, difference of a variable from a benchmark.

VaR Value at Risk, the α quantile of a distribution of profit/losses.

References

Alexander, C., (1999). Optimal Hedging Using Cointegration, from Mathematics of Finance, *Philosophical Transactions: Mathematical, Physical and Engineering Sciences*, **357**, 1758, pp. 2039–2058.

Alexander, C., Dimitriu, A. (2004). A Comparison of Cointegration and Tracking Error Models for Mutual Funds and Hedge Funds, *ISMA Centre Discussion Papers in Finance*, March.

Amenc, N., Giraud, J. R., Malaise, P., Martellini, L. (2004). The benefits of bond ETFs for institutional investors The natural vehicle for a core-satellite approach (EDHEC-Risk Institute Publication).

Amenc, N., Goltz, F., Grigoriu, A., Schroder, D. (2009). The EDHEC European ETF Survey 2009 (EDHEC-Risk Institute Publication).

Amenc, N., Martellini, L., Ziemann, V. (2009). Inflation Hedging Properites of Real Assets and Implications for Asset Liability Management Decisions, *The Journal of Portfolio Management*, Summer, pp. 94–110.

Anderson, N., Sleath, J. (2001). New estimates of the UK real and nominal yield curves, *Bank of England*, Working Paper Series, **126**.

Ang, A., Briere, M., Signori, O. (2011). Inflation and Individual Equities, Working paper.

Angelelli, E., Ortobelli, L. S. (2009). American and European portfolio selection strategies: the Markovian approach, chapter 5, *Financial Hedging* (Novascience: New York).

Bach, G. L., Musgrave, R. A. (1941). A stable purchable power bond, *American Economic Review*, **31**(4), pp. 823–825.

Bacon, C. (2008). Practical Portfolio Performance Measurement and Attribution (John Wiley & Sons: England).

Bank for International Settlements (2012). International banking and financial market developments, *BIS*, Quarterly Review, June.

Bardong, F., Lehnert, T. (2004). European inflation indexed government debt security markets: on efficiency, *Journal of Portfolio Management*, Special Issue, pp. 226–238.

Barro, R. J. (1997). Optimal management of indexed and nominal debt. *National Bureau of Economic Research*, Working Paper Series, **6197**.

Biglova, A., Ortobelli, S., Rachev, S., Stoyanov, S. (2004). Different Approaches to Risk Estimation in Portfolio Theory, *Journal of Portfolio Management*, **31**, pp. 103–112.

BlackRock (2012). ETP Landscape: Industry Highlights, *BlackRock Investment Institute* (Bloomberg).

Blitz, D., Huij, J., Swinkels, L. (2010). The Performance of European Index Funds and Exchange-Traded Funds, *European Financial Management*, doi:10.1111/j.1468-036X.2010.00550.x.

Blume, M., Edelen, R. (2004). S&P500 indexers, traking error, and liquidity: a complex answer to profiting, *Journal of Portfolio Management*, **30**(3), pp. 37–46.

Campbell, J. Y., Shiller, R. J. (1996). A Scorecard for Indexed Government Debt, *National Bureau of Economic Research*, Working Paper Series, **5587**.

Campbell, J. Y., Viceira, L. M. (2002). Strategic asset allocation: portfolio choice for long term investors, *Clarendon Lectures in Economics* (Oxford University Press, Oxford).

Cappiello, L., Guene, S. (2005). Measuring market and inflation risk premia in France and in Germany, *ECB*, Working Paper Series, **436**.

Cresson, J., Cudd, R., Lipscomb, T. (2002). The Early Attraction of S&P Index Funds: Is Perfect Tracking Performance an Illusion?. *Managerial Finance*, **28**, pp. 1–8.

Deacon, M., Derry, A. (1994). Deriving estimates of inflation expectations from the prices of Uk Government bonds, *Bank of England*, Working Paper Series, **23**.

Drenovak, M., Urošević, B. (2011). Exchange-traded funds of the Euro zone Sovereign debt, *Economic Annals*, **LV**(187), pp. 31–60.

Drenovak, M., Urošević, B., Jelic, R. (2012). European bond ETFs: Tracking Errors and the Sovereign Debt crisis, *European Financial Management*, doi:10.1111/j.1468-036X.2012.00649.x.

Drudi, F., Giordano, R. (2000). Wage indexation employment and inflation, *Scandinavian Journal of Economics*, **102**(4), pp. 645–668.

European Central Bank (2008). Covered bonds in the EU financial system, *ECB*, Report, December.

European Covered Bonds Council (2010). Financial Integration Report, *European Covered Bonds Council*, April, http://www.ecbc.org.

European Covered Bonds Council (2011). European covered bond Fact Book, *European Covered Bonds Council*, htt://www.ecbc.org.

European Covered Bonds Council (2012). European covered bond Fact Book, *European Covered Bonds Council*, http://www.ecbc.org,

Evans, M. (1998). Real rates, expected inflation and inflation risk premia, *Journal of finance*, **53**(1), pp. 187–218.

Farcia, J. A., Rixtel, A. (2007). Inflation linked bonds from a central bank perspective, *European Central Bank*, Occasional Paper Series.

Fischer, S. (1975). The demand for index bond, *Journal of Political Economy*, **83**(3), pp. 509–534.

Friedman, M., Savage, L. J. (1948). The utility analysis of choices involving risk, *Journal of Political Economy*, **56**, pp. 279–304.

Garcia-Zarate, J. (2012). ETP selection A Step-By-Step Approach, *NASDAQ OMX*, ETF seminar.

Goltz, F., Tang, L. (2012). The EDHEC European ETF Survey 2011, *EDHEC-Risk*, Institute Publication.

Gurkaynak, R., Sack, B., Wright, J. (2007). The US treasury yield curve: 1961 to the present, *Journal of Monetary Economics*, **54**, pp. 2291–2304.

Gurkaynak, R., Sack, B., Wright, J. (2010). The tips yield curve and inflation compensation, *American Economic Journal: Macroeconomics*, **2**, pp. 70–92.

Hordahl, P., Tristani, O. (2010). Inflation risk premia in the US and the Euro area, *ECB*, Working Paper Series, **1270**.

Hordahl, P., Tristani, O., Vestin, D. (2006). A joint econometric model of macroeconomic and term structure dynamics, *Journal of Econometrics*, **131**, pp. 405–444.

Houweling, P. (2011). On the performance of fixed income exchange traded funds, Working paper, http://ssrn.com=1840559.

Hunter, D., Simon, D. (2005). Are TIPS the real deal? A conditional assessment of their role in a nominal portoflio, *Journal of Banking and Finance*, **29**(2), pp. 347–368.

Issing, O. (1973). Indexklauseln und Inflation, *Vortrage und Aufsatze*, **40** (Walter Eucken Institut, J.C.B. Mohr (Paul Siebeck): Tubingen).

Jensen, J. L. W. V. (1906). Sur les fonctions convexes et les inegalites entre les valeurs moyennes, *Acta Mathematica*, **30**(1), pp. 175–193, doi:10.1007/BF02418571.

Kennedy, M. (2012). Exchange trade funds Guide, *about.com guide*, http://etf.about.com/od/bondetfs/a/Types_Bond_ETFs.htm.

Kondor, I., Pafka, S., Nagy, G. (2007). Noise sensitivity of portfolio selection under various risk measures, *Journal of Banking and Finance*, **31**, pp. 1545–1573.

Kothari, S. P., Shanken, J. (2004). Asset allocation with inflation procted bonds, *Financial Analysts Journal*, January/February, pp. 3–24.

Levy, M., Levy, H. (2002). Prospect theory: much ado about nothing?, *Management Science*, **48**, pp. 1334–1349.

Longstaff, F. A. (2004). The Flight-to-Liquidity Premium in U.S. Treasury Bond Prices, *Journal of Business*, **77**(3), pp. 511–526.

Markowitz, H. M. (1952). The utility of wealth, *Journal of Political Economy*, **60**, pp. 151–158.

Markowitz, H. (1959). Portfolio selection; efficient diversification of investment (Wiley: New York).

Martellini, L., Mihau, V. (2011). Optimal Design of Corporate Market Debt Programmes in the Presence of Interest Rate and Inflation Risks (EDHEC-Risk Institute Publication).

Nelson, C. R., Siegel, A. F. (1987). Parsimonious modeling of yield curves for U.S. Treasury yields, *Journal of Business*, **60**(4), pp. 473–489.

Nomura Global Economics, Europe Will Work, Nomura, March 2011.

Ortobelli, S., Rachev, S., Shalit, H., Fabozzi, F. (2009). Orderings and probability functionals consistent with preferences, *Applied Mathematical Finance*, **16**(1), pp. 81–102.

Pallaris, S. (2011).Swap-based Exchange traded funds, *Horizons ETFs*, Educational report.

Papp, G., Pafka, S., Nowak, M. A., Kondor, I. (2005). Random matrix filtering in portfolio optimization, *ACTA Physica Polonica*, **B**(36), pp. 2757–2765.

Pope, P., Yadav, P. (1994). Discovering Errors in Tracking Error, *Journal of Portfolio Management*, **20**, pp. 27–32.

Prokopczuk, M., Vonhoff, V. (2012). Risk premia in covered bond markets, *ICMA Centre*, Discussion Papers in Finance, DP2012-03, January.

Rachev, S., Ortobelli, S., Stoyanov, S., Fabozzi, F., Biglova, A. (2008). Desirable Properties of an Ideal Risk Measure in Portfolio Theory, *International Journal of Theoretical and Applied Finance*, **11**(1), pp. 19–54.

Ramaswamy, S. (2011). Market structures and systematic risk of Exchange traded funds, *BIS*, Working paper, 343.

Reschreiter, A. (2004). Conditional funding costs of inflation indexed and conventional government bonds, *Journal of Banking and Finance*, **28**(6), pp. 1299–1318.

Roll, R. (2004). Empirical TIPS, *Financial Analysts Journal*, January/February, pp. 31–53.

Rompotis, G. (2008). Performance and Trading Characteristics of German Passively Managed ETFs, *International Research Journal of Finance and Economics*, Issue 15, pp. 210–223.

Sarnat, M. (1973). Purchasing power risk, portfolio analysis, and the case for index linked bonds - a comment by Marshall Sarnat, *Journal of Money, Credit and Banking*, **5**(3), pp. 836–845.

Sharpe, W. F. (1994). The Sharpe ratio. *Journal of Portfolio Management*. Fall, pp. 45–58.

Standard & Poor's (2012). Covered Bonds Outlook 2012: Is the Shine coming off?, *Global Credit Portal*, Structured Finance Research, January.

Stoyanov, S., Rachev, S., Fabozzi, F., Ortobelli, S. (2008). Relative deviation metrics and the problem of strategy replication, *Journal of Banking and Finance*, **32**(2), pp. 199–206

Towned, J. (1997). Indexed linked government securities: the UK experience and perspective, in De Cecco, Pecchi, Piga (eds.), Managing public debt: index linked bonds in theory and practice, pp. 1–17.

Chapter 8

Credit Derivatives Market

(*Rosella Giacometti*)

8.1 Introduction

Credit derivatives are financial products which allow the transfer of credit risk associated with a specific asset or a pool of assets from one party to another without transferring the assets. It is not necessary that the reference asset must be held by either of the counterparties. The party that wants to sell the credit risk is called the protection buyer and the party that provides protection is called the protection seller. Credit derivatives generate cash flows which are linked to so-called credit events. Credit events may be bankruptcy, failure to pay or restructuring of a reference entity. The asset underlying the credit derivative is called the reference asset or obligation. The issuer of the reference obligation is the reference entity or the 'name' and is usually a corporation or a government.

Credit derivatives are traded Over-The-Counter (hereafter OTC) through a dealer network. They where introduced in the mid 90s. Even if relatively small in size when compared to other OTC derivatives, they have shown an impressive fast growth.

Credit derivatives are instruments which allow parties to take a pure position in credit risk or a joint position in credit risk and market risk. Credit Default Swaps (CDS) and Credit Spread Swaps (CSS) are pure credit risk instruments; Total Rate of Return Swaps (TRORS) allow the joint exposure to market and credit risk. Credit default and credit spread products respectively provide protection in case of default and of downgrading of the reference entity of the contract. The risk of downgrading is related to the risk that the negative variation of the creditworthiness of the reference entity causes a loss in the value of the reference entity. Single name credit default swaps are the most liquid and widely used products accounting in 2011 for 64% of the outstanding notional amounts in the credit default swaps market. According to Fig. 8.1, they account for 50% of the overall credit derivatives market. They are able to isolate and to provide a precise market price for the credit risk of a single reference asset. A driver of the the growth of these instruments is the ability to use them to express credit views.

The expansion of the CDS market was boosted by the introduction of CDS indices which allow to trade the credit risk of a standardised basket of names. Indices are standardised contracts and refer to a fixed number of obligors with common features as geographical area and creditworthiness. Investors can be long or short the index which is equivalent to being protection sellers or buyers. As an example the ITraxx Europe index is a portfolio of 125 equally-weighted CDS of European investment grade names. CDS indices provide an efficient tool to transfer credit risk of a portfolio of names. As a natural extension, the credit risk of the index can be traded in tranches so that it is possible to buy protection for a specific profile of credit risk. Another family of popular instruments are basket products: the *k-th* to default CDS offers protection against the *k-th* default in a basket of n obligors. It is less expensive than an index on the same portfolio of obligors since it offers protection only to the *k-th* default and not the entire basket.

Total Rate of Return Swaps (TRORS) transfer the total return i.e, all the gains and losses related to a credit event and to a market movement, between two counterparties: the total return receiver and the total return payer. The former creates a virtual position in the reference entity without having it in his portfolio and the latter pays a period fee to buy protection against credit and market risk on the same reference entity.

Finally, coupled with securitisation, credit derivatives have also been wrapped into investment products as Credit Linked Notes (CLNs) and Collateralized Debt Obligations (CDOs). Credit Linked Notes are structured products that are similar to high return bonds with an embedded credit derivative. CDOs are structured instruments backed by one or more classes of fixed income assets. Originally CDOs were based on portfolios of high-yield corporate bonds. More recently, CDOs have been based on other assets, including CDSs and even other CDOs. With securitisation a credit derivative is embedded in a capital market instrument and the credit risk is transferred into the capital markets which act as protection seller.

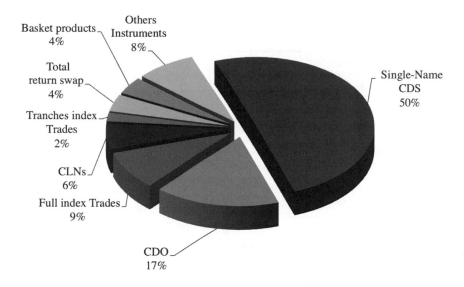

Fig. 8.1   Credit Derivatives by typology.

8.2   The CDS Market

8.2.1   *The single-name CDS*

CDSs are bilateral contracts in which a protection buyer agrees to pay a periodic fee (called a "premium") in exchange for a payment by the protection seller if one of a series of pre-defined credit events occurs for the reference entity. The contractual maturity is between one and ten years. The payment due by the protection seller in case of a default event corresponds to compensation of the loss caused by the default and it is equal to the Loss Given Default per unit exposure (LGD) times the notional value of the contract. The LGD is equal to $1 - RR$ where RR is the Recovery Rate (see Chapter 4). The exact value of RR is known only after the default. However for pricing reasons, it is estimated ex-ante on the basis of historical data, and it is generally provided by the Rating Agencies.

    When a default occurs there are two possible settlement methods: physical delivery of the underlying security or cash settlement. The difference is that in a physical settlement there is an exchange of the reference asset between the protection buyer and the protection seller against the payment

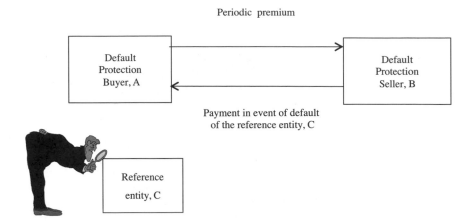

Fig. 8.2   Single name CDS.

of the par value of the bond; in a cash settlement the protection seller refunds the protection buyer for the incurred loss with a cash payment equal to the difference between the post default market value of the bond and the par value. Recently the market convention has switched predominantly from physical to cash settlement to avoid an effect on the prices known as 'short squeeze'. As an example, after the default of the Dana Corporation, in 2006, the price of the reference asset increased due to difficulty in finding the asset in the market for physical delivery.

These contracts are more precisely called "single-name CDSs" since they offer protection on a single corporate or sovereign reference entity. CDSs on Corporates account for 80% of the nominal values with respect to 20% on Sovereigns which have only recently seen an impressive growth. The terms of Sovereign CDSs and Corporate CDS are almost identical with the exception of repudiation or moratorium clauses commonly found in a Sovereign CDS.

A CDS contract can be used for hedging purposes: it provides the buyer of the contract, if he/she owns the underlying asset, protection against its default. However it is not necessary for the counterparties to hold the reference obligation. In this case the term naked position is commonly used.

CDSs are the most liquid credit derivatives and are able to isolate the credit risk of the reference entity. The market price of the premium is therefore an indication of the perceived risk related to the reference entity.

Before the introduction of credit derivatives, it was difficult to determine a price for measuring credit risk and as such there was no recognised benchmark. As the market has become more liquid, lenders and investors have been able to compare the pricing of cash instruments with credit derivatives. Further, investors are able to engage in relative value trades.

8.2.2 CDS as a measure of credit risk

CDS spreads reveal important information about the quality of Corporate and Sovereign bonds and other types of debt instruments. CDS spreads may frequently signal information about the credit risk of bonds before rating adjustments are made by Rating Agencies on underlying names. In essence, CDSs significantly contribute to credit market price discovery. This has important implications for the efficiency and stability of credit markets.

Although they account for less than 6% of all OTC contracts in 2011 in terms of notional value, they attract great attention by the media. They isolate and provide the price of the credit risk of one reference entity so an increase in the spread of CDSs is carefully monitored, especially for Sovereign CDSs. A Sovereign CDS is a controversial financial instrument and can be used by traders to speculate on the probability of a country failing to pay off its debt. Sovereign CDSs provide a simple mechanism for reflecting negative views of evolving credit risk in the market. CDS markets have emerged as a highly visible signal of a country's perceived credit risk.

In recent decades, the most widely followed barometer of Corporate and Sovereign stability has been the credit ratings published by Credit Rating Agencies as Standard & Poor's, Fitch and Moody's. A new entry amongst the top Rating Agencies is the Chinese Dagong, founded in 1994. Dagong is a Credit Rating Agency based in China and it is one of the few notable non-US based Credit Rating Agencies.

Despite their enormous importance to the markets, the ratings are notoriously slow in reacting to changes in market conditions. Like the yield spreads of corporate bonds, Credit Default Swap pricing often provides better and more timely information about the soundness of companies for whom a credit default swap market has developed.

A simple relationship is used by practitioners to link the price of a CDS with the default probability (see Appendix 8.A for further details). The default intensity implied from the market prices is

$$\lambda_{t_0,t_n} = p_\alpha(t_0, t_n)/(1 - RR) \tag{8.1}$$

where,

- α is the reference entity;
- $p_\alpha(t_0, t_n)$ is the periodic CDS premium (also called spread) to insure against the default of α over the period $[t_0, t_n]$;
- λ_{t_0, t_n} is the average default intensity or hazard rate on an annual basis for α over the period $[t_0, t_n]$. To keep notation simple, we omit α;
- RR is the Recovery Rate.

Assuming $t_0 = 0$, the default probability in t_n years is given by

$$F(t_n) = 1 - \exp\left(-\lambda_{0,t_n} t_n\right). \qquad (8.2)$$

However, this quick rule of thumb must be used with caution. An increase in the CDS spread cannot be completely attributed to an increase in the Probability of Default, especially in a period of crisis. Recovery Rates are assumed to be fixed, but there is empirical evidence of a negative correlation between the Default Rate and the Recovery Rate over the cycle. In a period of financial market stress, with a higher liquidity risk premium and falling Recovery Rates, CDS spreads may also be affected by other risk premia, such as jump-to-default risk and systemic risk. The canonical example of jump-to-default risk is the Lehman Brothers' default, i.e. the risk of a credit default occurring was so sudden that the market was not able to incorporate the increased default risk into the current spreads. Systemic risk, is the risk of the simultaneous failure of a number of institutions due to interconnections in the financial system.

Credit Default Swaps are generally used for hedging purposes, in addition to their function of information disclosure. Assume an investor holds a portfolio of risky bonds. It is possible to shift and eliminate the credit risk by buying the protection implicit in the relevant CDSs. This might be more desirable than simply selling the security if the investor only wants to reduce the risk exposure and not completely eliminate it. If a bank has a loan protected by a credit derivative its risk exposure is reduced. Because Credit Default Swaps enable banks to lend at lower risk, these contracts increase liquidity in the credit market. Credit Default Swaps thus significantly expand companies' access to capital from bank lending. In term of hedging, CDSs can be used to diversify the credit risk of a bond portfolio and to hedge the counterparty risk of dealers. As part of daily trading activities, dealers take unsecured exposure to other financial institutions which are the counterparties of their transactions. Part of this risk can be mitigated by CDSs.

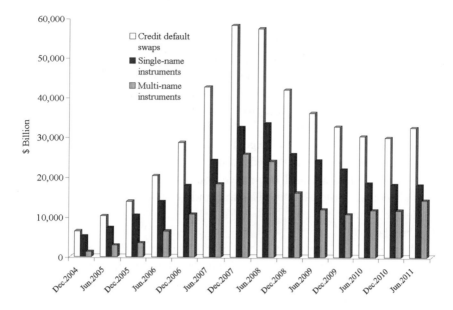

Fig. 8.3   Nominal amount outstandings.

CDSs may also be used for speculation or arbitrage. In normal conditions speculators and arbitragers have a positive effect on the market since they increase the liquidity of the market and eliminate pricing inefficiencies.

The European parliament voted in November 2011 to ban naked credit default swaps on sovereign securities. This rule will make it impossible to buy CDSs for the sole purpose of speculating on a country's default. Naked CDS instruments were prohibited in the Eurozone from December 1, 2011. Purchasing Italian CDS, for example, will now be possible only if the buyer already owns Italian government bonds or has invested in a sector which is highly dependent on the performance of these bonds, such as an Italian bank.

8.2.3   *Market features*

To understand the risks embedded in the CDS market, it is interesting to examine its features considering also their counterparty risk. A recent study of the European Central Bank [ECB (2009)], based on a quantitative and qualitative survey has pointed out four main features:

(1) Concentration:

The CDS market is concentrated around a few large Institutions: in 2008 these were JPMorgan, Goldman Sachs, Morgan Stanley, Deutsche Bank, Bank of America and Barclays. The 5 largest CDS dealers were counterparties to almost half of the total outstanding nominal amount and the top ten largest for almost 72%. In addition, the concentration of the CDS market is now higher than before the crisis, since some major players (such as Bear Stearns, Lehman Brothers, and Merrill Lynch) and counterparties that used to sell protection like credit derivative product companies and Insurance companies have exited the market. This concentration has increased liquidity risk in the event of another dealer failure.

(2) Circularity:

When we consider the top ten non-sovereign reference entities (see Table 8.1) we observe that six of them are also on the list of the major dealers. There is a network connecting protection sellers, protection buyers and reference entities. In other words financial institution sell protection against each other default. This means that instead of removing credit risk, banks may be replacing one type of risk i.e. credit risk with another, counterparty risk.

(3) Interconnectedness:

CDS contracts can be closed in 3 ways: by offsetting transaction, by novation — i.e. counterparty substitution- and by yearly termination, if it is included in the term of the contract. To offset a contract it is sufficient to have an equal and opposite position. In this way the two opposite positions are offset but not canceled. The effect of contract offsetting is that dealers are linked through chains of OTC derivative contracts, this results in increased contagion risk. The rush to unwind a vast array of interconnected contracts could create serious liquidity problems in the financial markets. The contracts between the interbank dealers are covered by ISDA and netting.

(4) Opaqueness:

The market for Credit Default Swaps is quite opaque. Because swaps are structured as OTC derivatives, they are largely unregulated. Among other things, this means that the details of particular swaps often go undisclosed. The main concern is the lack of transparency and information on volumes exchanged. In recent years, there was heated debate on the need to introduce a clearing house in order to guarantee a greater regulation and market transparency.

Table 8.1 Top ten non-sovereign reference entities on the basis of net protection amounts (USD billion; as at July 2009).

GE Capital	11.23
Bank of America	7.21
Deutsche Bank	7.17
JPMorgan	6.10
Morgan Stanley	5.95
Goldman Sachs	5.22
Merill Lynch	5.21
Berkshire Hathaway	4.95
Wells Fargo	4.87
The Royal Bank of Scotland	4.31

The size of the CDS market combined with the opacity, concentration and interconnectedness have created some shadows over these financial instruments because they could increase the systemic risk and contagion effects in financial markets

Despite these possible concerns, CDSs have been shown to be a very useful portfolio management and speculative tool, and they will continue to be an important and critical part of the financial markets.

8.2.4 *Factors determining the credit spread*

Especially during a credit crisis, market-based credit information helps participants to have timely indications of financial stress in the European banking industry. More recently, CDS spreads have also been closely monitored by regulatory authorities. Understanding the determinants of credit spreads is important for financial analysts, traders and policy makers.

Some recent research provides evidence that sovereign credit spreads are related to common global factors. As an example, Pan and Singleton [Pan and Singleton (2008)] suggest that the credit spreads for Mexico, Turkey, and Korea share a strong common relation to U.S. stock market volatility as measured by the VIX index. Such a common dependence could induce significant correlations among sovereign credit spreads. Longstaff et al. [Longstaff (2011)] analyzed the American CDS market using Principal Component Analysis and found that the first principal component affects 64 % of the variability in the period 2000-2010 and this value increases to 75% in the period 2007-2010. This principal component is highly correlated both with the US stock market return and with the VIX index. The same result does not hold when they consider the US stock market. Here the first principal component explains only 46 % of the variability in the period 2000-2010 and 62% in the period 2007-2010. In light of these findings they regress changes of CDS premia on macroeconomic factors to measure the possible relationship among these set of variables.

Fontana and Scheicher [Fontana and Scheicher (2011)] analysed the Eurozone (10-year CDSs spread relative to the ten-year swap rate for Austria, Belgium, France, Germany, Greece, Ireland, Italy, the Netherlands, Portugal and Spain) in the period 2006-2010, dividing it into two sub-periods in September 2008. The motivation is an observed massive repricing of risk which reached its first peak in the fall and winter 2008/2009 due to a decrease of risk appetite and a subsequent 'flight-to-quality' effect. They apply principal component analysis and found results similar to Longstaff et al. [Longstaff (2011)]. The first principal component account for 64% of the variability in the period 2006-2008 and subsequentially increased to 78% in the period 2008-2010. Overall, the analysis shows that a common factor plays a large role in the variation in sovereign CDS and that the variability explained by it has increased during a period of financial distress, augmenting the fears of contagion.

The presence of common factors indicates a need to investigate the determinants of the credit spreads. We present a non-exhaustive list of factors which affect both Corporate and Sovereign CDSs:

(1) Credit ratings: the most widely observed measure of credit quality of a specific debt issue or the issuing entity in general; numerous studies on credit ratings have shown that often changes in ratings are anticipated by the market, thus we expect that ratings have only a limited explanatory power for price changes. However other studies particularly on sovereign ratings (see [Cantor and Packer (1996)]) have shown that ratings efficiently include all the fundamental factors and also some additional ones. Related to credit rating of a country, there are a number of macroeconomic factors which must be considered such as budget deficits, debt-to-GDP ratio and current account balances which are positively correlated with rating variations.

(2) Stock Prices: they contain information on the underlying companies; negative information on the firm is reflected faster in the stock price than in the rating. The stock price reflects business conditions ahead of time, while a drop in the stock price can induce a higher leverage ratio.

(3) Financial Leverage: higher leverage leads to higher credit spreads and vice versa.

(4) Asset Volatility: credit spread is expected to increase with a higher volatility because it increases the likelihood that the default threshold is hit.

(5) Risk Free Interest Rate: it constitutes the drift in the risk neutral world; higher risk free rates lead to decreasing credit spreads. This negative relationship can also be explained in a macro-economic setting: interest rates are positively linked to economic growth and higher growth should imply lower default risk.

(6) Yield curve slope: it does not directly appear in most of the structural models, but its effects on the expected future short rate are related to future business conditions. A high positive slope anticipates improved economic growth, indicating higher future interest rates which implies lower credit risk.

(7) Risk Appetite: credit spreads not always compensate for pure expected loss and the spread may change due to a change in investors risk aversion

Other factors that can be relevant are liquidity, idiosyncratic factors, general business improvements and banking stability, for example. The Credit Rating remains the most important source of information on credit risk, even if all the other factors add significant information.

A first conclusion is that the determinants of bank CDS spreads vary strongly across time, which implies that the models must be re-estimated frequently in order to give the right 'signals' to supervisors and monetary policy makers. Different actions can then be adopted depending on whether changes are driven by credit risk, liquidity or business cycle factors. A second conclusion is that the listed variables became significant drivers of CDS spreads after the start of the crisis. This suggests that policy-makers should not rely only on financial institutions' CDS spreads to monitor credit risk, but they should be examined together with other market indicators to achieve an accurate assessment. A third conclusion is that a change in risk appetite was one of the causes of the repricing of the cost of sovereign debt. Finally, CDS market liquidity appears to have played a role both before and after the start of the crisis in explaining Euro area bank CDS spread changes, suggesting that CDS market liquidity should explicitly be taken into account when analyzing CDS spreads.

8.2.5   *Bond yield and CDS spread*

As a first approximation, CDS prices reflect the expected loss of the reference entity given by its default probability and the recovery rate. Additional risk premia are required to compensate for an unexpected default. Theoretically bond spreads should be equal to the CDS premium for the same reference entity. A portfolio composed of a risky zero coupon bond with maturity t_n and a CDS on that same bond with maturity t_n should replicate a synthetic risk-free asset.

For the sake of illustration, consider a reference entity α and let:

- $r(t_0, t_n)$ be the risk-free rate in t_0 for the maturity t_n.
- $y_\alpha(t_0, t_n)$ be the yield at time t_0 on a Zero-Coupon Bond (ZCB) issued by α with maturity date t_n.
- $s_\alpha(t_0, t_n) \equiv y_\alpha(t_0, t_n) - r(t_0, t_n)$ be the spread over the risk-free rate of the issuance cost of α, prevailing in t_0 and referred to the maturity t_n.
- $p_\alpha(t_0, t_n)$ be the periodic CDS premium to protect against the default of α within the period $[t_0, t_n]$.
- $p_\alpha(t_0, t_n) - s_\alpha(t_0, t_n)$ is the 'basis'.

Hence the ZCB yield $y_\alpha(t_0, t_n)$ minus the CDS premium $p_\alpha(t_0, t_n)$ should be exactly equal to the risk-free rate $r(t_0, t_n)$. The invoked equilibrium is ensured by the two following arbitrage strategies[1]:

- *Arbitrage Strategy 1:* $p_\alpha(t_0, t_n) < s_\alpha(t_0, t_n)$: the arbitrage strategy in this case consists of buying the bond, financing the purchase at the risk-free rate $r(t_0, t_n)$ and then buying the CDS at the premium $p_\alpha(t_0, t_n)$. The portfolio return is $y_\alpha(t_0, t_n) - r(t_0, t_n) - p_\alpha(t_0, t_n) = s_\alpha(t_0, t_n) - p_\alpha(t_0, t_n) > 0$.
- *Arbitrage Strategy 2* $p_\alpha(t_0, t_n) > s_\alpha(t_0, t_n)$: the arbitrage strategy in this case consists of short selling the bond, investing the proceeds at the risk-free rate of return $r(t_0, t_n)$ and selling protection in the CDS market to get the premium $p_\alpha(t_0, t_n)$. The portfolio return is $p_\alpha(t_0, t_n) + r(t_0, t_n) - y_\alpha(t_0, t_n) = p_\alpha(t_0, t_n) - s_\alpha(t_0, t_n) > 0$.

The absence of arbitrage should imply a zero basis. However, the basis is rarely zero. From 2007, the basis for corporate debt has been mainly

---

[1]The portfolio payoffs are guaranteed for each strategy if and only if the positions are kept until bond maturity or until the credit event occurs. Otherwise the strategy faces a roll over risk in the financing/investing positions linked to the volatility of $r(t_0, t_n)$.

negative for BBB rated reference entities and below and moderately positive for high-quality reference entities (Amadei et al. [2011]). The persistence of negative basis can be explained by the failure in implementing Arbitrage Strategy 1 due to difficulties with some or all of the following:

- buying the bond and financing the position at the risk-free rate, due to the presence of liquidity problems and high tensions in the interbank market.
- buying the CDS, either due to a lack of protection sellers or for a perception of a high counterparty risk linked to thd contract.

In contrast, we observe a positive basis for most countries. The main exceptions are found for Portugal, Ireland and Greece where we find a temporary negative basis in 2009 and early 2010. One possible explanation for the CDS spread exceeding the bond spread are 'flight to liquidity' effects', which specifically lower government bond spreads in periods of market distress. The reasons for the basis to be non-zero are mainly linked to differences in the liquidity of CDS and bond markets, to counterparty risk and other market imperfections. As an example of the latter we can mention the different reactivity of CDS and bond markets to new information on the issuer. A negative or positive basis can reflect a different degree of adjustment between the two markets since arbitrage strategies correct mainly over the long run.

8.2.6 *Pricing a CDS*

In order to calculate the equilibrium price, or the default swap premium, of a single name CDS it is necessary to specify the reference entity or the reference obligation, the maturity of the contract, the credit event and the Recovery Rate RR. We apply the idea of a 'zero sum game' to price a single-name CDS: when the contract is settled the two counterparties must face equal and opposite expected payments.

Let be

- t_i, with i=0..n, the points in time of the possible payments. Assume, for sake of simplicity, that a default can take place only at these points in time;
- t_0 the current time;
- $F(t_i)$ the unconditional default probability in (t_0, t_i) (see Appendix 8.A for further details);

- $S(t_i)$ the unconditional survival probability up to t_i;
- $v(t_i)$ the discount factor i.e. the present value of €1 in t_0.

The periodic premium $p_\alpha(t_0, t_n)$, computed in t_0, paid in t_i with i=0..n-1 by the protection buyer against the default of α for a CDS with maturity t_n is determined setting the present value of his/her payments (Premium Leg, PL_{t_0})

$$PL_{t_0} = \sum_{i=0}^{n-1} p_\alpha(t_0, t_n) S(t_i) v(t_i) \qquad (8.3)$$

equal to the present value of the payments of the protection seller (Default Leg, DL_{t_0}):

$$DL_{t_0} = \sum_{i=0}^{n-1} v(t_{i+1})(1 - RR)(F(t_{i+1}) - F(t_i)). \qquad (8.4)$$

Equating the two legs we obtain the premium

$$p_\alpha(t, t_n) = \frac{\sum_{i=0}^{n-1} v(t_{i+1})(1 - RR)(F(t_{i+1}) - F(t_i))}{\sum_{i=0}^{n-1} S(t_i) v(t_i)}. \qquad (8.5)$$

8.2.7   *Multiname credit derivatives: basket products and CDS indices*

There is a second category of CDSs which refers to multi-name entities that can be mainly distinguished in basket and portfolio default swaps. In Fig. 8.3 we can appreciate the evolution of the single and multi-name CDSs over time and the increasing importance of the latter. By basket products we mean *k-th* to default baskets. CDS basket products involve default correlation pricing. This makes them more opaque in terms of pricing techniques. The protection is provided for the *k-th* default out of a basket of n reference entities. So each of the reference names form part of the basket and the protection seller bears the risk of each of them, however the payment is due only for the *k-th* default. After the credit event, the swap is closed. For example in a *1-st* to default swap as soon as anyone of the reference entities defaults, the protection seller provides the due payment and the basket credit default is closed. In a *2-th* to default swap if anyone of the reference entities defaults there is no payment, but as soon as there is a second default the protection seller provides the due payment and the basket credit default swap is closed, and so on. For this type of contract to price this instrument and measure its risk, it is crucial to understand the existing default dependence between the various reference assets. As an example, in a *1-st* to default, the protection buyer is betting on the probability that if one of the names default, the probability that the others also default is minimal.

On the contrary a portfolio credit swap (also called an add-up portfolio) provides full protection on a pool of names. The end of the contract is its maturity date or the default of all the names in the pool,whichever comes first.

We highlight the four main differences between a basket default swap and a portfolio default swap:

(1) a portfolio default swap provides full protection on the entire portfolio whereas the '*k-th* default' default swap provides protection on the entire portfolio but limited to the *k-th* default,

(2) the *k-th* to default swap is cheaper than the portfolio default swap on the same pool of names,

(3) a *k-th* to default default swap is a default correlation product where the parties are taking a view on the underlying default correlation. In a portfolio of CDS the investors buy protection against all the possible defaults. This implies that there are no specific views on the default correlation structure,

(4) a *k-th* to default default swap expires with the *k-th* default whereas a portfolio default swap continues till maturity or until default of all the names in the portfolio.

Two notable and standardised examples of portfolios of CDSs are the indices Itraxx and CDX. Itraxx Europe investment grades is a portfolio of CDSs, where the basket is composed by 125 investment grade names in Europe; CDX.NA.IG is composed by 125 investment grade names in the North American area. Each entity in the index has the same portion of the notional amount within the portfolio. The protection seller makes a payment when one of the names defaults. The contract does not expire and keeps on being traded with reduced notional amounts. The notional value of the contract is reduced by $1/n$ where n is the number of contracts in the pool. The standardization and transparency of these contracts have both contributed strongly to the growth of the multiname CDS market. Indices are commonly used to create tranches i.e. to slice the risk into different layers. Each tranche is characterized by an attachment and detachment point that delimited the range of the losses, in terms of notional value that the seller of protection has to cover. As an example a tranche [3%-5%] corresponds to a protection from losses between 3% and 5% of notional value of the contract. Assume there are 125 names in the pool and each of them has a notional value of \$1, the buyer of the tranche [3%-5%] will be eventually refunded from the 5-th and 6-th defaults. This structure is also referred as synthetic CDO and it will discussed in more details in the next section.

8.3   Collateralized Debt Obligation

A Collateralized Debt Obligation (CDO) is a pool of debt contracts, housed within a Special-Purpose Vehicle (SPV), whose capital structure is tranched and resold based on differences in credit quality. CDOs can be distinguished as either cash flow or synthetic.

In a cash flow CDO, the SPV purchases a portfolio of outstanding debt issued by a range of companies, and finances its purchase by issuing its own financial instruments, including primarily debt but also equity. Credit Rating Agencies rate the various tranches of the SPV's debt, whose terms vary depending on seniority. The main parties involved in these contracts are the seller (Originator) who sells the underlying asset portfolio to a Special-Purpose Vehicle (SPV),which issues the tranches and uses earnings to pay the underlying portfolio, investors, and Rating Agencies who give a rating to each issued tranches. These tranches are usually organized as senior, with higher quality and lower return since they face the lower risk levels, mezzanine and equity, with lower quality and higher return since they face the higher risk levels. Between them there is the so called 'waterfall payment' principle, which means that only when the higher tiers have received all interest and principal payments the next and lower tier of creditors will begin to receive interest and principal payments.

We illustrate the structure of a CDO using the example in Fig. 8.4. A pool of bonds is held by a SPV. The nominal value is €1,000. Each year the portfolio generates interest equal to the *Euribor* + 100*bps*. Its capital structure is sliced in 4 tranches and resold offering different interest payment according to the different credit qualities:

- AAA: The senior tranche, with higher quality and lower return. It covers the losses above 8% of the notional value of the collateral portfolio. It is the last tranche that is eroded and the first one that receives interest payments. The interest rate payed is *Euribor* + 50*bps*. At creation the notional of the AAA tranche is €920.

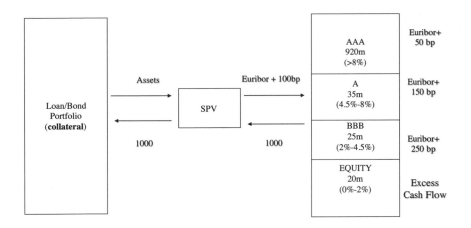

Fig. 8.4   CDO constructed on a bond portfolio of €1,000.

- A: this tranche covers the losses between 4.5% and 8%. At creation the notional of the tranche is €35 and the interest paid is $Euribor + 150 bps$.
- BBB: this tranche covers the losses between 2% and 4.5%. At creation the notional of the tranche is €25 and the interest paid is $Euribor + 250 bps$.
- Finally the Equity, the low quality tranche [0%-2%] covers the losses below 2% of the notional value of the collateral. It is the first tranche that is eroded (or attacked) and the last one that receives interest payments, if any are left; at creation the notional of the equity tranche is €20.

At the end of the first year, with no default in the underlying pool, the payment can be estimated. The interest rate generated by the collateral portfolio is the $Euribor + 100 bps$. We assume that the current level of Euribor is 3%. The interest earned by the portfolio is $(3.00\% + 100 bps) \times$ €1,000 = 40. This sum is used to pay the owner of the various tranches, net of the commission fees equal to $2 bps \times$ €1,000 = €0.2. In Table 8.2 we report the nominal value of the tranches and in Table 8.3 the interest paid applying the waterfall payment principle.

The first interest is paid to AAA. In fact we pay on the notional value of that tranche the interest rate of $3.00\% + 50 bps$. The second interest is paid to the A tranche and so on, till we reach the Equity tranche which receives the remaining sum.

Table 8.2　Nominal values of the tranches.

Tranches	Nominal Value
AAA [8%- 100%]	920
A [4,5%- 8%]	35
BBB [2%- 4,5%]	25
EQUITY [0-2%]	20

Table 8.3　Interest in case of no-default.

Tranches	Interest
AAA Interest	$(3.00\% + 50bps) \times 920 = 32.2$
A Interest	$(3.00\% + 150bps) \times 35 = 1.6$
BBB Interest	$(3.00\% + 250bps) \times 25 = 1.4$
EQUITY	$40 - 35.4 = 4.6$

Table 8.4　Residual nominal value after a default.

Tranches	Nominal Value
AAA [8%- 100%]	920
A [4.5%- 8%]	35
BBB [2%- 4.5%]	15
EQUITY [0-2%]	0

Alternatively let's assume that after one year 5 names, each with a value of €10, are in default and the RR= 40%. The loss is $(5 \times €10) \times (1 - 40\%) = €30$. The portfolio value decreases to €970 with a percentage loss of 3%. So the equity tranche is completely eroded as a part of the BBB tranche.

In Table 8.4 we report the nominal value of the tranches after the default and in Table 8.5 the interest payed on the updated nominal values.

The payments of interest follows a waterfall scheme: the difference with the payments estimated in the example above is evident starting with BBB which has a post default reduced residual nominal value of €15. The interest paid is €0.8. The Equity tranche receives the remaining sum.

In a synthetic CDO, the SPV does not purchase actual bonds, but instead typically enters into several Credit Default Swaps with a third party, to create a synthetic exposure to the outstanding debt issued by a range of

Table 8.5   Interest in case of default.

	Interest
Portfolio interest	$(3.00\% + 100bps) \times 970 = 38.8$
Fees	$2bps \times 1000 = 0.2$
AAA Interest	$(3.00\% + 50bps) \times 920 = 32.2$
A Interest	$(3.00\% + 150bps) \times 35 = 1.6$
BBB Interest	$(3.00\% + 250bps) \times 15 = 0.8$
EQUITY	$(38.8\text{-}0.2\text{-}32.2\text{-}1.6\text{-}0.8.) = 4$

companies. The SPV then issues financial instruments, which are backed by credit default swaps rather than by actual bonds.

8.4   Case Studies

In this section we present two case studies. The first is related to the possibility of extracting information from CDS premia and create non parametric mapping from CDS premia to an implied rating system(IRS) [Castellano and Giacometti (2012)]. The second shows how it is possible to extract information on the joint default probability from the CDS premia [Pianeti et al. (2012)].

8.4.1   *Forward-looking measures of default probabilities*

Recently, in parallel with the development of the credit derivatives market, the academic research began to explore the relationship between the Credit Default Swap (CDS) market and Rating Agencies events. Many papers provide evidence that CDS market is able to signal future Agencies' official rating changes and that CDS prices provide accurate estimates of the reference entity credit risk over short time horizons, (i.e. one year). A large body of literature has shown that the CDS market is superior to the bond market in signaling future agencies' official rating changes and that CDS quotes provide accurate estimates of the reference entity credit risk over short time horizons. The signaling power of CDS spreads reflects the crucial differences between the way markets and Rating Agencies work. Markets instantaneously incorporate all relevant news about an issuer. Rating Agencies take the same information into account, but with three important differences. The first is that a Rating Agency will often react at a slower pace than the markets, given the nature of the ratings process. Second, Rating Agencies strive to balance accuracy and stability, meaning that they should not change as often as market levels. Finally, Agency analysts might simply take a different view than the market on an entity's risk level.

We implement a CDS Implied Ratings (CDS-IRs) model which extracts information from CDS market quotes to create a non-parametric mapping from the official agency ratings to the market implied ones. We consider a historical data set of CDS daily market premia (*spreads*) from 2004 to 2009 and collect the rating announcements provided by the three major Rating Agencies (Moody's, Standard & Poor's and Fitch) for the same period. This allows us to analyze the differences between Agency ratings and CDS-IRs and compare how they have evolved over time. Furthermore we test whether CDS-IRs provide an early warning signal to anticipate future Rating Agency downgrades and defaults: this could be extremely valuable for investors to monitor and hedge their credit risk exposure.

Let assign to each CDS a rating class out of M possible values $\{c_1, c_2, ..c_M\}$, with $c_1 \leq c_2 \leq ... \leq c_M$. Starting from the official ratings provided by each of the three considered Rating Agencies (Moody's, Standard & Poor's and Fitch), we compute the CDS-IRs boundaries b_k for each rating class, c_k, given the number of CDS belonging to the kth rating class, N_k.

The boundaries of the CDS-IRs are obtained by minimizing the penalty function:

$$\min \sum_{k=1}^{M} \sum_{j=1}^{N_k} \frac{1}{N_k} \left[\max \left(p_{jk} - b_k^+, 0 \right) + \max \left(b_k^- - p_{jk}, 0 \right) \right] \qquad (8.6)$$

subject to:

$$b_{k-1}^+ = b_k^-, \forall k > 1 \qquad (8.7)$$

$$b_{k-1}^+ \leq b_k^-, \forall k > 1 \qquad (8.8)$$

where p_{jk} is the market premium of the j-th CDS in rating class k.

We compute the CDS-IRs on yearly basis and analyze the rating gaps, i.e. the difference between the CDS-IRs and the official ratings assigned to the reference entities by Rating Agencies. Ratings gaps are high and have been so since the summer of 2007, highlighting the CDS-IRs' ability to signal upgrade and downgrade risk. The main results of the analysis confirm the tendency of Agency ratings to move toward those levels suggested by the market implied ratings and the anticipation effects of the CDS quotes.

8.4.2 *Extracting joint default probabilities from CDS*

Systemic default risk — i.e. the risk of simultaneous default of multiple institutions- represents a key risk factor nowadays. To measure systemic risk is not a trivial task. In this section we estimate the joint probability of default for pairs of defaultable entities, belonging to different rating classes. Both bond and credit derivatives market convey information on the default probabilities: the former provides information on the marginal default probabilities whilst the latter on the joint default probabilities. The counterparty risk is reflected in the CDS price through the joint default probability of the reference entity and the protection seller. When the joint probability increases the CDS price decreases. Applying a no-arbitrage argument, we extract forward looking joint default probabilities of institutions operating in the CDS market. The analysis of the dynamic of the joint default probability can provide clear signals of an increase in systemic risk and danger of contagion.

In the previous sections we stated that the arbitrage-free value of the basis is zero. This holds when the counterparty risk is not explicitly taken into consideration. In the following, we relax this assumption: a negative basis, representing the counterparty cost, can still be consistent with an arbitrage free valuation and can be used to extract information on the joint default probability.

A formula for measuring the joint probability of default of two financial institutions is derived.

Consider two risky financial institutions and, for illustrative purpose, denote them as α and β. Consider a third party called γ and, for the sake of argument, assume that it cannot go bankrupt. Imagine that at time $t = 0$, the riskless entity γ builds a portfolio, according to the following single period strategy:

Strategy 1 (*Single-period case*):

- Buy a 1-year zero coupon bond (ZCB) issued by α,
- buy a 1-year CDS from β, the protection seller, on the reference entity α,
- finance the positions in the market with a 1-year loan.

All the contracts have a face value of $1. Since we assume that γ is risk-free, it can finance its positions at the current 1-year risk-free rate. On the contrary the interest rate offered by α on the bond issue is increased by a spread related to its creditworthiness. Now let:

- RR_α, RR_β be the recovery rates of α and β, respectively.
- Π_t be the value at time t of the portfolio built by γ according to Strategy 1.

The present value of the bond issued by α is $e^{-r(0,1)-s_\alpha(0,1)} \approx 1 - r(0,1) - s_\alpha(0,1)$ and the amount of money borrowed by γ is $e^{-r(0,1)} \approx 1 - r(0,1)$.

In Table 8.6 we report the value of the portfolio at two different points in time, $t = 0$ and $t = 1$, when all cash flows are exchanged. The second column summaries, at time $t = 0$, the present value of the financial instruments of the portfolio held by γ. The portfolio value at time $t = 0$ is therefore:

$$\Pi_0 = p_{\alpha,\beta}(0,1) - s_\alpha(0,1) \tag{8.9}$$

The other columns of Table 8.6 report the cash flows in the different states of the world at time $t = 1$. The dash on the name of a financial institution stands for the institution being in default.

Table 8.6   Cash flows of the static Strategy 1 at time $t = 0$ and $t = 1$.

	$t = 0$	$t = 1$			
		α, β	$\overline{\alpha}, \beta$	$\alpha, \overline{\beta}$	$\overline{\alpha}, \overline{\beta}$
Loan	$-(1 - r(0,1))$	-1	-1	-1	-1
ZCB	$1 - r(0,1) - s_\alpha(0,1)$	1	RR_α	1	RR_α
CDS	$p_{\alpha,\beta}(0,1)$	0	$1 - RR_\alpha$	0	$(1 - RR_\alpha)RR_\beta$
Π_t	$p_{\alpha,\beta}(0,1) - s_\alpha(0,1)$	0	0	0	$-(1 - RR_\alpha)(1 - RR_\beta)$

If α survives, independently from β, γ repays its loan using the money from the zero coupon bond, while the CDS expires. If α defaults and β survives, the position of γ is hedged by the CDS and the portfolio value is zero.

A non-zero cash flow is generated only when both α and β default, that is with a probability equal to the joint default probability of α and β. If the probability is zero, i.e. there is no counterparty risk, and the basis is zero.

Under the hypothesis that $0 \leq RR_\alpha < 1$ and $0 \leq RR_\beta < 1$, this would result in a negative present value of the portfolio in $t = 0$, i.e. $\Pi_0 < 0$.

The expected value of the portfolio at $t = 1$ is:

$$\mathbf{E}[\Pi_1] = -P_{\bar{\alpha},\bar{\beta}}(0,1)(1 - RR_\alpha)(1 - RR_\beta) \tag{8.10}$$

where we denote $P_{\bar{\alpha},\bar{\beta}}(0,1)$ as the risk-neutral 1-year joint default probability of α and β.

If we think in term of cash flows, γ implements such a strategy whenever the basis is negative, since he will receive $-\Pi_0$ from this strategy. The negative basis corresponds to the premium required for the potential loss due to the joint default of α and β. Thus within our framework we admittedly exclude the presence of a positive basis, since in that case γ would not implement such strategy. A positive basis typically conveys information linked to market imperfections, not explicitly modeled here.

Recall that in an arbitrage-free world, for every security with value f_t at time $t \geq 0$, it must hold that:

$$f_t = \mathbf{E}_Q[f_T]e^{-r(t,T)(T-t)} \qquad \forall t < T \tag{8.11}$$

where Q is the risk-neutral probability measure.

That is, excluding arbitrage possibilities, in our case we must have:

$$\Pi_0 = \mathbf{E}[\Pi_1]e^{-r(0,1)}, \quad \Pi_0 < 0 \tag{8.12}$$

Combining Eq. 8.9, 8.10 and 8.12, we obtain:

$$P_{\bar{\alpha},\bar{\beta}}(0,1) = \frac{\left(s_\alpha(0,1) - p_{\alpha,\beta}(0,1)\right)^+}{(1 - RR_\alpha)(1 - RR_\beta)}e^{r(0,1)} \tag{8.13}$$

where $(\cdot)^+ \equiv \max(\cdot, 0)$.

According to Eq. 8.13 and given RR_α and RR_β, the risk neutral joint probability of default is explained by the negative basis. In absence of counterparty risk and arbitrage opportunities, this difference is supposed to be zero. The presence of counterparty risk reduces the premium of the CDS and motivates a negative basis. The wider is this difference, the higher is the counterparty risk and the higher is the joint probability of default of the bond issuer α and the protection seller β. If the basis is positive, we set the joint default probability equal to zero since we attribute a positive basis to market imperfections.

Appendix 8.A. Unconditional Default Probability

In the appendix we provide a simple definition of the unconditional default probability, the conditional default probability, and the instantaneous and average default intensity or hazard rate.

Let be:

- T the time to default. It is a random variable representing the time before the default;
- $t_0 = 0$ the current time and consider $t \geq t_0$;
- $F(t) = Pr(T \leq t)$ the probability, seen in t_0, that the default event is at any time before t;
- $S(t) = Pr(T > t) = 1 - F(t)$ the survival probability up to t.

The unconditional probability to observe a default in the time interval $(t, t + \Delta t)$ is

$$Pr(t < T \leq t + \Delta t) = F(t + \Delta t) - F(t) \qquad (8.A.1)$$

The conditional default probability in time interval $(t, t + \Delta t)$ given the survival up to t is

$$Pr(t < T \leq t + \Delta t | T > t) = \frac{Pr(t < T \leq t + \Delta t)}{Pr(T > t)} = \frac{F(t + \Delta t) - F(t)}{S(t)}. \qquad (8.A.2)$$

Finally, we define the average default intensity on the time interval $(t, t + \Delta t)$ as

$$\lambda_{t,t+\Delta t} = \frac{Pr(t < T \leq t + \Delta t)}{Pr(T > t)\Delta t} \qquad (8.A.3)$$

The instantaneous default intensity or hazard rate is obtained as the limit for $\Delta t \to 0$

$$\lambda(t) = \frac{-S'(t)}{S(t)} \qquad (8.A.4)$$

The default probability can be re-written as

$$F(t) = 1 - \exp - \int_0^t \lambda(s)ds \qquad (8.A.5)$$

and the average default intensity in $(0, t)$ is

$$\lambda_{0,t} = -\frac{\log(1 - F(t))}{t}. \qquad (8.A.6)$$

Glossary

CDS Credit default swap. It is the most liquid credit derivative. The protection seller compensates the protection buyer in the event of a default against a periodic premium.

CSS Credit spread swap. The protection seller compensates the protection buyer in the event of a downgrading against a periodic premium.

OTC Over the counter. It is a market where financial instruments such as stocks, bonds, commodities or derivatives are traded directly between two parties.

TRORS Total Rate of Return Swap. It is credit derivative where the total return receiver creates a virtual position in the reference entity without having it into his portfolio. The total return payer pays a period fee and transfers all the cash flows of the bond to the former against credit and market risk protection.

CLN Credit link notes. It is structured as a security with an embedded credit derivative that allows the issuer to transfer a specific credit risk to credit investors.

CDO Collateralised debt obligation. It is an asset security backed by bonds.

Protection seller Who sells credit risk protection. One of the two parties of a derivatives contract;

Protection buyer Who buys credit risk protection. One of the two parties of a derivatives contract;

k-th to default basket It is multi-name CDS. It pays upon the k-th default in the reference basket.

CDS index it is a multi-name credit derivative used to hedge on a basket of credit entities. It is equivalent to an add-up portfolio of CDS on a standardised basket of names.

CDS-IR A CDS-IR model processes the collective marketplace view of firms' credit condition based on its current CDS pricing. It then calculates and converts these into implied ratings.

References

Amadei, L., Di Rocco, S., Gentile, M., Grasso, R., Siciliano, G. (2011). I credit default swap, *CONSOB*, Discussion papers, **1**.

Cantor, R., Packer, F. (1996). Determinants and Impact of Sovereign Credit Ratings, *Economic Policy Review*, Academic journal, (Federal Reserve Bank of New York), *2*(2), October.

Castellano, R., Giacometti, R. (2012). Credit Default Swaps: Implied Ratings versus Official Ones, *4OR-A Quarterly Journal of Operational Research*, **10**(2), pp. 163–180.

Covitz, M., Harrison, P. (2003). Testing conflicts of interest at bond ratings agencies with market anticipation: evidence that reputation incentives dominates, *Federal Reserve Board*, Finance and Economics Discussion Series, **68**.

European Central Bank (2009). Credit default swaps and counterparty risk, *ECB*, http://www.ecb.int/pub/pdf/other/ creditdefaultswapsandcounterpartyrisk2009en.pdf.

Fontana, A., Scheicher, M. (2011). An Analysis of Euro Area Sovereign CDS and their relation with Government Bonds, *European Central Bank*, Working Paper, **1271**, December.

Hull, J. C. (2006). Options, Futures, and Other Derivatives, 6th edition (Pearson Education).

Hull, J. C., Predescu, M., White, A. (2004). The relationship between credit default swap spreads, bond yields, and credit rating announcements, *Journal of Banking and Finance*, **28**(11), pp. 2789–2811.

Longstaff, F. A., Pan, J., Pederesenn, L. H., Singleton, K. J. (2011). How Sovereign Is Sovereign Credit Risk?, *American Economic Journal*, Macroeconomics, **3**(2), pp. 75–103.

Norden, L., Weber, M. (2004). Informational efficiency of credit default swap and stock markets: the impact of credit rating announcements, *Journal of Banking and Finance*, **28**, pp. 2813–2843.

Pan, J., Singleton, K. J. (2008). Default and Recovery Implicit in the Term Structure of Sovereign CDS Spreads, *The Journal of Finance*, **LXIII**(5).

Pianeti, R., Giacometti, G., Acerbis, V. (2012). Estimating the joint probability of default using CDS and bond data, *The Journal of Fixed Income*, Winter, **21**(3), pp. 44–58.

Schönbucher, P. J. (2003). Credit Derivatives Pricing Models: Model, Pricing and Implementation (John Wesley & Sons Ltd: Chichester West Sussex England).

Index